SMART
RUNNING

SMART RUNNING

The ultimate guide to becoming a fitter, stronger, more confident runner

Jen and Sim Benson

Vertebrate Publishing, Sheffield
www.adventurebooks.com

SMART
RUNNING

The ultimate guide to becoming a fitter, stronger, more confident runner

Jen and Sim Benson

First published in 2024 by Vertebrate Publishing.

VERTEBRATE PUBLISHING
Omega Court, 352 Cemetery Road, Sheffield S11 8FT, United Kingdom.
www.adventurebooks.com

A CIP catalogue record for this book is available from the British Library.

ISBN: 978-1-83981-047-3 (Paperback)
ISBN: 978-1-83981-211-8 (Ebook)

Edited by Helen Parry, design and production by Jane Beagley, Vertebrate Publishing.

Printed and bound in Slovenia by Latitude Press.

Vertebrate Publishing is committed to printing on paper from sustainable sources.

MIX
Paper | Supporting
responsible forestry
FSC® C106600

Acknowledgements

A huge thank you to the brilliant team at Vertebrate Publishing, including Kirsty Reade for commissioning this book and providing much-needed words of wisdom, both in the book and during the Arc of Attrition; Helen Parry for being an incredibly talented (and incredibly patient) editor; Jane Beagley for making it all look fantastic; and John 'Vader' Coefield for applying some much-needed time pressure to actually get it to print. Thank you to NoblePro treadmills, Suunto, mindfulness guru Danielle Frake (*www.thejourneyyogastudio.com*), Renee McGregor, James Barker at Endurancelife, and Nicola Frow at Beta Running/Ultimate Direction for much-appreciated support and advice.

Contents

Introduction

Recreational distance running is, perhaps, the most individual of all sports. We all have our reasons for taking up running, and our reasons for carrying on. Some run for competition – to beat others or better themselves – while for some it's entirely unrelated to competitive sport and more about movement or mindfulness, being outdoors or being with others. For many, the regular practice of running is closely tied to our identity, our sense of self-worth and well-being. Running is where we meet others and discover ourselves.

As a form of exercise, running's ability to fit in around other commitments, along with its time-efficiency and cost-effectiveness, make it perfectly suited to our busy, modern lives. Running can be what you want, when you want it. Running is therapy, relaxation, challenge, health, companionship, sightseeing, competition and much more.

This book is aimed at anyone wanting to improve their knowledge and understanding of the art and science of running. Covering a broad range of topics, relevant to all runners, and drawing on the latest research and evidence-based practice, our aim is to provide a clear, concise, detailed, yet accessible guide to all things running.

Compared with a few decades ago, runners tend to specialise less in the kind of running they do. Parkrun has made a weekly 5K commonplace for thousands, while running marathons for charity or a new PB, trail races as a way to explore new places, or an ultramarathon to explore our own limits, are all popular ways to spend a morning, a day, a weekend, or even longer.

Whether you're just starting out, contemplating your first marathon, aiming for a new personal best, training for a multi-day ultra, or simply enjoying exploring your local trails, this book covers everything you need to know to approach it at your best. It is the result of many years of experience and a lifelong passion for the subject, underpinned at every step of the way by solid, scientific evidence from a vast range of disciplines. It will help you to navigate the mass of often-conflicting information on areas as diverse as form, fitness, technology, technique, supplements and shoes, addressing and clarifying each topic to help you make better-informed decisions. You'll also discover the intricate interplay of body and brain in endurance sport, and learn how to hone these to work best for you.

Why run?

Having run for so many years ourselves, it can be hard to pin down and explain exactly why we head out for a run on most days, even if we've no races planned. We've both run regularly for so long that running has become a part of who we are, shaping and strengthening our bodies and our minds. Our daily escape to the trails has become an essential part of life.

The research on why people take up running, particularly later on in life, is pretty scarce. From our own ethnographic work, we've found that health-related reasons for taking up running are common. For many it's to try to lose weight and get fitter; for some it's following a health scare of their own or someone close to them; for others it's a desire to take on a new challenge, learn a new skill, or meet new people. Forming the habit to run can be hard at first; when our days don't have a space reserved for running and it feels like an effort simply to get everything together and make that first step out through the door. Once the habit is truly ingrained, though, to the point where it is perhaps no longer exactly a habit but instead a necessary part of feeling like the truest version of ourselves, it can feel like more of a struggle *not* to run.

In his book, *Running with the Pack: Thoughts From the Road on Meaning and Mortality*, philosopher and runner, Mark Rowlands, discusses running's 'inherent' or 'intrinsic' value – how the act of regular running benefits us in terms of physical and psychological health – alongside its meaning to us, as human beings. While research certainly backs up the idea that physical activities like running, particularly when undertaken in green environments, are good for our health, is this really the main reason why runners run? Rowlands suggests not. He thinks we don't run for any inherent value in running, and neither does he think it is much to do with enjoyment – for every moment of enjoyment during a run there are far more when it feels like a slog and yet we still keep at it. Those who race must always know there are many people faster and slower than they are – that performances and finishing times are all relative, all essentially meaningless – and only a very select few are good enough to begin to make a living from running. Rarely do we even run in order to get somewhere.

Perhaps, then, as Rowlands suggests, we run for running's own sake. For the places running takes us to *during* our run, rather than as a function of it. For the way running enables us to understand and remember who we are.

The world of running

At first glance, running is just running – one foot in front of the other, repeat. But when it comes to the kind of running we might want to do, there's a range of different disciplines, each with its own ethos, skill set and kit requirements.

Road running

Road running is considered by some to be a purist form of running, which might seem odd given that we spent a couple of million years evolving to run off-road. But the essence of road running lies in the fact that the terrain doesn't necessarily influence the outcome in the same way it does on the trails or in the mountains – as far as possible, it's all about the running. As long as the road is reasonably flat, times run for standard distances can be compared across any number of locations. Big city marathons are run on the roads for this reason, and because closed roads mean plenty of room for a lot of runners. Road running is the discipline where many runners start, inspired by friends, family or the vast crowds of runners and spectators filling the streets on marathon day.

Track running

Many runners have never set foot on a track, yet it's often track running – the battles to be the fastest over every distance from 100 to 10,000 metres – that dominates in the media. These floodlit arenas, populated by elite athletes wearing little more (and sometimes a little less) than their swimming kit, aren't where most recreational runners feel at home. And yet track running can be enjoyable and surprisingly varied, from weekly interval sessions to 24-hour track ultramarathons. Many running clubs have access to a track and club track nights can be both fun and beneficial to your running, so, even if running in lanes and circles doesn't sound like your cup of tea, don't knock it until you've tried it.

Cross-country running

Not to be confused with any other kind of off-road running, cross-country running is a specific discipline, mostly popular with schools, club leagues, and off-season track and road runners. Held over the winter months in a muddy field, it usually involves a large number of runners and the wearing of spikes, which are entirely different to the off-road running shoes worn by trail and fell runners. Cross-country races are usually short, fast and furious, and run in freezing cold conditions. They're a great way to maintain fitness and leg strength over the winter months.

Trail running

Trail running – following pre-made trails through a variety of landscapes – is a fast-growing running discipline, popular because of its sense of freedom and adventure, and its customisability. The number of trail races held globally has increased rapidly over the past decade, and the offering is vast from short, fast and flat to long, slow and mountainous. Trails offer a ready-made adventure for runners, with waymarked long-distance trails perfect for multi-day exploration (also called fastpacking) or timed challenges, aiming to claim the fastest known time (FKT) for a particular route. Trail races are usually waymarked, but can also be self-navigated.

Fell running

Originating in Scotland and the north of England, fell running (also known as hill running) usually follows off-trail routes over open, upland landscapes such as mountains and moorland. Sometimes courses are marked, but many races require runners to navigate themselves around a series of checkpoints. As with trail running, the distances, ascent and conditions vary widely, but the races tend to be more low-key, less expensive to enter, and more locally focussed. Fell races often take in short stretches of trail and/or road. Mountain marathons are usually two-day self-supported, self-navigated fell races for teams of two, with an overnight camp halfway round.

Ultrarunning

Another area of running that's seeing rapid growth in popularity, ultrarunning involves running any distance greater than a marathon – 26.2 miles (42.2 kilometres). Ultras can be run on trails, fells, roads, tracks or any other location that lends itself to being run over, around or through for a long time. Famous ultra races include the Spine Race, which has winter and summer versions and follows all 268 miles of the Pennine Way in the UK, and the UTMB (Ultra-Trail du Mont-Blanc), which encircles the famous mountain and travels through France, Italy and Switzerland along the way.

Our running journeys

Jen

Running is something I started doing even before I realised it was a *thing*. I ran in between riding my bike and climbing trees. I ran when I wanted to get somewhere more quickly than walking, which was often. I ran down hills with my arms spread wide, because it felt ... amazing.

The first time I remember running because somebody told me to was in my second year of secondary school at the age of 12. I was brand new to the school just in time for the annual cross-country race, something I'd never even heard of before. Nobody thought to mention to me that I should pace myself rather than front-running all the way, or that it wasn't very cool to finish covered in mud and sweat and then proceed to throw up over my shoes. But that's how I ran, and won, my first race.

Soon afterwards I again changed schools and started listening to those who told me it wasn't cool to get sweaty, muddy and sick running around a field. So, running and I had something of an on–off relationship until my early 20s.

Then, when a serious car crash left me unable to walk let alone run for a while, the incredible privilege of having a body that works really hit me. As I healed physically, I started running regularly; initially just for a slow five minutes at a time and gradually increasing my speed and distance. This process also helped me deal with the psychological trauma of the crash, and was the beginning of a love for running that has stayed with me ever since.

Running has been the background to many major life events, most importantly meeting Sim and the arrival of our two children. I've been lucky enough to run many races and even to win a few; I've run the London Marathon from the Championship start, as well as more than 60 other marathons; and I've experienced the full range of running challenges, including mountain marathons, fell races, fastpacking adventures, ultras, and the very special marathon that happens at the end of an Ironman triathlon. I've also been lucky enough to run through two pregnancies and experience the return to fitness that followed, running then becoming something that I juggled around childcare.

My career, too, has revolved around running. Firstly, as a musculoskeletal podiatrist, specialising in treating distance runners; then as a MSc and PhD researcher, looking at running biomechanics, injury, training habits and, more recently, the psychology, sociology and philosophy of running. For the past decade, together with Sim, I've been researching, writing and photographing content for our own running books and for major running magazines and the national press. We've also both gained our running coach qualifications, and we work together coaching a fabulous group of runners of a range of ages, experiences and backgrounds.

Over the years I've met and talked with countless runners: through work, friends, events, research projects, clubs and simply out running. I've seen many running trends come and go; records and FKTs broken; and inspirational people of all kinds telling their own running stories. This book has come about through the accumulation of all these things: personal experiences, scientific learning, and the wisdom, courage and expertise of others.

Sim

I grew up with outdoorsy parents. I remember long walks and sometimes camping out so we could link walks together – I loved it. As I grew older, I started riding my bike and following Dad around his local running loop, I'd race ahead on the downhill and he'd reel me in on the next ascent. In my early teens I occasionally ran with Dad around Haldon Forest near Exeter, but I was getting into mountain biking and soon took any opportunity of a lift to the forest to take my bike. A few years later we started climbing and that took over. Climbing got me back into the mountains and used to long days on my feet. I learnt to navigate and be self-reliant in the hills. In my early 20s, having finished an environmental science degree, I started running. Initially it was to keep fit for climbing and a good activity for the rainy days when I couldn't climb, but I found that at some point I was choosing to run rather than climb; I'd evolved into a runner.

Jen and I met while working at a climbing shop – she started just after I'd signed up for my first marathon and my first ultra. I knew she ran so I was keen to quiz her; we got talking, went for a run and we've carried on running together ever since.

The marathon went well and so did the ultra.

We ran, raced and explored together, ending up creating our first book, *Wild Running*, in 2014. We loved the process and dived into the outdoor writing and photography world. Since then, we've been writing regularly for several running and outdoor magazines as well as publishing more running, walking and adventure guidebooks.

Now I run to explore, and to challenge my body and my mind. I run because that's what I do and who I am; running helps me to relax and to think. I've never regretted going for a run. I'm particularly excited by new trails and connecting valleys or ridgelines on foot; I love the adventure. I've used running to connect easy climbing routes, creating amazing mountain days. I once spent a brilliant afternoon swimming the bays and running the headlands around Bryher in the Isles of Scilly. My racing has seen me chasing faster times on the road and rougher races on the trails. I've raced from parkrun to 110 miles, completing ultras, SkyRaces, mountain marathons, adventure races and an Iron-distance triathlon. I'm currently chasing Jen's half and full marathon times and researching long run–scramble links in the French Alps, along with working on my VO_2 max for some shorter, faster races I've got lined up. I'm not sure which I'm most excited by.

I'm a geek when it comes to running kit, maps and planning. We've been gear experts for a number of running and outdoor magazines over the past decade and we've worked on product development for a few brands. We've tried out and reviewed a lot of shoes, clothes, packs and equipment over the years. I know what works well in specific situations and what's lightest, but with increasing public awareness of the climate crisis I'm excited to see how brands are creating more durable, versatile products that work in a wider variety of terrain and conditions. It's so important that our running kit works brilliantly, lasts well and that it was made with minimal impact.

My walking, climbing and mountaineering background taught me to navigate confidently in extreme weather and terrain, with training and practice I've adapted these skills for the higher speeds of run navigation. I find inspiring and empowering other people to run incredibly rewarding and, as a qualified running coach and run leader, love taking groups out on the trails to explore.

About this book

The varied and fascinating world of running – the physiology, psychology, biomechanics, culture and philosophy that come together to make someone a runner – offers a vast resource from which to draw when putting together a book like this. Across each topic we delve into a range of disciplines, aiming to explore and understand the very essence of what it is to be a runner.

Scientific research, published in journals, holds many of the answers to the questions we wanted to ask, from optimising your training and racing so you can be the best you want to be, to the more nuanced aspects of running such as identity, well-being and inclusivity.

Whether your primary goal is to stay injury-free so you can run every day for health and well-being, to see how fast you can run a marathon, or to find out how far you can go in the world of ultrarunning, basing your training on the best available evidence gives you the best chance of success. In the chapters that follow, we bring together the most up-to-date and relevant research and present it in a way that's (we hope!) interesting, informative and useful to real-world runners. In addition, we've interviewed experts, clinicians and runners themselves to draw from the wealth of experience that only comes through many years of working with, and being, runners.

Though we think all runners will enjoy its content, this book is most relevant to endurance runners – those running distances of 5K or more – rather than sprinters. While we do address faster running, this is presented as speedwork to improve your running over longer distances, rather than specifically for sprinting.

Our guiding principles

The book is based on the following three guiding principles. We'll bring them up regularly throughout the book, as they're relevant to every part of running.

1 Running should be fun — at least retrospectively

There's a lot of information in this book. But the single most important thing to remember about running is that it needs to be fun. If you don't enjoy running – or at least the satisfaction of having done it – you won't be motivated to get through the door, day after day, month after month, year after year. Becoming a runner is a passion, a way of life, and we've written this book to help you nurture and grow that passion.

An important part of falling in love with running is learning to take the rough with the smooth. That doesn't just mean regular off-road adventures – although those definitely help. It also means accepting that not every run is going to be filled with endorphin-inducing, in-the-moment fun. Some runs do feel amazing – when you hit that elusive runners' high, or when it all just feels smooth, coordinated and almost effortless. But there will always be runs that are a slog from start to finish. If you can, try to find joy even in the bad runs. Learn to embrace type-II fun – that special type you only appreciate retrospectively – then enjoy those post-run moments when you can bathe in the satisfaction and smugness of having done something difficult and come out the other side. The tough days are when we learn the most about ourselves, and when we build up our reserves of strength and determination for future runs – or any other life events – that don't go as planned.

Having said all this, if you can't remember the last time you enjoyed a run it might be worth taking some time to think about your reasons for doing it. Perhaps you need some time off, or a change in your approach to running. Or perhaps you need to try another sport for a while – we've heard they exist – at least until your love for running returns.

2 Every runner is unique

It seems obvious to state that everyone is different: no two human beings on earth possess the same specific combination of genes, life history and psychology. But in the world of scientific research, particularly the quantitative, objective kind, it sometimes feels like this gets forgotten. One of the downsides of numbers-driven research can be that it doesn't embrace – or even consider – individual differences. Scientists can run experiments and draw conclusions, but these conclusions will only answer the specific questions asked and may only apply to those who most closely resemble the group that was studied. In countries like the UK and US, young, white, male university students and military recruits are generally keen to take part in research and easy to study, so it's no surprise that this is the population studied in much of the existing sport science literature. Those who can be more time-consuming to recruit or to study, such as people of colour, children, older people, females, pregnant people and trans people tend to be under-represented.

This doesn't mean the existing literature isn't valuable. Well-conducted research provides an excellent foundation on which to base an informed but more individualised approach. But, sadly, not every study is conducted as well as it should be. In the same way as it's wise to treat anyone who claims to have found *the one true way that everyone should run* with a healthy dose of scepticism, research findings should always be scrutinised to make sure the study was well conducted and included participants similar enough to you to be relevant before adopting the recommended approach.

In this book we draw from both quantitative research – the numbers-driven stats and data kind – and qualitative research, which is more interested in areas such as individual experience, motivation, confidence and the narratives we all carry around in our heads that frame how we think about ourselves and others. Using these solid foundations to work from, we then offer suggestions for how to make running work best for you.

On a similar but at the same time entirely different theme, it's well worth holding on tightly to the importance – and brilliance – of our individual differences when it comes to places like social media. Comparing and contrasting ourselves with others, or attempting to imitate how other people do things, is, at best, usually a waste of time. In all likelihood, you're only seeing a heavily curated snippet of an influencer's real life or the successes of a top runner's season. Some accounts are informative and inspiring to follow, and may well help to increase your knowledge and inspire your running. But be picky about who you listen to. Try not to let the inevitable comparisons that are a consequence of scrolling through a social media feed make you feel worse about your life or your running – instead, focus on what you love and value about *your* life and *your* running.

3 *You know you best*

We live in a world filled with data and metrics. Wearable and portable technology has changed everything, and running is no exception. At the press of a button, we can view detailed information about facets of our physiology we previously didn't even know existed – as well as how fast everyone else is running. But how useful is all this information? And how much of it do we really *need* to know to run as far and as fast (and as fun) as we want to?

Research underpins the fact that we're actually really good at knowing how hard we're working at any given time, without needing to rely on data – you'll find plenty more on this on pages 18–19, when we discuss measuring fitness. Additionally, *really* listening to ourselves – the signals we're getting from our minds and bodies – allows us to maximise each day for training or recovery. Regardless of what your watch is telling you, if you're feeling great, consider going further or harder. If you're not, ease back or perhaps consider taking a rest day.

Legendary ultrarunner Courtney Dauwalter is well known for her intuitive approach to training. As a full-time athlete she has the luxury of having all the time she needs to train, but she'll plan each day's training depending on how she's feeling before she heads through the door and while she's actually out on her run. Her training is high mileage (over 100 miles each week) and incorporates all the essentials – long runs, easy runs, hilly runs, fast runs, rest days and strength and mobility work – but by being flexible about where and how she does each of these things she's able to maximise the effectiveness of each and every aspect of her training. And if it works for Courtney ...

Some people enjoy interacting with data and there's nothing wrong with that, as long as you're aware of the limitations of what you're seeing. Remember that numbers are an *interpretation* of reality, often through a specific corporate lens, and not *actual* reality. Again, more on this later in the book. A good piece of advice to consider in your daily relationship with your wearable tech is that if it makes you feel worse about your run than you did before you looked at it, you're better off leaving it at home.

A note on sex and gender

Throughout this book we refer to the biological *sex* of runners as female and male. While this isn't perfect, and doesn't capture every experience, it allows for helpful exploration and understanding of the distinct physiological differences between the bodies of those who have gone through puberty under the primary influence of female sex hormones, most notably oestrogen and progesterone, and those who have gone through puberty under the primary influence of male sex hormones, most notably testosterone. We embrace *gender* as a far broader term, referring to self-identity.

A quick-start guide to running

Despite the wealth of literature and expert opinions on running – including those drawn on in this book – running really is very simple to start. If you're keen to get going right now, here's what you really need to know – you can peruse the rest of this book at your leisure. Each point (and much more) will be covered in greater detail later on.

1 The three magic ingredients

While this book covers a multitude of different aspects of running, becoming a better runner – the best runner you can be and want to be – boils down to just the following three things:

* **Running well**, which is all about striking that balance between running enough to stimulate the physiological and psychological changes necessary for meaningful improvement, and avoiding injury and burnout.
* **Sleeping well**, which is all about getting an optimal amount of high-quality sleep for recovery and adaptation after training, as well as overall health and well-being.
* **Eating well**, which is all about enjoying a diet that is sustainable (both ethically and personally) and that provides adequate energy and nutrients to support health, training and everything else in life.

2 Play the long game

When you start out running, think about improvements happening over years rather than weeks or months. While some improvements, such as those in cardiovascular fitness, might seem to happen quickly, longer-term physiological and biomechanical adaptations, as well as the knowledge and experience to run at your best, continue to improve over many years. So be patient, and plan to be in this for the long run.

3 You probably don't need a gait analysis

If you're brand new to running, or coming back to it after a long time off, a lot of changes are going to be happening in your body – and therefore your running gait – over the coming months. Your gait will change naturally as you get fitter, stronger and more efficient, so at this point a gait analysis isn't going to tell you much that's of use. If you're a more experienced runner and concerned about your gait, a more holistic approach to training, including strength and mobility work, running drills and trying not to spend hours at a time sitting down will all have far more positive effects on your running gait than attempting to change it based on someone's opinion of what running gait 'should' look like. We're all different, and we all run slightly differently. However, if you're suffering repeated and/or long-lasting pain or injuries, or struggling to find shoes that work for you, it's a good idea to seek expert advice.

4 Comfort is key

Before worrying about the tech specs of your shoes, or the weight of your waterproof jacket, make sure everything you run in, from socks and shoes to hats and sunglasses, fits perfectly and stays comfortable and in place for the duration of your run. If anything you're wearing rubs, pinches or falls off on the go, you'll be less likely to enjoy the experience and less likely to want to do it again.

5 Shoes aren't magic

The basic functions of running shoes are to provide protection and traction for your feet. Humans may not have evolved to wear shoes, but neither did we evolve to run on uniformly hard surfaces such as roads and pavements. Our feet evolved to sink into the earth, and need to do so in order to function effectively. Shoes with some cushioning and some heel–toe drop (see page 176) create an interface between foot and ground that mimics the soft surfaces we did evolve to run on.

Shoes can even make feet better than evolution, adding protection from undesirable encounters with anything from sharp rocks to dog poo, as well as studded outsoles for aggressive grip in muddy, slippery conditions. If you've ever tried to run barefoot over slippery mud, you'll appreciate what a difference this makes. Choose shoes that fit your feet perfectly, with a good thumb-width of space in the toe, and lace them with care so that there are no tight or loose spots anywhere throughout the length of the shoe. When buying running shoes for the first time, go for a model that doesn't over-promise: simplicity is good to begin with – and probably longer-term too – but we'll get on to that later.

6 Start (and finish) slow

Slow running is still running. Walk-running (also known as Jeffing after US Olympic runner Jeff Galloway, who 'invented' the technique) is still running. As long as you're getting what you want from your running, or at least moving in the right direction, you're already a runner. Every run should start and end slow, allowing your body to warm up and cool down properly. Even experienced runners start and finish slow – and if they don't, they should.

7 Be kind to yourself

There's very little doubt in the scientific world that, for most people, running is beneficial for our mental and physical health. But sometimes it doesn't feel that way, and that's an important thing to accept right from the start and resolve to be kind to yourself about. In an ideal world, running would always be fun. Every run would be a blast and we'd love each mile and finish wishing we could carry on forever. But, in reality, getting out for a run can sometimes feel like a monumental struggle in its own right. Sometimes, every mile feels hard-won when brain, body – or both – refuse to co-operate. Sometimes, the training plan starts to look more like a list of things to avoid doing.

Usually, coincidentally, this is the exact moment when everyone on social media chooses to celebrate their massive achievements with #medalmonday photos, screengrabs of epic weekend mileage and, of course, the ability to coordinate all their kit so they look totally amazing while doing so. These are the times to stop comparing and go back to why you wanted to start running in the first place. Plan a run to a favourite cafe; get some conversational miles in with a good friend; or learn some in-the-moment appreciation tips from the dog. These are the times to stop worrying about the training plan, Strava, or what everyone else is doing and just do it for yourself. If you find yourself here, the best plan is to leave your watch behind, switch off your phone and find joy in the simple act of moving – even better if you can do it somewhere scenic.

Our b
Our bod
Our bo
Our b
Our
Ou
O

Our bodies and systems

01

How we run: our bodies and the effects of training

Human running involves a brilliantly complex interaction between our bodies' various systems: our biomechanics, physiology, energetics (the utilisation of the energy we take in via our diet) and our brains. In this chapter we'll provide an overview of these systems, delving into each one individually and then stepping back to take a broader view on how they all fit together.

1: Biomechanics

It's not just our individual bodies that are shaped by running; it would be fair to say that running has been instrumental in shaping us as a species. Our early ancestors took their first steps towards running as we know it today around two million years ago. Researchers have looked at the specific features of our unique skeletons that inextricably link human evolution and distance running. The conclusions? We're remarkably good at endurance exercise and have evolved specific biomechanical and physiological adaptations allowing us to cover long distances on foot (Bramble and Lieberman, 2004).

The energetic cost of human locomotion, i.e. how much energy it takes for us to move at a walk or run, is similar to that of quadrupedal mammals of a similar size to us. That doesn't sound particularly impressive until you stop to consider that we're able to achieve this while only using two limbs, rather than four. And that's a huge advantage, as it allows us to carry food, drink and useful tools such as running poles and navigational devices as we go.

Quadrupeds use their rear legs for propulsion and their front legs for stability and shock absorption. Watch a dog, cat or horse moving at speed and you'll see it using its large, powerful gluteal muscles to power rear legs that act like springs, storing and releasing energy to propel their body ahead of them. Their front legs act like struts, supporting the animal's body weight as it moves over them, leaving the rear legs free to start storing elastic energy again for the next stride. Human legs have to do all of this during every step we take, both absorbing the impact of each foot landing, and then generating forwards propulsion as we push off.

Our amazing feet play a key role in our remarkable bipedal ability. Human feet are different from those of other primates, having lost their opposable 'thumbs' in favour of two arches – the obvious one along the length of the foot and a lesser-known one across the width – which allow us to walk and run upright. These arches act like the leaf-spring suspension in vehicles, deforming to absorb the impact of each foot landing, which, especially during fast and downhill running, can be many times our body weight.

As our body moves over our supporting leg, the small muscles within our feet work to stiffen the joints in the mid and rear part of the foot. This magically transforms the foot from a flexible shock absorber into a rigid lever, which our powerful leg and hip muscles can utilise to move us forwards.

Running isn't just a faster version of walking. Human walking gait has been described as being like an 'inverted pendulum,' our bodies vaulting efficiently – almost effortlessly – over each supporting foot via a series of smooth joint rockers, carried by our own momentum. As we speed up to a run – and start to incorporate an airborne or 'flight' phase into our gait – we use our muscles, tendons, joints and ligaments in an entirely different way, storing and releasing energy like a series of springs. Running is basically bouncing from one foot to the next, facilitated by the storage and release of energy from the elastic structures of our bodies. As well as having a flight phase, running results in a higher cadence (the number of strides taken per minute) and a longer stride length than walking.

Uphill and downhill running

Running up hills increases the amount of energy and oxygen required for forward progress, but it also changes our biomechanics. Even if we still look and feel like we're running, the flight phase of our running gait may disappear altogether on very steep uphill terrain – the 'bounce' that moves us upwards and forwards on the flat is instead absorbed into our movement up the incline.

Steep uphills demand rapid delivery of oxygen to working muscles. For this reason, like running faster intervals, our individual ability to keep running when we're ascending a steep hill is highly dependent upon our level of fitness – our VO_2 max, which we'll go into in more detail on page 18 – as well as other factors such as muscle strength and fatigability.

Should I walk or run up hills?

Many runners, especially those starting out or used to flatter road running, assume they should be running up every hill. But running isn't always the fastest, or the most efficient, way to get to the top. Once the gradient of a hill is steeper than about 15 degrees (27 per cent), walking is more efficient than running.

Most runners, especially in longer runs and races, switch regularly between walking and running on uphill sections, which both decreases the demand for fuel and oxygen to the working muscles and changes the loading patterns, reducing fatigue in specific muscles.

Whether you choose to walk or run a hill in any given situation also depends on more subjective factors, such as whether you're trying to win a race, how tired you're feeling, and how far you've got left to run.

Running up hills is a great way to improve cardiovascular fitness and muscle strength with – as long as the hills aren't too steep – a potentially lower injury risk than downhill or flat running. Interval sessions (see page 221) can be more effective when run on an incline compared with flat terrain, as they require more effort with less impact.

Downhill running, especially when done at speed, often involves an extended flight phase, combined with large impact forces as we land and braking forces as our muscles work hard to slow us down against gravity. Downhills can be a great opportunity to cover ground for relatively little effort; however, they can also increase the risk of injury, both from the increased risk of falling over and from the repeated high forces transmitted throughout the body.

Muscles in running

Muscles are amazing. Using energy from the food we eat and oxygen from the air we breathe, they contract to create movement in our bodies. From the smooth muscle of the heart, gut and blood vessels, which carries out its essential contractions without our conscious input, to the skeletal muscles, which are under our conscious control, muscle and its unique contractile properties keeps every part of us going.

Types of muscle contraction

When we think about muscles and how they work, it's easy to have a Popeye-esque view of each muscle shortening as it contracts to form a noticeable bulge. But in reality, and particularly during dynamic movements such as walking and running, our muscles most often act *eccentrically* – lengthening, rather than shortening, as they contract. In this way, rather than purely generating power, they often work more like a brake, slowing down and controlling the gravity and momentum-assisted motion of our body segments.

The term 'contraction' simply means the tensioning of a muscle, regardless of whether it's shortening, lengthening or staying the same length while doing so. Here's a brief summary of the different types of muscle contractions.

Concentric contractions generate force through the shortening of the muscle – like the biceps muscle during a bicep curl.

Eccentric contractions happen in response to an opposing force, and are generated by elongating muscles – like the quadriceps muscles on the fronts of our thighs during downhill running.

Isometric contractions generate force without changing the length of the muscle – such as when we're holding a child or a heavy box.

Thinking about muscles in this way, it's easy to see why fast, sustained downhill running, where the quadriceps muscles are working hard to control gravity-assisted movement through eccentric contractions, is a classic cause of delayed onset muscle soreness (DOMS) – see page 118.

Muscle recruitment

Muscular control is driven by motor units, which consist of one motor neuron (a movement-specific nerve cell) that stimulates a number of muscle fibres. Muscles consist of a number of motor units, with muscle fibres dispersed and intermingling with fibres from other units. The size principle of muscle contraction states that muscle fibres are recruited in sequence, based on the need for them. Lower demand – e.g. for slower running – recruits fewer muscle fibres, whereas a greater demand – e.g. for faster running – recruits more muscle fibres.

Smaller motor units produce slower-twitch contractions, while larger motor units produce faster-twitch contractions. The stronger and faster the muscle contraction required, the more and therefore larger motor units which are recruited.

Muscle fibre types

Type 1 fibres, or red muscle, are our slow-twitch fibres. They are red due to their large number of capillaries, providing them with a plentiful, oxygen-rich blood supply. These muscles are also home to millions of *mitochondria*, the power houses of our cells, which burn carbohydrate and fat in the presence of oxygen to provide energy for endurance exercise. Athletes with a predominance of type 1 fibres tend to be best at endurance events, as their muscles are able to keep going for long periods of time.

Type 2 fibres, or white muscle, are our fast-twitch fibres. They lack the rich capillary network and therefore blood supply of type 1 fibres and have far fewer mitochondria. They produce short bursts of powerful activity, such as those required for sprinting and heavy weightlifting. Type 2 fibres also opt for an anaerobic bio-chemical pathway of energy production, rather than the aerobic pathways favoured by type 1 fibres – we'll cover the different energy production pathways later (see pages 10–11). Athletes with a predominance of type 2 fibres tend to be good sprinters, but may be less predisposed to longer, slower efforts.

The relative percentage of type 1 and type 2 fibres in our bodies is predominantly genetically determined. However, the type of training we undertake can influence both the type and distribution of our muscle fibres. This is likely to be due to the presence of **type 2a fibres** – intermediate fibres, which are a mixture of red and white fibres and exhibit qualities of both types. These fibres are more adaptable than either type 1 or type 2 fibres and, with specific training, can change into a redder (more aerobic) or whiter (more anaerobic) state, thereby adding to the effective percentage of slow- or fast-twitch fibres an athlete has. It's also thought that while muscle fibres cannot change their type, their function can be subtly changed through specific training to greater resemble the other, enabling them to contribute to performance in their non-specific domain. Regular endurance training therefore both increases the percentage of red fibres compared with white fibres in our adaptable type 2a fibres, as well as improving the efficiency of our existing type 1 fibres, increasing the overall endurance capability of our muscles.

WHAT ARE MITOCHONDRIA?

Mitochondria are tiny, sausage-shaped organelles located deep within our cells that are best known for their role as our cells' powerhouses. They break down food molecules, mix them with oxygen from the air, and turn out adenosine triphosphate (ATP), a molecular fuel that provides energy for the rest of the cell – a process known as the Krebs cycle (see pages 10–11). As well as energy production, mitochondria also carry out many other important biological processes, making them central to the optimal functioning of our cells.

Muscle function in running

When we're running, our calf muscles – the two bulgy heads of *gastrocnemius* on top and the flatter *soleus* underneath – start to fire as soon as our foot makes contact with the ground. The calf muscles' main job here is to slow down the progress of the leg as we move forwards and downwards on to and over our supporting foot. Gastrocnemius, which is a longer muscle than soleus and crosses the knee, also works at this point to prevent the knee joint from hyperextending. At the midpoint of stance, when the body is approximately over the top of the foot, the calf muscles stop firing. The elastic energy they have cleverly stored up during the eccentric 'stretching' contraction is then released as we leave the ground again to generate push off.

In our upper leg, the quadriceps muscle on the front of our thigh eccentrically contracts to slow down the bending of our knee as we absorb the impact of landing; without it our knee would keep bending until it collapsed. The big thigh muscle is also busy storing up elastic energy during this lengthening process, ready to forcefully extend the knee and provide propulsive power during push-off.

At the back of the thigh, our hamstrings work eccentrically to slow down knee extension and to prevent overextension of the knee joint – a thoroughly unpleasant experience if you've ever accidentally done it. They also fire powerfully during propulsion, forcibly pulling our body over our stationary foot as if trying to bend the knee against the resistance of the ground. It's this massive, short-duration force production during propulsion that leads to the hamstring injuries commonly experienced by sprinters.

Moving upwards brings us to the hips and pelvis, important areas for muscular control during running. The pelvis acts as a connection point between the legs below and the body above, providing movement through rotation and tilting, stability and shock absorption, and power generated by the hip flexor and gluteal muscles. These include the mighty gluteus maximus, the largest and heaviest muscle in the human body, which is specialised for our bipedal gait, both keeping us upright and generating power for lower limb function.

THE UNDERAPPRECIATED MUSCLES

While it's often the big players like the calves, quadriceps, hamstrings and gluteus maximus muscles that get all the credit for powering us through a run, without our numerous smaller muscles acting to stabilise, support and protect our moving bodies we wouldn't get far at all. Often overlooked, the piriformis and gluteus medius muscles provide essential stability and protection to the pelvis and hip joints. In particular, the combined action of these two muscles provides protection and strengthening to the femoral neck – a common site of stress fractures in runners and other highly active individuals, as well as the elderly.

Specific exercises aimed at strengthening these muscles (see chapter 19) help to keep this potentially vulnerable part of the skeleton strong and healthy, and the whole pelvic complex working effectively during running.

Good pelvic stability, provided by strong stabilising muscles, affects the direction of forces experienced at other joints including the hip and knee. Lack of strength, mobility and stability in the pelvic girdle – the muscles in and around the pelvis, hips, lower back and lower abdominals – has been implicated in many common overuse injuries experienced by runners. Running-specific strength and mobility work should include a strong focus on the core and pelvic area and, when done well, has the potential to both improve running performance and protect against many common running injuries (see chapter 6).

The upper body in running

During running, the upper body provides rotation and counter-rotation to enable optimal power generation for the lower body. We'll take a deeper dive into running posture and form later (see page 23), but maintaining a good upper body posture allows our bodies to carry out these functions as well as possible. Our heads are heavy, weighing in at an average of five kilograms, so it makes sense that keeping this weight nicely balanced at the top of the spinal column is going to be beneficial for everything that's going on further down – whether we are running, walking or sitting at a desk. Relaxation through the face, shoulders, arms and hands is important in order to avoid pointless energy use – there's no benefit to tightly clenching your fists.

Summary: biomechanics

* Our musculoskeletal system offers protection, support and the production of movement.
* Running gait is substantially different from walking gait, with a distinct, airborne, 'flight' phase (other than in steep uphill running) and a bouncing motion produced by the storage and release of elastic energy.
* While running, our feet act both as flexible shock absorbers (on landing) and rigid levers (on pushing off).
* Skeletal muscles can contract concentrically (shortening), eccentrically (lengthening), or isometrically (staying the same length). In dynamic movement, eccentric contractions predominate, with unaccustomed levels of eccentric loading resulting in muscle damage and DOMS.
* Skeletal muscle fibres can be slow-twitch (type 1), fast-twitch (type 2) or intermediate (type 2a), but some adaptation in either direction is possible with specific training.

2: Physiology

It's fascinating to explore how the musculoskeletal system works so beautifully together to create the efficient, coordinated movement of running. But none of this could happen without the body's complex and highly developed management system: our physiology.

The physiology of living things is based around a single, very important principle. One which guides everything our bodies do in order to keep themselves alive and functioning optimally. The principle of homeostasis.

What is homeostasis?

From the Greek words for 'same' and 'steady', the term *homeostasis* was coined in 1926 by Walter Cannon, an American physiologist. It captures the idea that biological processes, such as those happening all the time in our bodies, require a certain set of conditions in order to function optimally. When all of these conditions are met, we exist in a happy state of equilibrium. But venture far outside these closely regulated parameters and the overall functioning of the organism – in this case us – starts to fail. Ultimately, it is the careful and constant controlling of homeostatic mechanisms that maintains life.

Pretty much everything we do – from eating and drinking (or not eating and drinking), to getting too hot or too cold, to anxiety and sleep deprivation – results in a physical stress. These stresses, and the resulting changes, are monitored by multiple receptors located throughout our bodies. Depending on the effect of the stressor, an action is carried out by or within the body in order to bring the system back to a state of normal, optimal functioning – a state of homeostasis. Detecting and responding to deviations from optimal functioning involves a united response by all of our body's systems.

Exercise places large amounts of stress on our bodies. The more intense the exercise – the harder we work – the greater the disruption in homeostasis. When we go for a run, the following things happen, all controlled by our homeostatic mechanisms:

* Increased oxygen demands from our muscles stimulate an increase in our breathing rate in order to draw in more oxygen from the surrounding environment.
* Increased fuel demands from our muscles stimulate an increase in uptake of glucose from our blood – the resulting decrease in blood glucose in turn stimulates an increase in glucose being released from the liver to restore optimal blood glucose levels.
* Cardiac output increases (the heart pumps more strongly and rapidly) and blood vessels dilate to supply oxygen and fuel to the muscles more quickly.
* Blood is diverted away from areas of the body less critical for exercise, such as the stomach, prioritising oxygen and fuel delivery to the muscles.
* A sudden drop in temperature as we leave the house stimulates a shivering response to raise our body temperature.
* After a mile or so of running, our elevated body temperature stimulates sweating to increase heat loss through evaporative (and other forms of) cooling.
* Increased fluid loss as a result of sweating and increased breathing stimulates a sensation of thirst, telling us to drink in order to restore fluid balance.
* Decreased glycogen stores – the body's way of storing glucose – stimulate a sensation of hunger, telling us to eat.

As well as these obvious signs that our bodies are busy maintaining homeostasis, more subtle but equally essential biochemical balancing equations are going on deep within and around our cells, keeping the pH (acid/alkali balance) and concentrations of sodium, potassium and calcium ions stable. Through our all-day, everyday actions of breathing, eating, drinking, sweating, shivering and excreting, and through the complex action and interaction of our internal systems, we keep our bodies happy and functioning optimally.

A basic understanding of homeostasis is essential for understanding how training (and many other things we do) affects our running performance. Short-term stresses on our bodies, such as a single training session, result in a short-term response. Long-term stresses, such as regular, consistent training, result in long-term adaptations. This process begins during exercise but mostly occurs during the 24 hours afterwards. We'll discuss more on the specific adaptations to exercise throughout the body later in this chapter (see pages 15–17).

Summary: physiology

* Homeostasis is a state in which our biological processes are operating optimally – our bodies constantly aim to keep conditions within an optimal range.
* Stresses – such as heat, cold, high altitude and training – result in disruptions to homeostasis, which the body acts on to normalise as quickly as possible.
* Short-term stressors = short-term responses.
* Long-term stressors = long-term adaptations.

3: Energetics

No amount of running would be possible without the energy our bodies obtain from the food we eat. We'll look further into the fascinating world of sports nutrition and the specific recommendations for a runner's diet in chapter 2, but for the time being let's take a quick, introductory tour of our body's energy systems, the three macronutrients of which all our food is comprised, and how they combine to move, maintain and mend our bodies.

Usually measured in kilocalories (often simply referred to as calories or kcal), all of our energy needs must be met by the food and drink we take in. Exact requirements vary from person to person, depending on factors as various as body weight, sex, climate, age, health and body composition. How active we are and the type of activity we're undertaking have a big effect on our energy requirements. It's also worth noting that our energy requirements remain elevated during recovery from a hard bout of exercise, fuelling the repairing and renewal processes required for improvement.

Regardless of our training status, our diet must provide us with sufficient energy to fuel physical activity (sporting and otherwise), our brain and metabolic functions. In the short term, too high an intake can result in unhelpful, and potentially unhealthy, weight gain, whereas an insufficient intake can result in poor performance, motivation and recovery. Longer term, an imbalance in either direction can have serious negative impacts on our overall health.

How our food fuels our bodies

Energy we take in through food and drink is made up of three macronutrients: carbohydrate, fat and protein, with most foods being a combination of these. Energy from alcohol is treated separately, but still counts as part of our overall energy intake. Macronutrients are broken down during digestion into different subunits, providing energy for metabolism and movement, and the materials essential for growth, development and maintenance of the human body. Once eaten and digested, the energy we take in from our diet is converted into adenosine triphosphate (ATP), the body's energy currency, via a process called the Krebs cycle. ATP is produced in our cells' powerhouses, our mitochondria (see page 6). One of the results of physical training is *mitochondrial biogenesis* – the making of new mitochondria. The more mitochondria we have, the more ATP we can produce, so making sure we include specific types of training that promote this process is a good thing.

HOW IS ATP USED IN OUR BODIES?

Once produced, ATP is used in our bodies to power three energy systems, which are all used in slightly different ways:

The **aerobic system** is responsible for the majority of our energy production for daily life. It is highly flexible, having the ability to utilise all the macronutrients as fuel, and is also by far the most efficient system.

The **anaerobic or lactic acid system** provides rapid energy for intensive activity such as running up a hill, sprinting for the finish line or lifting a heavy weight. It is faster than the aerobic system, but it is less efficient and produces the metabolites responsible for the infamous lactate 'burn'.

The **immediate energy or ATP-PC system** is used for explosive bouts of activity lasting less than 10 seconds. Out running, this might be jumping over a stream or out of the way of a car, but probably wouldn't be the primary energy system for a finishing sprint in a race. The supply of ATP in this system is highly limited, but extremely useful for moments when quick reactions are needed.

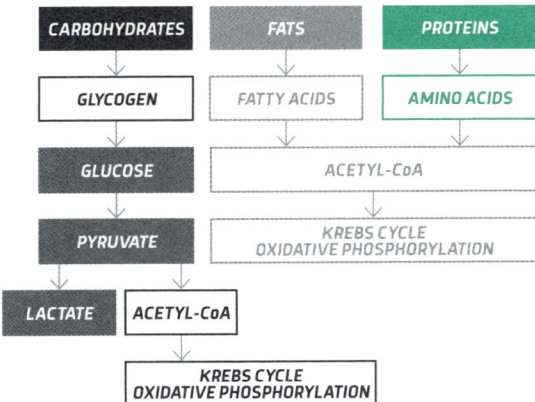

How the three macronutrients are broken down in the body to produce energy.

Our slow-twitch muscle fibres obtain the majority of their energy through the aerobic system, whereas fast-twitch fibres rely more heavily on the ATP-PC system. However, it's important to bear in mind that, while it's easy to imagine our three energy systems as separate entities each with a clearly defined role, in reality they all work together continuously to harmoniously and seamlessly provide energy for all activities, with each one coming to the fore when required as the primary source of energy production while the others continue to work in the background.

Summary: energetics
* Energy from the food we eat is converted into ATP – the body's energy currency – by mitochondria in our muscles.
* We need to consume sufficient food to fuel our training/racing, daily activities and metabolic functions.
* Chronic low energy availability is likely to be detrimental to both health and performance.

4: The brain

From coordinating our movements, learning new skills, and monitoring and regulating many of our internal conditions, to providing us with the motivation to train and race, our brains are integral to everything we do. In fact, rather than considering the body and brain as two separate entities that work together, it's more accurate to view them as entirely integrated and inseparable. It's only through our bodies – through moving and sensing – that our brains, locked away in our skulls, know anything at all. Right from birth, we explore, discover and feel using our bodies, building a picture of our world and our place within it. At the same time, having voluntary control over body movements is the only way we can interact with people, objects and our environment in order to discover things. Our brain-coordinated bodily movement isn't just about us controlling arms and legs during activities such as running, it also enables our head and eyes to visually explore the world, our facial expressions to display emotions and our vocal (or phonatory) system to communicate.

The motor system (the system involved in movement) sits mostly in the frontal lobes of the brain. Premotor areas plan and coordinate movements, while the primary motor cortex sends information down the spinal cord to create contraction and movement of specific muscles. The left motor cortex controls movement on the right side of the body, while the right motor cortex controls movement on the left side of the body. While all this is happening, sensory neurons all over the body send sensory information from the outside world to the brain.

Neuroplasticity is the ability of the brain to establish and strengthen neural pathways, and is how we learn new skills, or improve on existing ones. By repeating actions over and over again through practice or training, the neural connections related to those actions become stronger. The brain connections in our motor system strongly reflect the actions we practise most, so if you want to get better at running downhill, on technical terrain, or simply as smoothly and economically as possible, regular practice is essential. Training isn't just about getting fitter.

Our body-brain connection is also how we experience and regulate our emotions, and how we experience enjoyment, (dis)comfort, pain, fatigue, interactions with others, and even our sense of self and possibility. As well as delivering sensory signals about the outside world to the brain, our body feeds back information about its internal state – a process called *interoception*. Interoception is the communication link between the internal body and the brain, including signals from your internal organs and your cardiovascular system. Interoceptive centres in the brain interpret these signals, using past experiences, context and a host of other factors to inform a response. Interoception is the basis for our emotions, interpreting our bodily sensations and making sense of them in the context of the situation. Tense muscles and a racing heart could, in one context, mean fear, and, in another, excitement. An understanding of interoception is important for runners as it's the basis for the way we 'feel' when we're running. This awareness, and knowing how to manage it optimally, can help everything from race day nerves to mid-run fatigue or long-run fatigue.

Running changes our brains in some intriguing ways, too. In a study (Longman *et al.*, 2023), researchers from Loughborough University looked at the brains of ultrarunners during two 5-day, 250-kilometre ultramarathons. They found that, under conditions of energy deficit, runners improved in tasks relating to navigation and location information, allowing them to more successfully find available food. The runners' reaction times remained the same, while their ability to recall inform-ation about specific events decreased. This demonstrates our evolved ability to prioritise certain cognitive functions according to specifics of our environment and situation, improving our chances of survival.

Summary: the brain

* Our bodies and brains work together inseparably to explore and make sense of the world around us.
* Motor (efferent) neurons carry signals from the brain to our muscles to drive movement, while sensory (afferent) neurons collect sensory information from our environment and deliver it to the brain.
* Neuroplasticity describes our brain's remarkable ability to change its structure and function to optimise both performance and survival.

Bringing it all together – what does training do?

Earlier on, we explored the principle of homeostasis (see page 8) – the body's self-regulating process by which it strives to maintain the internal conditions necessary for survival. Homeostasis not only keeps us alive and functioning optimally, it also forms the basis of all adaptations to regular exercise, both in endurance and strength training.

Short-term stressors lead to short-term responses, while long-term stressors, such as those we exert during regular, long-term training, result in long-term adaptations. This underpins the **progressive overload** principle.

Progressive overload

In simple terms, at a point in time we start off at a specific fitness and performance level and undertake a training session. The stress from this training session results in a short-term decrease in our performance, but, as long as we allow sufficient time for recovery between sessions, our performance will recover, and our fitness will improve. If we keep on applying appropriate stresses and allowing sufficient recovery, our fitness and performance will gradually improve over time.

The progressive overload principle is what we need to use each day to become better runners. Improvements in athletic 'fitness', whether that's muscular strength, running speed or endurance capacity, require a *gradual* and *systematic* increase in training load, alongside sufficient time between training sessions to allow for both *recovery* and *adaptation* to take place.

If you decide to start running and simply apply the same stresses to your body week after week, month after month, you'll see an initial adaptation phase, followed by a plateau. If your training doesn't change, then you won't get any fitter or stronger. Knowing how the progressive overload principle works, and therefore how best to structure your training, means you'll get the most benefits from every session you do.

The *progressive* component of progressive overload means planning your training so that the load, which, for running, is a combination of volume and intensity, gradually increases over time. This creates a stimulus for your body to continue to adapt, rather than simply working within its pre-existing limits. The *overload* part reflects the need for training load to exceed your current physical and physiological capacity by an appropriate amount.

Overloading creates damage, whether that's by creating microscopic tears in your muscle and tendon fibres, increased stress on your heart and lungs, or a metabolic imbalance. During the recovery period after the overloading exercise, the body repairs this damage. These repairs will include reinforcements and adaptations to protect against the same damage occurring again – a process known as *supercompensation*. The result is stronger, more resilient muscle and tendon fibres, and altered homeostatic responses that will be quicker and more effective next time.

While each person's response to overloading exercise will be individual, factors such as age, biological sex, overall health and lifestyle factors will all play a part in how quickly, and by how much, your body is able to adapt. Older runners, for example, may need to leave a little more time between harder sessions as repair processes slow down as we age. Our diet should also support these adaptations, for example by including high-quality protein in order to maximise the repair and adaption of muscle, and sufficient carbohydrate to replenish glycogen stores and support metabolic functions.

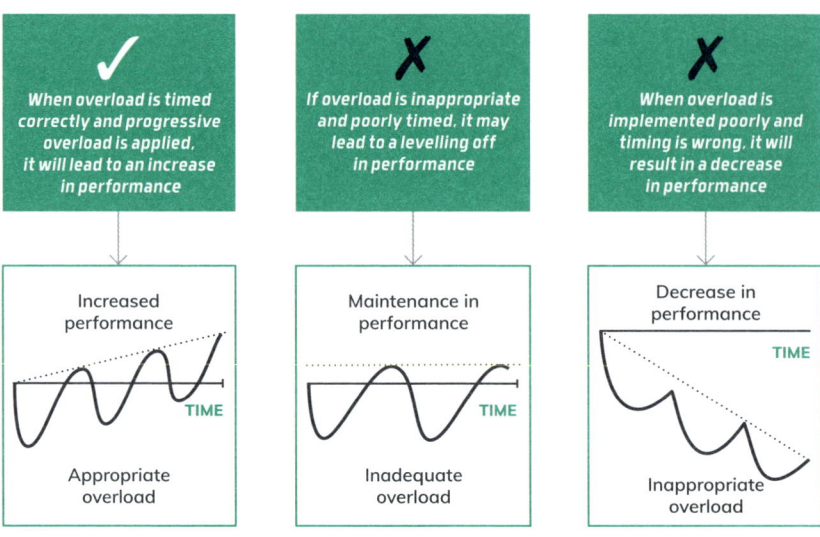

✓	✗	✗
When overload is timed correctly and progressive overload is applied, it will lead to an increase in performance	If overload is inappropriate and poorly timed, it may lead to a levelling off in performance	When overload is implemented poorly and timing is wrong, it will result in a decrease in performance
Increased performance	Maintenance in performance	Decrease in performance
TIME	TIME	TIME
Appropriate overload	Inadequate overload	Inappropriate overload

Progressive overload leading to increased performance, and the impact of inadequate or inappropriate overload.

Top tips for using progressive overload in training

* For progressive overload to be effective, both the rate of progress and the degree of overload have to be appropriate for your body. This means it must be sufficient to stimulate adaptations but without causing injury or excessive fatigue.
* Progressing and overloading too slowly or too little won't create sufficient stimulus for the body to adapt, so you won't see much progress in your fitness, strength or performance.
* Progressing and overloading too rapidly doesn't allow sufficient time for the body to adapt in order to withstand the increased loads, increasing the likelihood of injury, fatigue and an associated lack of progress.
* Increase training load gradually – no more than 10 per cent each week – is a standard rule that appears to work well.
* Increase either the volume (distance or duration) or the intensity of runs each week, not both.
* Allow sufficient time for recovery and adaptation between hard sessions. Some runners may be able to do three hard sessions each week without any issues, while others may only be able to tolerate a maximum of two.
* Progressive overload won't work continuously forever. *Periodising* your training – i.e. having periods of higher and lower training load across the year – and seeing progress and improvement as a long-term project – will give you the best long-term results.

The importance of specificity

Regular training – overloading a system repeatedly in order to facilitate long-term adaptations, and therefore improvements – is highly specific. Doing biceps curls every day for several months will result in adaptations in the structures involved in doing biceps curls, making you better at – you guessed it – biceps curls, but it won't improve cardiovascular fitness or increase leg strength. It sounds obvious, but it's amazing how often runners are told to do exercises that won't in any way improve their running.

One caveat to this is those exercises specifically designed to strengthen and stabilise muscles to improve efficiency and power and reduce the likelihood of injury during long-distance running. Examples include core and pelvic exercises and those to stabilise the ankle, knee and hip joints. While these might not directly improve your running, they may well enable you to sustain higher training loads and more regular running and racing, which will in turn improve your running. You'll find much more on strength, conditioning and mobility for runners in chapter 6.

The specificity principle applies to the intensity, distance and terrain you're training to run on, too. In order to run a faster (or more enjoyable) road marathon, you need to repeatedly stress the specific systems and structures involved in road marathon running, conditioning your body to the relatively high pace, hard but consistent road surface and number of hours' duration that you'll be required to run on race day. This will, over time and to a point, result in a gradual improvement in marathon running ability. To run a mountainous ultramarathon however, you need to train specifically for big ups and downs and long days out on your feet at a slower pace, which marathon training just won't do. While regular, consistent, specific training results in specific adaptations and improvements, it's worth

remembering that the same happens in reverse if you stop training. Removing the stimulus to adapt will return your fitness to pre-training levels – and alarmingly quickly. Use it or lose it as the old saying goes.

How our bodies adapt to training

As well as being specific, adaptations to training are highly individual. We can predict that regular, running-specific training will result in improvements in running, but the speed and magnitude of responses vary widely between people, and even for the same person over the course of life. Bear this in mind before comparing yourself with others, or even comparing yourself with your former self, and strive to be the best runner you can be *right now*.

While the speed and degree of changes varies between individuals, there are a number of general, longer-term, system-wide adaptations that occur with regular endurance training.

Cardiovascular adaptations

Our cardiovascular system circulates blood around the body, delivering oxygen and nutrients to organs and cells and removing waste products. It regulates blood flow according to the body's needs and regulates body temperature by altering blood flow to the skin.

Short-term effects of exercise on the cardiovascular system include:
* heart rate increases;
* cardiac output increases;
* blood pressure increases.

Longer-term effects of exercise on the cardiovascular system include:
* cardiac hypertrophy (enlargement of the heart muscle), which means the heart is able to pump out more blood during each contraction;
* resting heart rate usually decreases.

Pulmonary (lung) adaptations

When we exercise, our breathing rate increases in order to increase both the rate of oxygen extraction from the air for our heart to pump around our bodies to fuel our working muscles, and the rate of carbon dioxide removal from the blood. With training, adaptations occur to improve the efficiency and effectiveness of this process; the precise mechanism by which this occurs is debated.

Research findings suggest that high-intensity endurance training stimulates greater improvements in lung function than low-intensity training, providing another good rationale for including some higher-intensity work in your training plan (Dridi *et al.*, 2021).

Gastrointestinal adaptations

Our digestive system mechanically and chemically breaks down the food we eat, absorbs nutrients and removes waste via the gastrointestinal tract. Exercise speeds up the rate of digestive transit – the food's journey from start to finish – and the rate of absorption of energy, nutrients and fluid from the intestines. Combining regular exercise with a varied, unprocessed diet also improves the body's ability to be flexible in the type of fuel it uses for energy, increasing the percentage of fat used to generate energy at higher intensities, thus allowing carbohydrate stores to last for longer.

Digestive system problems are a common source of discomfort for runners. Longer races, warmer conditions, altitude and rough terrain all add to the likelihood of gastrointestinal problems. Training your gastrointestinal system is just as important as training any other part of your body, so it's essential to practise with the food, drink and, as close as possible, the conditions you'll encounter on race day.

Neuromuscular adaptations

Our muscles support, protect and control many aspects of our bodies. While they're often described as separate entities, skeletal muscles and tendons form muscle–tendon units, which function as a whole, contracting and relaxing to produce and control movement by exerting forces on our bones and around our joints.

Regular training increases the strength, size and specificity of our muscles. In our slow-twitch, red muscles it also increases the number of mitochondria in muscle cells and improves blood supply and therefore oxygen delivery through the formation of new blood vessels. An increase in stored carbohydrate, and in the number of intracellular transporters, which transport glucose from the blood into the muscle cells, also occurs, facilitating more rapid delivery of fuel to working muscles.

Endurance training also improves the muscles' ability to use fat as fuel, increasing fat stored within our muscles, increasing the amount of fat used at higher intensities, and sparing intracellular carbohydrate stores.

Adaptations that occur in response to endurance exercise decrease our reliance on less efficient energy production, increase our reliance on more efficient energy production and make our muscles more resistant to fatigue.

Skeletal adaptations

Our bones offer structure and protection to the soft parts of our bodies. Joints – the meeting points of bones – act as pivot points around which bones are moved by our muscles and tendons. Bone is a dynamic tissue, which is in a constant cycle of breakdown and formation. The specific stresses placed upon our bones cause them to remodel in such a way as to accommodate these stresses best.

The long bones in our legs such as the femur (thigh bone) and tibia (shin bone) are highly adapted to withstand compressive forces, which we exert upon them every day through walking, running and jumping. This, combined with their cylindrical shape, means they're far less able to withstand bending forces, however. Exerting forces on bones in a direction they have not adapted to withstand, continually stressing bone without allowing sufficient recovery time for adaptations to occur, or failing to meet energy – and in particular carbohydrate – requirements needed for bone adaptation, can all lead to bone injury. These range from stress reactions in the bone to stress fractures and larger fractures.

Integumentary/exocrine system adaptations

The integumentary system comprises our skin, hair, and nails, along with our exocrine glands. These are glands that release substances through a duct or opening to the body's surface, including sweat glands, tear ducts and digestive glands. Regular endurance training particularly affects our sweat response, stimulating earlier onset and higher rates of sweating, and therefore more effective cooling.

Immune function adaptations

Our immune system defends us against pathogens that may harm the body. Regular exercise, optimal sleep and recovery, and a healthy diet have all been shown to support immune health; however, heavy training, particularly in the absence of optimal sleep, recovery and diet, can negatively impact immune function. Our immune system is typically depressed for a few days after a hard race or training session, so particular attention should be paid to staying away from potential sources of viral infections during this time if possible.

Body composition adaptations

Everyone's predisposition to a certain body composition – the proportion of overall body mass made up by fat and lean tissue – is individual, and determined by factors such as our genes and physical history. But we can also have a large effect on our body composition through our diet and the type and amount of physical activity we undertake. With regular, consistent training supported by an optimal diet, body composition will shift towards a higher proportion of lean mass.

Summary: training adaptations

* Our body systems react to stresses such as heat, cold and physical exertion in order to maintain optimal functioning, a process called homeostasis.
* Short-term stress results in short-term reactions; long-term stress results in long-term adaptations.
* Adaptations are specific to the stresses placed upon them, so training for an event should mirror the specific demands of that event.
* Long-term appropriate training, in combination with a healthy lifestyle, has numerous, measurable beneficial effects throughout the body.

Measuring fitness: physiological thresholds and capacities

During lab-based exercise testing, physiologists set specific, measurable thresholds that can be assessed at various time points throughout a block of training in order to establish the starting point, progress and race-readiness of an athlete. Where your individual thresholds lie determines much of your performance capability, both currently and in the future. They are also what allows you to divide training intensity up into different zones.

While there are numerous different thresholds and numerous different names even for the same threshold, in practice, the main three – **VO₂ max**, **lactate threshold** and **critical speed** – provide all the information we need for effective training.

These three distinct thresholds can also be 'felt' during a run, meaning they require the least amount of measuring, analysis or interpretation. Through consistent and specific training, all three thresholds can be increased which, whether or not we ever actually have them measured in a lab, is an excellent sign that our training is progressing as it should be.

VO₂ max

A person's VO₂ max is a measure of cardiovascular fitness. It represents their maximal or peak oxygen uptake, either as an absolute value in litres of oxygen per minute, or as a relative value in millilitres of oxygen per kilogram of body weight per minute. The latter value is most useful for sports such as endurance running and cycling, where power-to-weight ratio is important. VO₂ max is the variable most commonly used to understand current and potential levels of performance.

VO₂ max in runners is measured using a 'ramp test', which is usually undertaken on a treadmill with the runner wearing a mask to collect and measure inhaled and expired gasses. The treadmill speed, and therefore exercise intensity, is gradually increased,

and oxygen usage steadily increases in response. At some point, oxygen use plateaus, and this is the point at which the body is unable to use any more oxygen, even if exercise intensity increases. Shortly after this point, runners either hit the stop button on the treadmill or fly off the back!

Average VO₂ max values for young, sedentary males are around 45ml/kg/min, while values for highly trained male athletes may exceed 70ml/kg/min. Females tend to have a VO₂ max that is 8–10 per cent lower than males.

Genetic factors determine a person's initial VO₂ max value, which varies widely between individuals, along with their ability to increase this value through training. With appropriate training and a genetic propensity for training adaptations, VO₂ max values can be increased by up to 50 per cent. Age also has a notable impact, with VO₂ max decreasing by around 10 per cent each decade after the age of 35.

Maximising your available VO₂ max is worthwhile, even if you're an ultramarathon runner who rarely exceeds 60 per cent of that maximum in training or racing. The higher your VO₂ max is, the faster and more economical 60 per cent of that maximum is.

Reaching, or getting close to, your VO₂ max while running feels like you're pushing as hard as you can at a pace you can hold for between six and ten minutes. You should be breathing hard and only able to talk in single words.

Lactate threshold

Lactate is a normal by-product of muscle cell metabolism that has, in the past, been demonised for everything from the 'burn' felt during hard running to soreness the day after a big race. In reality, lactate is a useful source of energy for many organs, including our hearts and brains.

It's important to note that, during intense exercise, the inevitable rise in blood lactate is due to physiological processes which lead to muscle pain and fatigue, rather than the lactate being the *cause* of pain and fatigue. Once exercise intensity is reduced, any accumulated lactate rapidly disperses – massage does not speed up this process.

During gentle exercise, the lactate produced by the muscles is resynthesised by the body, so blood lactate levels don't rise. During more intense exercise, when we can no longer resynthesise the lactate produced during exercise as fast as it is being produced, blood lactate levels begin to rise. The point at which lactate levels start to accumulate rapidly is referred to as our *lactate threshold*. This is also the point at which our muscles switch from using predominantly fat for fuel to predominantly carbohydrate for fuel. A lactate threshold test measures the muscles' metabolic ability, i.e. how well the muscles are able to use the oxygen delivered to them.

You don't need a lab to be able to put this into practice – lactate threshold occurs at around the point when we transition from easy to comfortably hard running. This can be assessed while running through the simple 'talk test' – the point at which you go from being able to comfortably hold a conversation to only being able to get through a single sentence at a time before needing another breath. Tempo runs are great for improving lactate threshold – see page 224.

Critical speed

Critical speed lies somewhere between our lactate threshold and our VO$_2$ max. It occurs at around 80–85 per cent of VO$_2$ max and is the point at which running begins to feel unsustainable, due to the physiological changes that occur at this point. In his book, *Scientific Training for Endurance Athletes*, exercise physiologist Philip Skiba describes critical speed (or critical power if you're cycling) as 'the threshold between what you can do for a long time and what causes predictable fatigue'. Most people can continue at critical speed for 20–40 minutes, or between 5K and 10K race pace.

Critical speed can be easily gauged by 'feel' during training – the point at which you know your time at that intensity starts to become severely limited – and improvements can be measured through 5K or 10K time trials or test races. When your weekly parkrun time improves, it's probably in large part due to improvements in your critical speed.

Do I need lab-based measurements?

While the measurement of thresholds, limits and other physical capacities is interesting for sport scientists and anyone interested in the physiology going on in the background while we're training at different intensities, how much the exact values actually matter for the vast majority of recreational athletes is debatable.

When it comes to measurements, it's always worth remembering the McNamara fallacy, which reminds us that not everything that can be measured matters, and not everything that matters can be measured.

Where these thresholds do come in useful, however, is in determining the intensity levels at which we should train in order to optimise fitness and performance gains. But these can be fairly accurately determined by feel, so you don't need to book yourself in for physiological testing. We'll come back to this when we discuss planning your training in chapter 4.

Fatigue

When it comes to endurance performance – whether it's the kind of endurance you need to get through a Sunday long run, a multi-day ultramarathon or writing a 100,000-word book – keeping going is all about winning the battle against fatigue. As Alex Hutchinson, author of *Endure: Mind, Body and the Curiously Elastic Limits of Human Performance*, puts it, 'the struggle to continue against a mounting desire to stop'. Hutchinson actually attributes this quotation to professor of sport science, Samuele Marcora, who developed the psychobiological model of fatigue (see below).

We're all familiar with the sensation of fatigue – those dragging, hyper-gravity moments when all you want to do is slow down or stop. It seems obvious that running a long way can elicit this feeling, but how about mental fatigue from sitting through a long and complicated lecture; emotional fatigue from difficult life events; or the kind of fatigue you get after a long day's travelling even if you've only walked a few steps? While the sensation is similar – predominantly a mounting desire for it all to stop – the causes are vastly different, and the mechanism is still poorly understood.

Fatigue we experience during endurance exercise can be divided into three distinct types (Marcora and Staiano, 2010):

* Muscle fatigue, which is defined as an exercise-induced impairment in muscle performance, measured by a reduction in the force or power our muscles are able to produce.
* A progressive increase in our perception of effort during endurance exercise – i.e. how hard it feels.
* Exhaustion or task failure, when we are simply unable to produce the speed or power required to continue.

THE PSYCHOBIOLOGICAL MODEL OF FATIGUE

Developed by Samuele Marcora and others (Marcora and Staiano, 2010; McCormick *et al.*, 2015), this model aims to explain why our perception of effort increases over time, and how this interacts with various motivational factors to determine how long we can maintain a given speed.

Utilising the psychobiological model of fatigue, to effectively reduce our sensation of fatigue – suppressing that mounting desire to stop – requires both reducing our perception of effort and having strong motivating influences.

This starts before a race, by keeping psychological stressors as low as possible through careful planning, and not obsessing over last-minute issues like poor sleep the night before the race. Careful race selection is really important too – choose races and/or causes that you really care about, enough that when the going gets really tough you'll still have the motivation to continue. There is more on the principle of 'knowing your why' later in the book (see pages 133–134).

Other ways of reducing our perception of exertion include eating, taking in caffeine, putting on some energising music, smiling, positive self-talk, cheerful supporters, or even, on really long races, taking a trail nap. Sometimes you just need to hang on in there and hope that either the feeling passes, or you reach the finishing line quickly.

It's also important to understand and accept your normal circadian rhythms, which aren't going to take a day off just because you have a big race planned. Running a long way is, of course, going to elicit feelings of fatigue in its own right, but if you're running all day (and even all night) there will be times when you would naturally feel fatigued even if you weren't running. While highs and lows in energy vary between individuals, classic struggle times are the post-lunch afternoon slump and the 3 a.m. sleep monsters, both of which are mediated by natural fluctuations in hormone levels that make us feel sleepy. There's no reason for this not to happen when you're running, or when circumstances dictate that you need to do your run or race at a time of day when your mind and body would far rather be tucked up in bed.

If you know you'll be running during a time of day that's usually suboptimal for you from an energy and enthusiasm perspective, have some interventions planned to combat them. Perhaps a favourite trail snack, an audiobook or podcast you've been looking forward to, or some strategically positioned fans. It's also well worth mixing up your training times so you get used to running at odd times of the day. If you enjoy running first thing in the morning, and that's when you run at your best, it's easy to only ever run first thing in the morning. But if your race starts in the afternoon – or is long enough to take you through an entire day – practising beforehand will help you feel more confident on the day. Running home from work, when you're fatigued from a day in the office and the last thing you want to do is run, is fantastic mental training that will pay dividends on race day.

Top tips for fighting fatigue

* Regular or chronic fatigue can be a good sign you need to slow down, take a rest day or look at your sleep and/or nutrition.
* Fatigue in long races is inevitable but often simple to deal with. As soon as you spot the signs – slowing down, low mood, irritability, sleepiness – step in with a snack, caffeine or some motivating music or a podcast. Practise in training so you know what works for you.
* Expect to feel more fatigued at certain times of the day – often mid-afternoon – and either accept this or pre-emptively deal with it.
* We all feel fatigued on a fairly regular basis – learn what helps your specific personality and situation. Sometimes a run after a stressful day at work can be the perfect fatigue fighter; at other times you might be better off having a quiet night in.

Form and technique

Scan any list of running books, flick through magazines or listen to the latest running technique guru and you'll discover a wealth of conflicting advice on running form and technique, often selling a quick fix for injured or underperforming runners. While maintaining good posture is undoubtedly important in running, as it is in walking, standing and sitting, there is no one specific running technique that will make you a faster, more efficient, less injured runner.

While for a very small number of people, changes in running gait may help reduce specific forces that can lead to injury, for most people, changing how you run via any method other than regular, consistent, long-term training is likely to be counterproductive. It's easy to look at elite runners and assume that their prowess is due to their perfect running form, but like any other perfected art it's actually the result of thousands of hours of practising running. Good running form is important to think about, but it is a product of, rather than a precursor to, good training.

Our running form is as unique as everything else about us; it is a result of many things, including our biomechanics, our physiology and our physical history. It changes as we become more experienced at running, as our bodies adapt to the many and various stimuli of regular training, and as we age. Research has found over and over again that our bodies are incredibly good at finding the most economical way for us to run.

We often hear that adopting the form of the world's best runners is a good way to improve our own running. In reality, adopting their approach to training and lifestyle would bring us far greater benefits. Years of high-quality training and avoiding spending hours each day sitting at a desk are exactly the reason the best runners run as they do – it is these things we need to try to incorporate into our lives, rather than attempting to superimpose another body's style of running on to our own. Watch the elite runners in a marathon and you'll see a vast range of different running forms, as each body gets itself from start to finish in the fastest and yet most economical way possible. Each runner has spent years evolving a running style that works brilliantly for them and no one else.

Footstrike

An integral part of running form, footstrike is another area that's seen more than its fair share of attention over the past decade or so, both in the media and research literature. Thankfully, we're moving away from the advice for everyone to artificially adopt a forefoot strike, but there are still many mixed messages out there. As is so often the case, our bodies and brains are fantastically complicated and highly adapted, able to make judgements, decisions and continuous micro-adjustments to our gait. Like so many other unconscious processes, these have evolved over millennia of crossing the earth's terrain on foot, and therefore exist to enable us to navigate the line between being as efficient – and as safe – as possible. Like so many other unconscious processes, we get into trouble when we underestimate just how good our interconnected brains and bodies are at looking after us, and try to interfere.

It's a fact of biomechanics that the faster we run, the further forwards on our foot we need to strike the ground. Being on our toes locks the joints at the midfoot, creating a more rigid foot. This allows us to maximise the mechanical leverage of the full length of our foot, combined with the full stretch and recoil of the muscle–tendon units in our legs. When we need to sprint, we prioritise speed and power over economy and injury prevention. If you've ever run away from something as fast as you possibly can (usually cows in my experience) you might recall that whole-body tension that results from a massive surge of adrenaline. If you'd had time to look at your feet, you might have noticed that one of the first things you did is get right up on your toes to run.

Another time we naturally adopt a forefoot strike is on very technical terrain, when foot stiffness and precision is important for injury prevention. A forefoot strike allows for more precise foot placements, making it less likely that we'll trip over and hurt ourselves.

When we know we need to run a long way, we self-select a slower pace, our bodies prioritising energy conservation, economy and injury prevention. Walking is the ultimate economical pace, using the rolling motion of our rounded heels and the balls of our feet to progress forwards with as little energy requirement as possible. As we progress to a slow run, continuing to utilise these natural rockers in our feet makes sense. It's true that modern running shoes with a built-up heel can make our heelstrike even more pronounced, as the heel of the shoe makes contact with the ground fractionally before a naked heel would do. But running barefoot on soft, uneven ground would result in a similar foot position to running in a cushioned shoe on a flat surface.

Interestingly, when we run on a hard surface barefoot, we initially adopt a forefoot strike, which allows for greater precision as our bodies work out and adapt to the new stresses being applied to our bodies. This response is sometimes provided as a rationale for runners to adopt a further-forwards foot-strike – it's what we do barefoot so it must be our natural gait, right? But over time, even barefoot runners running on hard surfaces will begin to strike further back on their foot, as their bodies become accustomed to the new surface. Running slowly on soft, even ground, whether we're shod or not, most of us will naturally adopt a heelstrike.

Next time you're out for a run, particularly if it's an off-road one with hazards from rooty singletrack to savage dogs (or cows), try 'listening' to your feet, allowing them to do what they naturally do and simply taking note. Or watch how kids use their feet as they run about: tiptoeing when they want to be quiet; using the forefoot for maximum control and precision; using a rear- or midfoot strike for general running about; and then switching back to the forefoot when they want to run away at top speed. Rather than telling your feet what to do, notice how they adapt, self-selecting the footstrike that's optimal for each individual step with all its multitude of specific variations.

Top tips: running form

* Good posture is important for healthy and optimal function of our musculoskeletal system, whether we're walking, running or sitting.
* There's no single form or technique that works for every runner.
* Try to stay relaxed through your upper body, especially the jaw, shoulders, arms and hands. Tensing these muscles while running is common but an unnecessary use of energy.
* 'Perfect' form is the result of many years of good training and a healthy lifestyle. To improve your running emulate the training and healthy lifestyle of top athletes, rather than their technique.
* Don't get hung up on footstrike. Your body will naturally change which part of the foot you land on depending on a multitude of factors. Training on a variety of surfaces and at varying speeds will help you stay flexible, adaptable and injury-free far more effectively than trying to force your body to land in a specific way each time.

Running techniques for different scenarios

While the simple act of well-structured training, week after week, month after month and year after year, will stimulate the body-wide adaptations that enable you to run in the way that's most efficient for you, there are times when adopting and practising specific techniques can help you to run more effectively, especially during races. Learning techniques for running up and down steep hills and on technical terrain, and then practising and perfecting these in training, will help you to become a stronger, faster and less injured runner, wherever your running takes you.

Running uphill and downhill

Hills – runners either love them or they hate them. But, either way, knowing how to approach training and racing on hills is going to make you better and more confident when you come to run them.

Top tips for running uphill
Don't think (or look) too far ahead
A long hill – especially the kind you'll find in the bigger mountain ranges, which can go on for two hours or more – can feel daunting. One approach is to break the climb up into smaller 'chunks' – look ahead to the next rock or tree, the next plateau, or even the next time you have to stop to catch your breath and simply keep going to that point. Then choose the next goal. Don't look ahead to the next segment until you've finished the one you are on. Another approach is simply to 'be' in the climb, focusing on each step and each moment as you go. Worrying about how long it's going to take to get to the top, or whether your legs have what it takes to get there, is pointless. Simply take it one step at a time and reaching the summit will take care of itself.

Use your arms
Your arms can be surprisingly helpful when it comes to steeper climbs. If you're confident using poles for running, these can be used for digging into the slope ahead of you and pulling yourself up and/or to push yourself forwards by anchoring your poles behind you. You'll find more on choosing and using running poles on pages 183–184. If you're not using poles, placing your hands on your thighs allows you to push down with each step, adding bracing and even a little power to the knees and large quadriceps muscles. Driving with your arms when running up steep hills can also help keep momentum going, and counteract the rotational forces happening in your lower body.

Vary your stride length
On steep but even terrain, try shortening your strides. Taking shorter strides helps to keep your momentum moving upwards and forwards, whereas longer strides result in having to lift your weight in an arc over your planted foot. Shorter strides also allow you to utilise the storage and release of elastic energy in your soft tissues, which act like springs. When the terrain is rocky or stepped, however, taking longer strides will allow you to find the best foot placements. Practise both approaches in training, so you can call on whichever technique works best for the stretch of hill you're on.

Look ahead
Try not to focus on your feet when you're running uphill. Keep looking ahead and lean slightly into the hill, maintaining balance and engaging your quadriceps and gluteal muscles most effectively. Hunching over also makes it harder to fully fill your lungs with air – something that really helps when you're working hard. If you're wearing a pack on a long climb, loosening the chest straps so they're not restrictive also helps.

It's OK to walk

When you're climbing steeper hills, mixing running with walking – or even walking (also called 'power hiking' in ultrarunning circles) the whole thing – can often be far more efficient than trying to run it all (see page 4). Listen to your body and pay attention to its cues for when to walk and when to run. This will enable you to more effectively cross very technical sections by slowing down, maximise your pace on slightly easier terrain, and vary the stresses on your muscles as you go.

Top tips for running downhill
Do it regularly, but not too much

Running downhill is a skill that demands quick reactions, agility, strength and a little bit of crazy. By running hills regularly, you'll gradually build up your comfort and confidence on the downhills. But downhill running also brings with it a greater risk of injury – both from the increased repetitive forces your body must withstand from gravity-assisted descents and from the risk of falling over or twisting an ankle, especially on technical terrain. Make time on your training runs to practise downhills, starting out on gradual, smooth descents and building up your confidence and speed, then moving on to steeper gradients and rougher terrain. As well as helping to improve your technique, this graduated approach helps manage the fear and anxiety many runners feel about fast, tricky descents. But don't overdo downhill running, especially the harder, faster kind. A little downhill running goes a long way, so practise it deliberately, but not too much.

Don't look down!

It's tempting to fixate on your feet when running downhill, but this can actually make you more likely to slow down, stumble and trip over what's immediately in front of you. Instead, try to look a few metres ahead, so you can plan your next foot placements before you hit them. As you become more confident and adept at running downhill, you'll find you can look further ahead, and the whole process feels more like a flowing,

natural movement. You'll have more time to make decisions on both foot placement and route choice, both of which are essential for fast, safe and enjoyable descending.

Build stronger legs

Regular strength training, including specific exercises designed to strengthen and stabilise your legs for the demands of downhill running, is hugely beneficial. Plyometric exercises, such as squat jumps and dynamic lunges, and those that directly mirror the actions of climbing and descending, such as step-ups and step-downs, can be done in the privacy of your own home, or in the gym if you prefer, ready to take out on to the hills. There are some good leg strengthening exercises on pages 231–233.

You'll also probably find you have a preference for landing on one leg over the other – try practising landing on your non-dominant leg, so you're happy with stepping down on to either. And don't forget your core and pelvic stability work, as all these muscles play important roles in controlling and stabilising movement in both uphill and downhill running.

Use your arms

Watch elite fell and mountain runners descending, and you'll see they use their arms to balance and control their movement as they go. It can look a little like flailing, or windmilling, but give it a try – it's surprisingly effective at keeping you balanced during this highly dynamic and rapidly changing movement. Try to stay relaxed and let your arms move in a way that 'feels' right, rather than attempting to do the 'right' thing.

Choose your route

Especially when you're not following pre-made trails, route choice can make a big difference to your speed and safety downhill. The most direct line down a hill may not always be the fastest, so choose your route carefully. Avoiding rocky or other particularly technical terrain in favour of a more runnable but longer alternative route can be quicker and more efficient. Practising running on unfamiliar hills is a great way to improve your ability to spot the best line and react on the go. If you are preparing for a race that includes tricky downhill sections, try to recce these in advance so you can take the best lines on race day.

Running on varying terrain

Even when you're not on hilly ground, technical, varying terrain can slow you down if you're not used to it. But running regularly on different types of terrain during training has many benefits, including varying the stresses experienced by your body, building strength and agility, and learning to be flexible and adaptable, whatever your run throws at you.

Top tips for running on variable terrain
Mud

If your route is going to be muddy, choose shoes with deep, widely spaced tread for the best grip. Take short, fast steps so that if you do slip, you're already on to the next step rather than sliding along on one foot. On any slippery terrain, keeping your weight forwards on your foot will give you the best grip. It can be tempting to lean back, especially running downhill on slippery ground, but you'll very quickly find yourself sitting down.

Rocks and boulders

Running fast through rocky terrain is all about being reactive and adaptable. You'll be changing direction rapidly and often, landing on surfaces at different angles, and potentially on rocks that move as you land on them. Try to stay light and agile, picking your line as carefully as you can while not overthinking any single move. If a rock moves when you land on it, rather than panicking and coming to a halt – when you'll almost certainly fall over – try to absorb the movement into your step and carry on to the next one. Good exercises to train for running on rocky terrain include dynamic lunges, especially round-the-clock lunges (see page 232), drills (see right) and simply spending more time on rough ground, building your speed up as you gain confidence.

Long or tussocky grass

Keep your knee-lift high to reduce drag when running through long grass. Be aware of ankle-twisting dangers, such as rocks and holes, lurking out of sight.

Ice and snow

Choose shoes with metal studs, or wear nano-spikes or microspikes (see page 180) over your shoes for the best grip. Take short, fast strides to reduce propulsive forces and help you catch yourself quickly if you do start to slide.

Running drills

Drills are great for improving your ability to run over all kinds of terrain, as well as improving muscle recruitment, strength and the ability to store and return energy. Do them after an easy couple of miles' warm-up on a soft but not slippery surface – short grass or an athletics track are ideal.

* **Skipping:** remember when you were a kid and you skipped along instead of walking? Recreate that movement, taking powerful strides and using your arms for balance and drive. This is one of the most underrated non-running, running-specific exercises there is, combining everything: power, muscle recruitment, balance, eccentric loading and fun all in one perfect, plyometric package.
* **Side skipping:** skip sideways, stepping your legs first apart, and then together again. Be sure you go in both directions.
* **Bounding:** run using exaggerated strides, powering off each stride and landing in a controlled way. Again, use your arms for balance and momentum.
* **Fast feet:** take very short, fast steps – great for increasing leg turnover and improving muscle recruitment.
* **Hopscotch:** you don't need to draw out the boxes, but playing around with the classic single-foot, double-foot hop/jump movements is great for agility. This is a great one to do on pavements, avoiding the cracks.

What makes a great runner?

Many runners seem to be constantly striving to get that elusive edge. To find the magic session, wearable device, supplement or shoe that will propel them to the very best of their ability, and ideally beyond that of their competitors. In reality, being the best runner you can be is all about training well and consistently, and supporting this training with a healthy diet, good quality sleep, rest and recovery days, and good mental health. It sounds so simple but, in the real world of relationships, jobs, illness and injury, it's rarely easy.

Away from those of us who juggle running with everything else in a busy life, elite runners pushing the boundaries of human performance provide a perfect opportunity for scientists to identify the key attributes that come together to make a really great runner.

On 12 October 2019 in Vienna, Austria, Eliud Kipchoge and the INEOS team made history by breaking the two-hour marathon, crossing the line in 1:59:40.2. Aged 34 at the time, Kenyan runner Kipchoge was the 2016 Olympic marathon gold medalist and went on to win the 2020 Olympic marathon. He also set the world record for an 'official' marathon (which the INEOS 1:59 project did not count as) of 2:01:09 at the 2022 Berlin Marathon.

When it came down to the very best candidates for breaking two hours for the marathon distance, all were from eastern African countries. The dominance of great runners from this region of the world is likely to be due to a combination of genetics, an active lifestyle from early childhood onwards, living and training at altitude, the ability to develop superb running economy based on body biomechanics, optimal skeletal muscle fibre composition, a traditional plant-based diet that is low in ultra-processed foods and alcohol, distance running culture and infrastructure, and economic motivation.

While we may not all have the perfect blend of all the factors required, or the time to devote to training, in order to run at our best, knowing how to make the most of what we've got is a powerful tool. Here are some of the lessons learned from INEOS 1:59 that we can all adapt to improve our running.

Training volume

Most elite distance runners run between 100 and 120 miles per week. Few train much less or much more than this, suggesting this is the mileage that, for the best runners at least, manages to tread the line between maximising performance benefits and minimising the risk of injury, illness or burnout. There's lots of very good evidence to suggest that higher weekly mileage is associated with all three, so it's a line we all need to tread carefully.

Training intensity

Kipchoge is quoted as having said he rarely exceeds 80 per cent of maximum effort in training, saving his hardest runs for race day. However, it's also well documented that Kenyan runners incorporate lots of running drills, interval sessions and hard, hilly running into their regular training. They're also known for gradual warm-ups and knowing the value of good quality rest and recovery.

Experience

Research shows that, up to marathon distance, elite running performance peaks at around the age of 28. So why did the INEOS performance team choose a runner well into his 30s, and how is Kipchoge still smashing records even now he's approaching 40? The wealth of experience he's gained along the way may well be the answer. More experienced runners know their bodies, improving their ability to pace longer races well. They've had time to develop psychological strategies to combat stress, doubt and fatigue. Perhaps there's also a sense of urgency present in older runners, knowing their opportunity to perform at their very best may soon come to an end; knowing they have less to lose by pushing themselves harder than those earlier on in their careers.

Running and health – is running good for us?

It seems intuitive that running is good for our physical and mental health. But the reality – as is so often the way with human beings – is a little more complicated.

Mental health and well-being

If you're someone who already runs regularly, you're probably no stranger to the feelings of life-affirming joy that running can produce. It's why most of us do it. As busy, self-employed parents we both know we'll be happier, nicer, more patient and more productive for the rest of the day if we've started it with a run. No matter how hard it might feel to get through the door in the first place, barring injury, illness or some other misadventure along the way, we're always glad we made the effort. There's a lot of truth in the saying that no one ever regretted a run. Running is a great way to meet and spend time with like-minded people, or to escape and destress after a busy day at work, or to zone out to music or a good audiobook. Best of all, running is endlessly flexible and customisable to fit around our busy lives and to undertake at whatever level we want.

Regular physical activity, especially when done outdoors, does appear to be overwhelmingly beneficial from a psychological point of view – those who participate regularly are less likely to suffer from depression and anxiety and more likely to report a better quality of life.

But there's a dark side to this, too. What about when we can't run? When we don't perform well or even fail to finish a race? When illness, injury, family commitments or work gets in the way? When not being able to run isolates us from our social groups? It's really good for us, as humans, to have a passion. But, like any passion, it's possible to become too dependent on running – to miss out on life's other joys for the sake of running, or to measure our self-worth by how far, fast or frequently we run. It's a difficult balance, and there's no single right way for everyone. But if you're someone who makes a habit of turning down other opportunities because they might negatively affect your running, it's well worth bearing in mind.

There's also far less evidence on the benefits of running for people with certain existing mental health problems. Particularly those for whom undertaking physical activity isn't straightforward for social, cultural, physical health or other reasons, exercise isn't necessarily the quick fix it's sometimes touted to be. As passionate runners it's all too easy to extol the virtues of our favourite pastime to everyone we meet, but it's certainly not an answer to all of life's challenges.

Physical health

When it comes to the more easily measured physical benefits of running, there's a lot more data available. There's overwhelming evidence that regular physical activity of any kind is hugely beneficial to our health. Starting with large-scale epidemiological studies in the 1980s, backed up by lab-based physiological research, the 1990s saw a firm stance taken by government health advisors advocating for an active lifestyle. Today, we know that because of the adaptations that take place with regular training, exercise not only reduces our risk of cardiovascular disease, but also provides direct cardiovascular protection (Li *et al.*, 2020).

How about running specifically? Longitudinal cohort studies follow a large number of regular runners for many years, comparing numerous health-related variables with similar groups of non-runners. A review of several of these types of studies found that runners have a 30–45 per cent lower risk of dying from any cause than non-runners, including up to a 70 per cent lower risk of dying from cardiovascular disease and up to 50 per cent for cancer (Lee *et al.*, 2017). The researchers also found running to be protective against neurological conditions, such as Alzheimer's and Parkinson's diseases, metabolic disorders like diabetes, and respiratory infections. Long-term runners see the greatest health benefits, adding, on average, 3.2 years to their life expectancy.

Too much of a good thing?

That all sounds like good news for regular runners, but how much running is enough – and how much is too much?

Purely from a health point of view, the sweet spot for running seems to fall between one and three hours per week – less than an hour is better by far than no exercise but doesn't maximise running's benefits. For many runners, three hours of running each week works well, but how about those who are keen to do more? Research also suggests that, particularly when it

comes to heart health, there may be an upper limit to the recommended amount of running, beyond which these benefits may either disappear or even turn into higher risks (Lee *et al.*, 2017). Recommended upper limits for running range from 30 to 60 miles (50 to 100 kilometres) per week across different studies, but the researchers all acknowledge the lack of available evidence to support these numbers.

Many athletes, including elite distance runners, average over 100 miles (160 kilometres) of running per week for years, seemingly without harm, so there's certainly plenty of room for interpretation. The likelihood is that differences in health and running history, genetics, the ability to rest and recover between runs, and running environment all strongly influence how much running an individual can safely tolerate, but it's well worth considering how much might be *too much* for your specific set of circumstances, particularly if you or a close family member has a history of heart problems.

The more obvious short-term risks of overdoing it with running include increased susceptibility to illness and injury, low mood, and a lack of motivation. For runners still early in their running journeys, this is usually down to increasing training load – a combination of distance, intensity and frequency – too rapidly. For more experienced runners the cause is more likely to be down to the chronic over-stressing of physical and psychological resources, usually a result of inadequate recovery including, crucially, good quality sleep, and/or poor or inadequate nutrition (see chapters 2 and 5).

Top tips for healthy running

* Regular running is great for our bodies and brains, so keep doing it!
* To maximise running's health benefits, run for one to three hours each week.
* Above 60 miles (100 kilometres) of running per week may not be beneficial for all runners.
* If you have a history of medical problems, seek advice before starting or increasing exercise.
* Support your running with good sleep, nutrition and recovery.

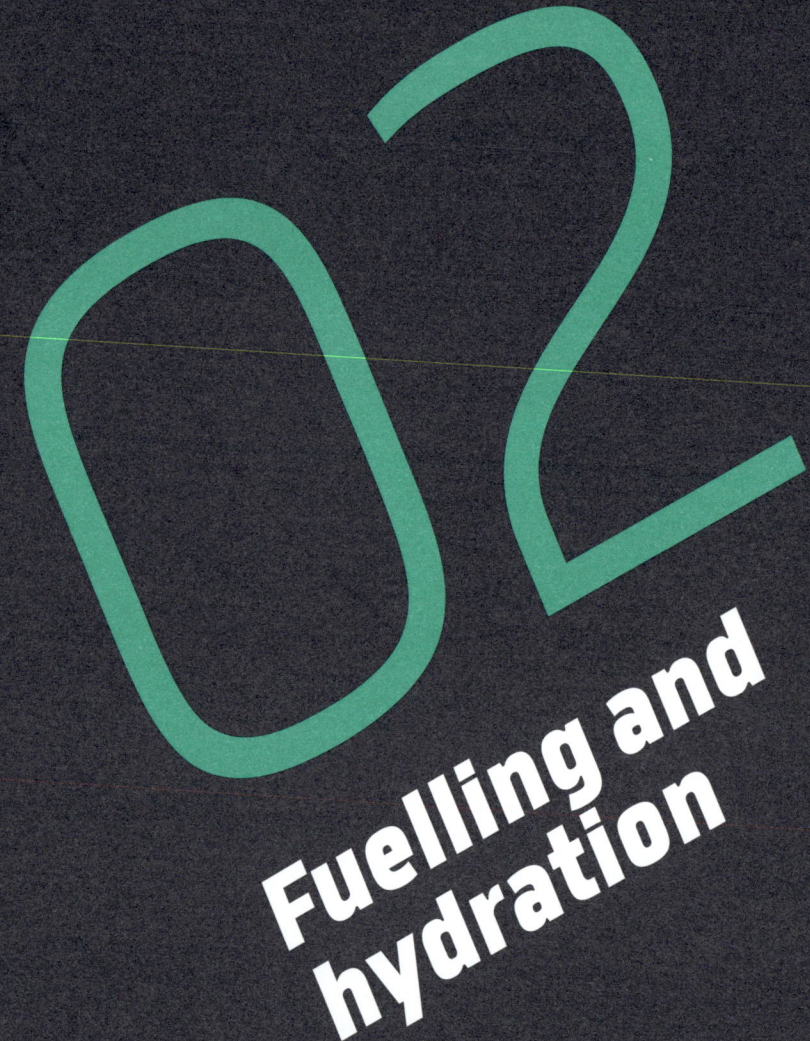

02

Fuelling and hydration

Fuelling the constantly changing needs of training and racing throughout our different life stages is one of the biggest challenges of running. Food is many things to many people, intricately tied up with our history, culture, emotions and relationships, as well as simply a source of energy. In this chapter, we'll start with an overview of what the food we eat 'does' in terms of supplying energy to our exercising bodies, and then move on to a practical look at how we can use this knowledge to support both our health and our running performance.

Macronutrients

The food we eat is made up of a huge variety of different nutrients, many of which have essential roles in the body. The three essential nutritional macronutrients – carbohydrate, fat and protein – are the nutrient groups we use the most, forming our primary sources of energy for our bodies to move, grow and repair. Water, oxygen and fibre are also classed as essential macronutrients, necessary for life but not as a nutritional source of energy.

Carbohydrate

Carbohydrates are molecules formed from carbon, oxygen and hydrogen, and are also known as *saccharides*. The simplest carbohydrates are *monosaccharides*, which cannot be broken down into smaller units. All carbohydrates are broken down into monosaccharides during digestion before being absorbed by the gut. The length of the saccharide chain determines how long each type of carbohydrate takes to be broken down in the body, which is why it's important to consider the type of carbohydrate we're eating at a given time.

* **Shorter-chain or 'simple' carbohydrates** are great for quick hits of energy – for example during a race – and include foods such as sweeter fruits, gels, sweets, energy drinks and refined grains such as white bread.
* **Longer-chain or 'complex' carbohydrates** provide their energy over a longer period of time as they take longer for the body to break down into useable monosaccharide units. These include starchy and fibrous foods such as wholegrains and many vegetables.

GLYCAEMIC INDEX

The glycaemic index (GI) assigns a number between 0 and 100 to different foods to represent the rise in blood glucose levels two hours after consumption, and therefore the insulin response to that rise.

Pure glucose has been assigned a GI value of 100, while a (theoretical) food that caused no rise in blood sugar would be assigned a GI value of 0. The GI value of a food depends primarily on the quantity and type of carbohydrate it contains, but it also depends on numerous other variables including the fat and protein content of the food, whether it is cooked and, if so, the method of cooking.

GI tables allow you to estimate the value of specific foods (note that it should be considered a rough value only, as responses to carbohydrate ingestion are highly individual).

Low GI food is considered to have a GI value of 55 or less; mid-range is 56 to 69; and high GI is 70 or more.

Although fat produces more ATP (adenosine triphosphate – the body's energy currency – see page 6) per gram than carbohydrate when broken down in the body, carbohydrate produces more ATP per unit of oxygen than either fat or protein, making it a more efficient source of fuel. As well as fuelling our muscles, carbohydrate is essential for brain and nervous system functioning, along with numerous other metabolic processes including bone metabolism and hormonal regulation.

Once processed, the glucose is either immediately used or stored in the following ways:

* some glucose circulates in the bloodstream, providing ready energy for immediate conversion into ATP;
* some is converted into glycogen and stored within skeletal muscles to be used as fuel to produce ATP by the muscle itself;
* some is stored as large glycogen molecules in the liver.

Total carbohydrate stores within the body vary widely, depending on factors such as recent diet and activity, and body composition.

Each gram of stored carbohydrate – glycogen – is stored with three grams of water, the loss of which is why people adopting a low-carbohydrate diet often lose a lot of weight in the first few days.

Release of glucose from glycogen stores in the liver is carefully controlled by the hormone insulin in order to regulate blood glucose levels, as levels that are either too high or too low can be damaging to the body.

In addition to fuelling activity directly, carbohydrate ingestion aids fat metabolism, as carbohydrate is required in order for the body to break down fats. Restricting carbohydrate intake therefore has the (presumably unintentional) knock-on effect of limiting fat metabolism. Consuming adequate carbohydrate to fuel exercise also prevents the body breaking down the protein in our muscles and organs, or using dietary protein, when other fuel sources run low. Protein from our diet is far better utilised for building, maintaining and repairing our bodies than as an inefficient fuel source.

Fat

Fat is an essential part of our diet, forming parts of the structure of brain tissue, cell membranes, bone marrow and the insulating sheaths around our nerves. It provides important fat-soluble vitamins A, D and E, along with essential fatty acids such as Omega-3, which is involved in oxygen delivery to working muscles and may also reduce inflammation and help speed up recovery after exercise. Public health guidelines suggest fat should make up around 35 per cent of our daily energy intake, although this may necessarily be slightly lower in some athletes due to higher carbohydrate requirements to fuel training and racing.

Because fat takes longer to digest than carbohydrate, adding fat (and/or protein) to foods high in carbohydrate lowers their glycaemic index. However, be aware that foods containing a combination of fat and carbohydrate, particularly if sugar and/or salt is also added, are notoriously difficult to stop eating – a fact capitalised upon by the processed food industry.

Protein

Protein is broken down during digestion into its building blocks – amino acids. These are utilised in the body for growing, maintenance and repair, but can also be used for fuel.

Protein is not stored in the body in the same way as carbohydrate and fat – i.e. as a ready fuel source. However, the protein that makes up our muscles can be broken down and utilised as fuel during the later stages of prolonged exercise when other fuel sources are running low. In this case, amino acids from skeletal muscle can be converted into glucose through a process called *gluconeogenesis*, which occurs in the liver and kidneys. While this is a normal way for the body to maintain blood glucose levels between meals, the extent to which it may be required during prolonged exercise without adequate carbohydrate ingestion can lead to excess breakdown of muscle tissue.

Macronutrient use during exercise

During exercise, the majority of energy required comes from burning a combination of carbohydrate and fat. Both sources continually supply energy for the production of ATP, but the relative contribution of each varies according to the following factors.

Intensity of exercise – at higher intensities the body utilises a higher percentage of carbohydrate as fuel, in the form of muscle glycogen, via the ATP-PC and anaerobic systems (see page 10). This is because it is faster and more efficient to utilise than other sources when energy is required rapidly. As exercise intensity decreases, the relative contribution of fat as an energy source increases.

Duration of exercise – as our carbohydrate stores can only fuel a maximum of about 180 minutes of endurance activity – less if the intensity is high – once our glycogen stores are depleted, the body needs an alternative source of energy. At this point, protein can be utilised, by breaking down muscle proteins in order to maintain blood glucose levels.

Fitness level and previous training – regular aerobic training increases the body's ability to utilise fat as fuel, as well as increasing overall metabolic flexibility (i.e. the ability to switch between fuel sources as required). Also, women use a higher percentage of fat as fuel than men.

Fasted training – training with depleted glycogen reserves by not fuelling beforehand forces the body to rely on fat and protein for energy. While it may, if used carefully, be a useful part of training for some people, for many, including women for whom carbohydrate depletion quickly affects hormonal regulation, it isn't recommended.

Energy availability

Energy availability, a relatively recent concept in research, is useful for understanding how our bodies utilise the energy we take in:

**energy availability
= energy intake – exercise energy expenditure**

Our **energy intake** is simply energy we take in via our diet; our **exercise energy expenditure** is *all* the physical activity we undertake – training, racing, walking the dog and everything else. The remaining energy, our **energy availability**, is what's available for our body to perform all its other *essential functions* to keep us healthy and happy, including hormone regulation, metabolic processes and brain function.

Any excess energy taken in surplus to these require-ments will be stored as fat – an essential part of survival

for our hunter-gatherer ancestors for whom periods of abundant food were often interspersed by periods of food scarcity. Unlike the food-abundant world many of us live in today, for most of human history being readily able to store fat and access these fat stores during exercise would have been key to survival.

RED-S
When there is insufficient energy left over after the fuelling of physical activity, the body is not able to carry out its metabolic processes as normal. While various physiological and psychological mechanisms, such as a reduction in our metabolic rate – our rate of energy expenditure at rest – and a decreased desire to expend energy, can allow us to cope with short periods of energy deficit, a chronic lack of available energy can lead to poor performance and eventually poor health, conditions covered by the umbrella terms of overtraining syndrome and relative energy deficiency in sport (RED-S).

People often use the terms *energy availability* and *energy balance* interchangeably, but they are in fact quite different concepts. When we have sufficient energy availability, we have enough energy to fuel both our training and the healthy and optimal function of our various body systems. When energy is restricted, our metabolic rate reduces in order to conserve energy. Alongside this reduction, hormonal changes result in reproductive system suppression in women (babies aren't a great idea when food is scarce), reduced testosterone in men and other adaptations to reduce the overall requirement for energy. For this reason, from a purely 'energy in versus energy out' point of view, we can be in energy balance while still failing to have sufficient energy availability to fuel optimal physiological functioning.

Energy expenditure
Because we're all different, calculating our daily energy expenditure based on things like our body mass index, age, biological sex or activity level is difficult and inexact. Scientists can accurately measure energy expenditure in natural environments using the doubly

labelled water method. This uses isotopes of the hydrogen and oxygen in water to measure the average daily metabolic rate of a person (or other organism) over a period of time. Thanks to this technique, we now know that human metabolic rate is carefully maintained within a relatively small range, a mechanism described by the constrained energy theory of metabolism.

Constrained energy theory

This theory (Pontzer *et al.*, 2016), is based on extensive research of the energy expenditure of global populations, including the Hadza people of Tanzania, one of the world's few remaining hunter-gatherer communities.

It states that the combined action of our body and brain will work to adjust our metabolic rate according to whether food is plentiful or scarce. As a result, our daily caloric expenditure will stay in a very narrow range, regardless of how much we exercise.

Potentially life saving for our ancestors during times of food scarcity, this mechanism often works against us in the modern world when food is not only plentiful but pushed upon us by advertising at every available opportunity and made highly palatable through ultra-processing. Alongside this, time- and labour-saving devices mean that movement that once would have been necessary for everything from obtaining food and collecting water to carrying children and building shelters has been removed from our daily lives.

This theory explains part of the reason why many people find losing weight so difficult, particularly when undertaken by energy restriction alone – in this case, our metabolic rate slows so that our resting metabolic rate is lower. This means that our bodies' essential processes use less energy than they would if we were taking in more energy.

Estimating energy expenditure

Doubly labelled water isn't something that's available to most of us, but it can be helpful to work out an estimate of our daily energy expenditure, and there are calculations that enable us to do this. When calculating our daily energy requirements, we need to account for both our overall energy expenditure, and the energy required for physical activity.

Our **total energy expenditure (TEE)** is the total amount of energy we expend during a 24-hour period. It is made up of the following three components.

* **Resting energy expenditure**, also known as **resting metabolic rate**, is about 10 per cent higher than our basal metabolic rate (our metabolic rate at complete rest) and is easier to measure. This is the energy we require to maintain our basic metabolic activities.
* **Thermic effect of food**, which is the energy required for food digestion, absorption, transport and metabolism, storage of nutrients, and elimination of wastes. It represents about 10 per cent of our total daily energy expenditure.
* **Activity energy expenditure** is the most variable among the components of TEE. It can account for less than half of TEE in sedentary people, and up to 80 per cent in athletes and heavy labourers.

Our TEE can be measured in a number of different ways, some more accurate than others. But our bodies are good at allocating energy and nutrients where and when required, so unless you're carrying out a controlled scientific study, a rough estimate is sufficient. Many of the common methods for measuring energy expenditure are inaccurate or impractical – wearable gauges such as those on our sports watches tend to have low levels of accuracy.

Body composition (fat, muscle and other lean mass, and bone) varies between individuals but, with training and a balanced diet, it will shift towards what is optimal for that individual and the type of activity they're doing. Many runners worry about their weight, but in fact an optimal body composition is far more meaningful than a number on a scale. Ways of measuring body composition range from bio-impedance scales (hugely inaccurate) to DXA scan (gold standard but expensive) and skinfold measurement (less expensive; accurate if carried out by an experienced practitioner).

Estimating your total daily energy expenditure (TEE)

To estimate your TEE (which, along with the energy you get from food and drink consumed, is measured in kilocalories (kcal)), you first need to calculate your **resting metabolic rate (RMR)**, using the Mifflin-St Jeor equation (which gives the most accurate results when compared with the gold standard doubly labelled water method).

RMR (males) = (10 x weight in kg) + (6.25 x height in cm) – (5 x age in years) + 5

RMR (females) = (10 x weight in kg) + (6.25 x height in cm) – (5 x age in years) – 161

Next, you need to estimate your **physical activity level (PAL)**, using the following numbers:

PAL (inactive/sedentary) = 1.2
PAL (fairly active: walking and other exercise once or twice a week) = 1.3
PAL (moderately active: exercise two to three times a week) = 1.4
PAL (active: higher intensity exercise more than three times a week) = 1.5
PAL (very active: higher intensity training on most days) = 1.7

Finally, multiply them together:

total daily energy expenditure = RMR x PAL

ESTIMATING YOUR TEE – EXAMPLES

For an 80kg, 180cm, 38-year-old, very active man:

RMR = (10 x 80) + (6.25 x 180) – (5 x 38) + 5 = 1,740kcal

PAL = 1.7

TEE = 1,740 x 1.7 = 2,958kcal

For a 60kg, 172cm, 25-year-old, active woman:

RMR = (10 x 60) + (6.25 x 172) – (5 x 25) – 161 = 1,389kcal

PAL = 1.5

TEE = 1,389 x 1.5 = 2,084kcal

It's well worth bearing in mind that these are estimates only. As well as using these figures as a guide, long-term weekly weighing (daily, and even monthly, fluctuations in body weight are normal), and logging how you're feeling in yourself and during training will offer the best insight into your specific circumstances.

If you regularly run out of energy while you're out running, often feel hungry – especially if it wakes you up at night or you're constantly thinking about food – or have any of the classic signs of chronic under-fuelling (including persistent fatigue, repeated injury or illness, muscle loss, reduced performance or lack of improvement in training, slow recovery, emotional disturbances, or hormonal disruption (loss of menstrual periods in females, loss of libido or changes in sexual function for males and females)), consider increasing your energy intake to avoid health problems.

Remember that insufficient energy intake slows our resting metabolic rate, meaning we burn less energy at rest than a sufficiently fuelled person. Increasing your energy intake if you're currently in energy deficit won't, therefore, cause you to gain weight, but it will improve your health, well-being, and performance.

Food to help you run well

Aside from being how we fuel our bodies, our personal relationships with food are all unique, shaped through our childhood years, experimented with through our teens and early adulthood, and then, perhaps, evolving into more stable habits as adults. Mealtimes are often about so much more than food. In our house it's a meeting time, a catching up time, a time to talk about the day that's been, and a time for planning for the days ahead. It's not always straightforward – sometimes conversations get heated and emotions overflow at the table – but, by the time the meal is finished, they're almost always positive emotions.

The food we eat is closely tied in with who we are; our choices are shaped by our parents, friends, beliefs, culture, tastes and then the wider influences that expand outwards as we explore and create our own versions of the world. But, surrounded as we are by near constant and often conflicting messaging around our food choices, in a world of sponsored fad foodstuffs and synthetic assimilations that bear little resemblance to anything our great-grandparents would recognise as being edible, how can we make the best choices for our own health, including optimally supporting our training and recovery, and that of the planet and the other life we share it with?

As explained in our section on energetics (see page 9) the basic function of the food we eat as runners is to provide the energy and nutrients we need to keep our bodies healthy and as active as we want to be.

Consuming more than we need to the point where we're carrying around excess, and potentially unhealthy, weight is obviously counterproductive. But so too is consuming insufficient energy to meet both the energy demands of our sport and those of a healthy, optimally functioning body.

As with many other aspects of training, the 'right' diet is highly individual. Runners, like the general population, vary widely both in daily energy requirements and optimal balance of macronutrients (carbohydrate, protein and fat) and micronutrients (broadly, vitamins and minerals) depending on our overall activity levels, age, biology and individual genetics, and life history. Importantly, we also vary in what we enjoy eating. Nutrition is one of those highly polarising subjects that regularly sees high-profile fads, fuelled by celebrities and social media influencers, feeding into an increasingly contradictory cloud of advice, most of which has little scientific basis. The good news is that recent, well-conducted studies – and in particular some larger-scale reviews of the literature – are finally establishing some much-needed clarity on the subject. The even better news is that the overarching advice is pretty simple.

General principles for a healthy diet for runners

* Provided you have a reasonably healthy relationship with food, i.e. you're not currently living with or recently recovered from disordered eating or an eating disorder, **listen to your body and be guided by its cues to your hunger**. This also applies to thirst in the majority of cases (see pages 52–53).
* **Expect to be hungrier as you train** more and ensure you're meeting your increased requirements for fuel and nutrients, but try to avoid the post-training blowout.
* **Fuel for the work to come** is good advice for distance runners, encouraging you to think about the quantity and content of meals and snacks prior to running. The bulk of your energy should come predominantly from carbohydrates ingested at least a couple of hours before training, topped up with an easily digested carb-rich snack just before the session begins in order to stabilise blood glucose level and avoid the dreaded bonk.
* If you have a longer race or training session coming up, you may wish to **increase your carbohydrate intake** for a couple of days before in order to ensure your

body's glycogen stores are replete. Taking on carbohydrates in food or drink form as you run also helps to maintain circulating levels of easily available glucose. During early morning runs, this approach may be better tolerated by those who suffer from gastrointestinal issues than trying to eat beforehand.
* **Refuel after training** with a mix of carbohydrates to replenish glycogen reserves and protein to aid recovery.
* **Optimal intakes of macronutrients and micronutrients** varies according to individual requirements. Older people, for example, should include more protein in their diets in order to facilitate muscle protein synthesis, which slows with age.
* **Eat good quality produce** with minimal ingredients and processing. Buy organic if you can; you're likely to be ingesting fewer harmful chemicals and you'll be supporting more sustainable methods of food production. Veg box schemes are a great way to get fresh, seasonal, organic fruit and veg delivered to your door.
* Minimise food waste and impulse purchases by **planning your meals** and only buying what you need. Keep a good staples cupboard with herbs, spices, stocks and sauces to add flavour to anything and everything.
* **Cook from scratch** whenever possible – that way you know what you're putting into your body.
* **Avoid ultra-processed foods**, many of which contain additives with little long-term scientific testing on their safety in humans. Many of these foods contain combinations of fat, salt and sugar which may override your natural ability to tell when you've eaten enough, adding large amounts of energy to your diets often for very little nutritional benefit and making you less hungry for healthier foods.

Running on low-fat and low-carbohydrate diets

At low levels of physical activity, our bodies burn predominantly fat, but, as our exercise intensity increases, so does our need for carbohydrate. As well as being our bodies' preferred means of fuelling training, being broken down most easily into the simple sugar units that are combined with oxygen in our mitochondria to produce energy, our brains are heavily reliant on carbohydrate for energy. Our requirement for carbohydrate increases when we're sleep deprived, at altitude and, for females, at certain times during the menstrual cycle. But carbohydrate has had some bad press over recent years, and there are some good reasons why.

Back in the 1940s, some studies showed a correlation between high-fat diets and high levels of cholesterol in the blood. As high blood cholesterol was considered to be a risk factor for heart disease, it was theorised that high-fat diets might increase heart disease risk, and therefore a low-fat diet might help to prevent heart disease in high-risk patients. Over the decades that followed, despite there being no clear evidence that a low-fat diet either prevented heart disease or promoted weight loss, by the 1980s it was the recommended approach for everyone, promoted by doctors, governments, the food industry and the media.

Ironically, since then obesity and diet-related diseases have steadily increased. Part of this is likely to be down to replacing fats with sugars to overcome the lack of flavour, alongside a rapid increase in ultra-processed convenience foods.

So entrenched was the low-fat ideology that it took until the Atkins revolution in the early 2000s to swing the balance entirely unhelpfully in the polar-opposite direction. Suddenly, carbs became the enemy, and low-fat cookery books disappeared off the shelves and were replaced with low-carb versions.

Low-carb diets even made their way into the endurance world, aiming to tap into the plentiful reserves of energy even the leanest humans have stored as fat compared with our limited glycogen (carbohydrate) stores.

Thankfully, moderation seems to be the overarching message emerging in current times, along with eating not just for our own health but for that of our planet and the other lives we share it with. We now know that fats aren't necessarily bad, as long as you steer clear of the hydrogenated variety (also known as trans fats), and are in fact essential for many biological processes, including immune function, and keep us feeling fuller for longer after eating.

Running on vegetarian, vegan and plant-based diets

As with an omnivorous diet, there's far more to a vegetarian or vegan diet than whether or not they contain animal-derived products. While the consumption of meat and dairy undoubtedly has huge environmental and welfare impacts, many meat and dairy replacements are highly processed and packaged – not great for you or the planet. A recent report found that a third of supermarket products labelled 'vegan' contained animal derivatives.

Vegetarian and vegan athletes, particularly menstruating females and those spending time at altitude, may need to pay more attention than meat-eaters to their iron levels (see page 51). Vegans may also need to add a vitamin B12 supplement to their diet (see page 51).

Whatever type of diet you follow (omnivorous, plant-based, vegetarian or vegan), a balanced, nutrient-dense diet that provides enough energy for all your exercise and metabolic needs will support your training well.

Cooking meals from scratch if you can, and using high quality ingredients, is the best way to make sure you know what's going into your body.

Measuring our food intake

Armed with the knowledge that the basic aim of nutrition is to provide the right quantity and quality of fuel for our bodies and brains to function optimally at whatever level of activity we choose, how can we measure the energy we take in?

Energy intake, via our food and drink, is often measured in kilocalories (kcal), and calorie counting is the mainstay of many diets and nutrition plans. (Confusingly, kilocalories are commonly referred to as simply 'calories'.) Most energy information displayed on foods is calculated based upon standardised values of protein, fat, carbohydrate and alcohol, or from published tables of values for different ingredients. The resulting number quoted on the packet usually falls within about 10 per cent of the actual value.

While these nice, neat numbers might appear to make working out our energy intake pretty straightforward, the reality is somewhat more complicated. This is because the number of calories we see on a packet or list doesn't take into account how our bodies use the different types of food and drink we ingest, or the changes that occur through processes such as cooking.

Regardless of the caloric value of a food as printed on a list or packet, the amount of energy our bodies can extract from different foods varies. Foods that are high in insoluble fibre, such as whole grains, celery, nuts, fruit and vegetables – particularly those with their skins on – have less useable energy available to us than foods that have already been processed. Insoluble fibre is essential for our gut health but, after it has done its good work promoting free movement of matter through our digestive tract and improving the diversity of the gut microbiome, it is passed out of the body mostly undigested. Additionally, foods that are high in protein require more energy for the process of digestion than carbohydrates or fats, so the net energy gain is lower than might be expected.

Highly processed foods – usually a super-palatable mixture of sugar, salt, fat and refined carbohydrates – provide us with energy that is easily and almost instantly available for absorption, straight into the bloodstream. This might be a good thing halfway through an ultramarathon when maximum calories for the least effort is just what's needed, but, for everyday consumption, processed foods are worth limiting to minimise their negative impacts throughout our bodies and brains. Processing foods also helps to bypass our satiety responses – our evolved mechanisms for telling our brains when we are full – making them all too easy to overeat. Great for sales, but disastrous for global health.

At the start of this chapter, we ran through a rough calculation of the daily energy requirements for a very active 80-kilogram man and an active 60-kilogram woman. The results were along the lines of the government's recommended daily caloric intake of 2,500 calories for men and 2,000 calories for women, plus a bit extra for training. Wearable technology offers an estimated daily energy expenditure, but studies show smartwatches and fitness trackers are usually out by a minimum of 20 per cent – and in some cases up to 80 per cent – compared with actual energy expenditure (Shcherbina *et al.*, 2017). As we discussed previously, the only accurate way to measure energy expenditure is using the doubly labelled water method, along with weighed, lab-prepared food, a lab and a bunch of scientists, so most of us have to make do with what we've got: paying attention to our bodies and their hunger cues, aiming for a diet that supports health and training, and not being overly restrictive – if you can't enjoy a pastry with your coffee then, frankly, what's the point?

Periodising nutrition

The idea of periodising our nutrient and energy intake draws from the most up-to-date science on sports nutrition, moving from generic nutritional advice to a dynamic and tailored approach that addresses an individual athlete's needs and requirements according to daily training and recovery to help them maximise their performance and progression.

As training will always involve a mix of higher and lower intensities – and harder and easier days – it makes sense for nutrition to follow suit. On easy days, when you may purposely want to train your body to use a higher percentage of fat as a fuel, it's fine to consume less carbohydrate. This method of 'training low' can be effective but should be employed with care and not more than once or twice each week. On harder days, when the quality of your session is important and you want to train as optimally as possible, it's important to fuel with sufficient carbohydrate beforehand. If you're training more than once per day, refuelling with carbohydrate in between sessions is important, but it's likely you will still have lower carbohydrate availability for the second session of the day, so plan your harder sessions when your stores are fully topped up.

In relatively sedentary individuals, the evidence for the effects of the timing of meals on health, body weight and body composition is inconclusive. But for those undertaking regular training, knowing what to eat and when to eat it can make a big difference to both the quality of training (or performance in racing) and the body's ability to adapt, repair and recover in response to exercise.

Top tips: macronutrient timing
Here's a useful summary of the main points that are helpful for runners who want to periodise their nutrition (Kerksick *et al.*, 2017).
* The timing and ratio of macronutrient intake may enhance repair and recovery, increase muscle protein synthesis, and improve mood following a high-volume and/or high-intensity exercise session.
* The body's glycogen stores are depleted by high-volume exercise and so, for those undertaking regular training, a high-carbohydrate diet (8–12 grams of carbohydrate per kilogram of body weight per day) will ensure carbohydrate stores are adequately replenished.
* In cases where rapid restoration of glycogen is required, for example for multiple training sessions during a single day, or during ultramarathons and multi-day challenges, increasing carbohydrate intake to 1.2 grams per kilogram of body weight per hour if tolerated, prioritising carbohydrate sources that have a high glycaemic index (see page 32), adding caffeine (3–8 milligrams per kilogram of body weight), and taking in some protein alongside carbohydrate can all help.

* During extended periods of high-intensity exercise (more than 70 minutes at more than 70 per cent VO_2 max), when both fuel and fluid need to be rapidly replenished, carbohydrate should be consumed at a rate of approximately 30–60 grams per hour in a 6–8 per cent carbohydrate–electrolyte solution (6–12 fluid ounces) at regular intervals throughout the session.
* During exercise lasting more than four hours, such as ultramarathons, carbohydrate ingestion should be increased to 60–90 grams per hour, and can be taken as a mixture of solid foods, sports nutrition products (gels, chews) and drinks.
* Consuming carbohydrate during standard full-body resistance exercise sessions has been shown to regulate blood sugar levels, increase muscle glycogen stores, reduce muscle damage and facilitate better short- and long-term training adaptations.
* Adequate protein intake, ideally evenly spaced throughout the day (20–40 grams (or 0.25–0.40 grams per kilogram of body mass) of protein approximately every three to four hours is suggested), is important for those undertaking regular training. This should include the essential amino acids to maximise muscle protein synthesis.
* Post-exercise ingestion of protein (up to two hours afterwards) increases muscle protein synthesis – this can be a normal meal that includes a high-quality source of protein rather than a specific protein recovery product.
* Consuming casein protein (approximately 30–40 grams) prior to sleep can acutely increase muscle protein synthesis and metabolic rate during the night.

Carbohydrate availability

An interesting recent finding is the role of carbohydrate not just as fuel, but as an important mediator for various hormones, including those regulating mood, immune function and bone health. This means that, as well as ensuring our diet provides sufficient overall calories to meet our health and exercise needs, it's important to ensure enough of this intake is made up of carbohydrate.

Recent research has found that a short-term ketogenic (low-carbohydrate, high-fat) diet impaired markers of bone modelling and remodelling, and that only a marker of resorption recovered after carbohydrate was restored, indicating that even in the short term, low-carbohydrate diets may have long-term consequences for bone health (Heikura *et al.*, 2020). In a separate study, it was found that athletes on a ketogenic diet which met overall energy requirements had worse markers of bone health than athletes on a high-carbohydrate diet that did not meet overall energy requirements (Fensham *et al.*, 2022).

How much carbohydrate do I need?

Carbohydrate requirements vary widely depending on the type, duration and intensity of exercise, but the following is a guide.
* For low-intensity or rest days you'll require about 3 grams of carbohydrate per kilogram of body weight per day.
* For moderate-intensity training (one hour per day) this will increase to 5–7 grams per kilogram of body weight per day.
* For heavier training (one to three hours per day) you'll require 6–10 grams per kilogram of body weight per day.
* For multiple training sessions (four hours or more per day) requirements are 8–12 grams per kilogram of body weight per day.

EXERCISE-INDUCED HYPOGLYCAEMIA

Have you ever experienced that horrible low blood sugar feeling three to four miles into a run, even though you've eaten plenty before running? Exercise-induced hypoglycaemia (also known as rebound hypoglycaemia) is a common complaint in endurance athletes and occurs when high GI foods (easily digested sugars such as those present in sports drinks and sweets – see page 47) are consumed before a run, but not immediately beforehand. Especially if the food is combined with caffeine, the sudden influx of glucose into the bloodstream stimulates the release of insulin, which facilitates the movement of glucose into cells. When this spike in insulin combines with exercise, the effect is to greatly increase the removal and utilisation of glucose from the bloodstream, resulting in low blood glucose levels. Associated unpleasant symptoms can include nausea, shakiness, confusion, visual disturbances and lethargy – in effect, what athletes term 'bonking'.

It's easy to avoid this by making sure you take on your high GI food or drink within the final few minutes before you set off. This will mean glucose will enter your bloodstream once you've already begun exercising, levelling off the insulin response and reducing the likelihood of the dreaded bonk.

hydration plan right can be running out of energy due to insufficient fuelling, feeling bloated and nauseous due to too much or the wrong kind of fuelling, dehydration, or overhydration.

Top tips for race-day nutrition

* **Plan ahead** – the specifics will depend on the distance and timings of your chosen race, but planning your nutrition strategy in advance means one less thing to worry about as race day approaches. Plan everything carefully, including your meals on the night before and the morning of your race, any nutrition you'll be using during the race, and your post-race recovery.
* **Practise** – never try anything new on race day. Practise your race-day nutrition strategy in training, so you know what you'll want to eat, and what works best for you, when it matters. If you know there will be a specific brand of sports nutrition product available at the race, experiment with this in training to make sure it works for you. If not, you can always take your own.
* **Be flexible** – if the unexpected happens and you end up having to eat something different for your pre-race meals, or needing to rely on unfamiliar in-race nutrition, don't panic. Accept the situation, stick to what's closest to what you've trained with, and remember most gels/chews/drinks have the same basic ingredients, just a different label.

Race-day nutrition

Getting your nutrition and hydration right is a key ingredient in successful racing. It might seem like a minefield, with so many different variables and options, but with a bit of time, patience and practice you can come up with a plan that will allow you to perform at your very best, supporting your race day energy requirements so you can focus on putting all that training into practice.

The results of not getting your nutrition and

Shorter races – optimal nutrition and hydration strategy

For shorter races – from 5K up to half marathon distance – not getting it wrong before the race is more important than what you do during the race when it comes to nutrition. These distances are not going to problematically drain your body's glycogen reserves, but when you're running faster, gastric discomfort is more likely, so have a small, easily digested breakfast at least two to three hours before the race starts. Stopping drinking two hours before the start of a race is a good strategy to avoid needing to pee halfway round. A sports drink (or water and a gel or a couple of sweets) just before you set off will provide the hydration you need for the race, plus a blood glucose boost to stave off exercise-induced hypoglycaemia.

Marathons – optimal nutrition and hydration strategy

Marathons present perhaps the greatest need for precision when it comes to fuelling and hydration. This is because we store sufficient fuel in our body's reserves for shorter distances, while over ultramarathon distances the slower pace makes it easier to fuel on the go. For the vast majority of marathon runners, the body's glycogen reserves will run out at some point before the finish line – one of the primary causes of the infamous 'wall' we tend to hit somewhere at the far side of 18 miles.

Running a marathon can take anything from two to six hours (or longer), burning between 2,200 and 3,200 calories of energy along the way. This figure varies substantially with body weight but very little with pace – it takes about the same amount of energy to run 26.2 miles in 2.5 hours as it does in five hours (although it would obviously require far more energy to run for five hours at a 2.5-hour marathon pace).

Regardless of the exact number of calories you burn, it will exceed the number you have stored as easily accessed glycogen, meaning that unless you take on fuel as you go, you may experience hypoglycaemia (low blood sugar) and its associated symptoms of light-headedness and loss of power. This is especially likely if you're running at a higher pace that prioritises burning carbohydrate over fat. At the very least, you'll experience the loss of performance resulting from insufficient readily available fuel for your working muscles, and find that you need to slow down.

An optimal fuelling strategy for a marathon ensures there's adequate carbohydrate stored in your muscles and liver by the time you line up at the start, along with adequate carbohydrate replacement during the race itself.

Two days before a marathon

Start increasing your intake of carbohydrate and slightly reducing your fat intake in the two days before the race to ensure your glycogen stores are full by the start line. This, alongside your taper (see pages 143–144), will allow your muscle stores to replenish. Intensive carb-loading practices of the past have not been shown to have any advantage, and may add the disadvantage of starting out heavy and uncomfortable from unaccustomed levels of carbohydrate and the water stored alongside it.

In the final couple of days, steer clear of too many high-fibre foods, sticking with white or refined versions of carbs such as pasta, bread and rice. It's a good idea to have your main meal earlier than usual the day before the race to allow plenty of time for digestive transit to be complete by the time you're ready to run.

If you're prone to gastrointestinal issues, pay particular attention to your food the day before and on the morning of the race, as well as during the race itself. *Never* try anything new at this point – stick with tried-and-tested favourites. A mild vegetable curry with rice is our absolute go-to meal the day before a big race of marathon distance or longer.

Carb-rich foods for the day before, and morning of, your marathon
* Refined grains such as white rice, pasta, bagels and bread
* Low-fibre cereals such as puffed rice and corn flakes
* Porridge
* Pancakes
* Yoghurt
* Cooked, peeled vegetables (go for seedless types)
* Cooked, peeled potatoes
* Ripe bananas
* Cooked, peeled fruits and fruit purees
* Rice cakes
* Honey, jam and syrup
* Smooth fruit and vegetable juices

On the morning of a marathon

Liver glycogen stores are depleted overnight as it's from these supplies that a steady blood glucose level is maintained. It's therefore essential to replenish these on race morning with a small, easily digested, carb-rich breakfast, around three or four hours before the race.

Optimal hydration for marathons means starting the race hydrated but not to the point where you're wasting precious minutes popping to the Portaloos halfway round. Stop drinking two hours before the race begins, then aim to take on 20–30 grams (80–120 calories) of carbohydrate with 90–180 millilitres of water in the final 15 minutes before the start. This will top up both carbohydrate and fluid levels, without risking exercise-induced hypoglycaemia (see page 43).

During a marathon

Drink if you're thirsty when you pass a water station. It works well to take a gel just before a water station, so you can wash it down (and off your teeth) with plain water, but if there's a sports drink available, and you're confident it's compatible with your stomach, these can provide hydration and some carbohydrates too. Electrolytes aren't usually necessary for marathons; however, drinks which contain a small amount of sodium may increase palatability and absorption.

Carbohydrate can improve performance in events lasting more than two hours, ingested at a rate of around 60 grams per hour. With training, some athletes can improve their ability to absorb carbohydrate during exercise, with amounts in excess of 90 grams per hour – and even up to 120 grams per hour – reported in some studies. It's worth noting that many of the studies were undertaken on cyclists – runners may be less able to tolerate such high quantities than cyclists due to the repetitive movement of running making digestion more difficult than in cycling. The carbohydrate source you use depends on personal preference, with research showing no benefits of one kind over another, and can be achieved through a combination of water, sports drinks, gels, chews, bars and, if you can handle them at the pace you're running, real foods.

Ultramarathons – optimal nutrition and hydration strategy

Legendary ultrarunner Ann Trason once said, 'ultra-marathons are just an eating and drinking competition with a little bit of running thrown in.' If you're going to run a long way – ultras can be anything from 50K up to the world's longest footrace, the Self-Transcendence 3,100-mile race in New York – you need to constantly keep your body topped up with the energy and hydration it needs to carry on.

Unlike over shorter distances, nausea and flavour fatigue can be big issues in ultras. Many hours of jostling the stomach, extensive tissue damage, extreme fatigue and sleep deprivation all play their part in disrupting our normal ability to eat. It's therefore essential to plan ahead and make sure you have your nutrition strategy as dialled, tried and tested as possible. Gastrointestinal issues are one of the main reasons for runners dropping out in ultras.

Train your gut

Just like the rest of our bodies, our digestive system adapts as a result of repeated stresses, so practise your race-day nutrition on your long runs in training.

Little and often

Digesting food requires blood to be diverted to our digestive system, but running demands blood to deliver oxygen and fuel to our working muscles. Eating a small amount every 30–40 minutes when racing or out on a long run is therefore optimal for delivering fuel while minimising the risk of gastrointestinal issues.

Mix it up

While a few elite ultrarunners can get through 100 miles on gels alone, for most people a mix of different foods works well, and allows you to take cues from your body about what it needs, and when. Have a mix of sweet and savoury foods available – most people find they go through phases of wanting one or the other over the course of an ultra. Be cautious with dry foods such as crisps and nuts, which may be difficult to eat later on due to a dry, and even sore, mouth. It can be hard to know what you'll crave deep into an ultra, so a good tip is to plan a stop at a supermarket a few hours into a long training run and see what calls out to you. That's how we discovered cheese sandwiches made with hot cross buns – an absolute winner during an ultra but not something we'd have ever thought up otherwise.

Disaster management

Unfortunately, vomiting is a fairly common event in longer ultras. It's often just your body's way of getting rid of excess food or fluid that it doesn't have the capacity to process at that moment. If you do find yourself in this position, try not to panic. Slow down, and try to keep some food and water going in, little and often. Sipping on some salty broth or sucking on a boiled sweet can both help if you're struggling to get anything in.

Fuel for the long run

Start fuelling right from the start of an ultra, and keep it up throughout. Many longer ultramarathon races offer hot food at checkpoints, and this is well worth trying to eat a little of at each opportunity. If you're aiming for a certain number of calories and/or grams of carbohydrate per hour, bear in mind this is likely to differ over the course of the night and day – some hours you might be able to happily take in more than your goal, other hours you might be able to take in very little. A good aim is around 60–70 grams of carbohydrate per hour. Increase this if you're a larger athlete, or if you're working at a higher intensity, such as in a track race. You may need to decrease it a little if you're a smaller athlete and/or working at a very low intensity.

Hydration

Hyponatraemia (see pages 53–54), caused by over-drinking, is a bigger risk in ultramarathons than shorter races. Drink to thirst in the early hours of the race, and then continue little and often throughout. The amount you'll need to drink will be hugely dependent upon the conditions, and will be far greater in hot, dry weather than in cold, damp weather.

Should I mix my carbs and hydration?

Drinking your carbohydrate is a common strategy, and the basis of many sports drinks. While it's convenient and can work well, especially if you're struggling to stomach food, it can also lead to problems. For example, if you're experiencing hunger, and drinking carbohydrate-containing beverages to satisfy your hunger, you may end up overdrinking. On the other hand, if the weather is warm and you're very thirsty, the high levels of carbohydrate you'll be taking in as you drink may result in stomach problems. Having access to drinks that also provide energy, such as squash, sports drinks, fruit juice or milkshakes, is a great idea during ultramarathons, but should be taken occasionally, rather than as a primary strategy.

Electrolytes

Over the course of a longer ultra, we'll lose large quantities of electrolytes (salts) as we sweat – most importantly sodium. Thanks to homeostatic mechanisms, our bodies are very good at maintaining an optimal electrolyte balance, and will let us know if we need to take in more salt via cravings for salty foods. While snacking on salty foods during a race will provide sufficient sodium in most cases, if you're out for many hours, you're suffering from vomiting and/or diarrhoea, you're a heavy sweater running in a hot environment, or you're only using gels containing little or no electrolytes, you will need to have a strategy in place to replace lost electrolytes. These can be added to drinks or taken as tablets.

Sports nutrition products

Sports nutrition products are designed to either deliver fast, easily-digestible energy before and during exercise, or to support recovery afterwards. Energy products deliver carbohydrate in the form of simple sugars, such as glucose, sucrose (which is glucose and fructose) and dextrose, conveniently packaged for ease of use on the go.

> Sports nutrition products are developed for use in competition, but should definitely be trialled in training to make sure that:
> * you like them (you won't use a product you don't like the taste of); and
> * they work for you in terms of energy delivery and digestion.

Taking in energy products that contain a mixture of different simple carbohydrates has been shown to be most effective for absorption and utilisation during exercise. While a 2:1 glucose to fructose ratio was at one time considered to be optimal, recent research suggests a ratio of 1:0.8 or even 1:1 may be even better (Podlogar and Wallis, 2022).

Sports drinks typically contain around 60–70 grams of carbohydrate per litre of fluid, usually a mixture of sucrose, dextrose or glucose, plus sodium and other electrolytes to aid palatability and fluid absorption. Higher carbohydrate versions are available, which may be useful in longer events. Due to their concentrated nature, you will also need to drink water with these.

Gels are a concentrated source of carbohydrate energy, usually designed to be taken with water. Generally individually packaged in easy-open sachets, they typically deliver a shot of 20–25 grams of carbs on the go. Gels can also contain caffeine, taurine, electrolytes and other substances. Gels differ in texture, flavour and sweetness – which one is best for you depends entirely on personal preference, but should be tested thoroughly during training. Bear in mind that the gel flavours you love during a marathon may become completely unpalatable during the later stages of an ultramarathon. Some gels are also full of less helpful ingredients like artificial flavourings and sweeteners, and emulsifiers. Some of these additives have been found to have negative effects on our gut, altering absorption and microbial content, so are well worth steering clear of.

Chews are jelly-like chewable sweets containing many of the same ingredients as gels, although overall with noticeably fewer weird additives. Some runners may find them more pleasant to eat, and they can be nibbled at if you're struggling to get food in. Chews typically contain 7–10 grams of carbohydrate each, so you'll need to eat three or four to get the same amount you'd get from a gel. Whether they offer any benefits over well-known brands of chewy sweets is unknown but unlikely.

Energy bars are chewy bars packed with an assortment of high-carbohydrate ingredients along with, depending on your bar of choice, protein. A bar might pack in 30–40 grams of carbohydrate, but in a format that's harder to eat and digest on the run than sports drinks, gels or chews. However, during a long run or ultra they may be more satisfying and easier to stomach.

Bananas deliver a totally natural and unprocessed 20–30 grams of carbs each along with water, potassium, and even a little protein, all in a biodegradable package. Unless you like them black and squidgy, they're not ideal to carry a long way, but they're a perfect aid station or pre-run snack.

Recovery products deliver a high dose of protein along with some carbohydrate, and are usually in the form of a drink. Taken after hard and/or prolonged exercise, they help to support recovery and repair, replenish glycogen stores and rehydrate. If you include dairy in your diet, flavoured or plain milk offers many of the same benefits.

Supplements

Referring to sports supplements in a podcast interview, eminent sports physiologist Philip Skiba once said, 'if it works, it's probably not legal'. By the same token, if it's legal (as long as what's in the product actually matches what's on the ingredients list) it quite likely doesn't work.

> The sports supplements industry is a predominantly unregulated area in Europe, as supplements are counted as foods, and so do not require the strict testing and safety standards of medicines. The claims made by supplements companies have no requirement for scientific research to back them up.

Like expensive recovery products with big promises but little evidence, many people view supplements as being worth a go – as long as they're not doing you any harm, then maybe they're worth a try, right? But the reality is far darker. Many supplements manufacturers don't know where the ingredients in their products come from. Many supplements don't contain the amounts of active substances that they say they do – or are contaminated with something else entirely. Do you really want to put amino acids from completely unknown sources into your body? Or accidently ingest tetrahydrocannabinol (THC), the psychoactive (and banned) component of the cannabinoids from which CBD (an all-the-rage cannabidiol) is extracted?

However, supplements can be useful in some circumstances. They can be used in the following ways:
* To manage or protect against micronutrient deficiencies.
* To provide convenient forms of energy and macronutrients.
* To provide direct benefits to performance.
* To provide indirect benefits to performance by supporting hard training.

Many different vitamins and minerals (micronutrients) play important roles in the regulation of processes underpinning both health and sports performance, ranging from energy production to making new cells and proteins. Many people take a daily multivitamin as an insurance policy against possible deficiencies. But a good, varied diet should provide everything your body needs to function healthily – dieticians call this the 'food first' approach.

Too much of a good thing?

While they can be helpful in restoring existing deficiencies to healthy levels, vitamin and mineral supplements aren't benign and can cause harm if taken in excess. Research has found links between high levels of beta-carotene supplementation and an increase in lung cancer risk, and high vitamin E intake with an increased risk of prostate cancer. While many people take vitamin D with the aim of improving their bone health, taking too much has actually been found to decrease bone density. Vitamin D overdoses have been reported to cause symptoms including drowsiness, high blood pressure and kidney problems. Taking too much iron can result in gastrointestinal problems from nausea and diarrhoea to stomach ulcers, while overdosing on calcium can leave you with kidney problems.

> If you're struggling with low energy, low mood or poor immune function, ask your GP about the possibility of deficiencies. Testing for and treating deficiencies should always be done in conjunction with addressing the underlying cause, which might include a poor or insufficient diet or underlying health condition.

Performance-enhancing supplements

The International Olympic Committee's consensus statement on dietary supplements for athletes (Maughan *et al.*, 2018) suggests that the list of performance-enhancing supplements that 'might, at the present time, be considered to have an adequate level of support to suggest that marginal performance gains may be possible' is quite short: caffeine, nitrate, sodium bicarbonate, creatine and (possibly) beta-alanine.

Caffeine

Caffeine is a stimulant, which works on the peripheral and central nervous systems by blocking the action of adenosine, a sleep-inducing hormone. As a result, caffeine can increase alertness, improve concentration and reduce our perception of effort, thus enabling us to work harder for longer before fatigue sets in. Used

wisely, caffeine can be a powerful tool for runners, improving performance over every distance, from increasing our ability to tolerate the pain of running a fast 5K to keeping us awake on the night sections of an ultramarathon.

Caffeine is classed as a drug rather than a food, as it has a demonstrable pharmacological effect. Until 2004 it was listed as a banned substance by the World Anti-Doping Agency, when it was removed not because it doesn't work, but because everyone's on it, and methods for distinguishing illegal from normal usage are unreliable.

Many athletes use caffeine before or during a race to improve their performance, and there's good scientific evidence to back up its effectiveness. However, there are known to be large differences between individuals in tolerance and response to caffeine. People are either super-responders, responders or non-responders. You'll likely know which one you are as non-responders can happily drink coffee in the evening and still sleep well, whereas super-responders may need to stop their caffeine intake at midday to ensure its effects have worn off by bedtime. Relatively small amounts of caffeine (about 3 milligrams per kilogram of body weight; 200 milligrams for a 70-kilogram person) are thought to be required in order to elicit optimal effects. A daily maximum of 400 milligrams of caffeine from all sources is recommended for most people, with significant reductions for those who are pregnant or breastfeeding.

> ### Timing of caffeine intake
> It takes between 30 and 90 minutes to absorb caffeine into the bloodstream after ingestion, so it's important to consider timing carefully when planning your caffeine intake, especially in a race setting. Studies have shown that drip-feeding caffeine over the course of a longer race can maximise its effects, but even caffeine ingested late on in a race can still provide benefits. The best approach for each athlete is highly individual, and should be established by trial and error; however, it's generally recommended that the caffeine consumption for a race shouldn't far exceed a person's normal intake of caffeine.

ROUGH GUIDE TO CAFFEINE CONTENT
* Espresso coffee: 80–100 milligrams per shot
* Caffeinated energy gels: 25–50 milligrams per gel
* Cola drinks: 33 milligrams per 330-millilitre can
* Energy drinks: 50–100 milligrams per 250-millilitre can

Nitrates

Nitrates are found naturally in foods, and people with a varied, plant-based diet are probably already getting plenty. Beetroot juice is particularly nitrate-rich and is a handy source of concentrated nitrates for those whose diets may not be optimal, as well as for scientists undertaking research on nitrate supplementation.

Nitrate is converted into nitrite by salivary bacteria, and then into nitric oxide in the body. Its positive effects on sporting performance are thought to be due to an improvement in contractile or mitochondrial efficiency in our muscle cells, reducing the oxygen cost of physical activity. A meta-analysis of the previous research into nitrate supplementation with beetroot juice (Senefeld *et al.*, 2020) found an improvement in endurance performance of around 3 per cent. More recent studies (Tan *et al.*, 2022), have also linked supplementation with improvements in sprint performance.

Creatine

Creatine is a naturally occurring nutrient, consumed in our diet and synthesised in our bodies. Creatine supplements have been found to increase lean muscle mass and aid recovery during hard training, however supplementation may also result in an increase in overall body mass. As with all supplements, it's essential you know the full ingredients list and where the creatine is sourced from before considering taking it.

Omega-3

Omega-3 fatty acids are important for brain health and muscle recovery. In our diets, oily fish is the most bioavailable source of Omega-3; vegetarian and vegan sources include flax, chia and walnuts, but these aren't utilised in the body as effectively. Promising results have recently been found in Omega-3 extracted from algal sources, so this is likely to be the best source for those who do not eat fish.

Collagen

Collagen supplementation has been found to be associated with increased collagen production, thickened cartilage and decreased joint pain, but more research needs to be carried out in athletic populations to establish any performance benefits.

Sodium bicarbonate

Already present in our blood, sodium bicarbonate acts as a pH buffer, maintaining the alkalinity of the blood. During intense exercise, blood pH falls (the blood becomes more acidic), limiting exercise duration. But the theory goes that bicarbonate 'loading' can slow this rise in acidity, thus allowing us to work hard for a little longer. Some studies have found beneficial effects in performance at events lasting up to 10 minutes, so it's unlikely to help endurance athletes.

Natural anti-inflammatories

Natural anti-inflammatories such as turmeric and tart cherry juice are appealing as you can be reasonably sure they're free from potential contaminants and won't have negative side-effects. Drinking cherry juice during the days before and after a race may help to reduce delayed onset muscle soreness (DOMS). Unlike high-dose antioxidants, which may affect the body's normal mechanism of inflammation necessary for adaptation to training, studies on cherry juice have not found negative effects and some have been favourable. As with nitrate supplementation, the largest effects are likely to be in those with a diet lacking in nutrients and a better approach would be to improve the overall quality of your diet first, then consider trying cherry juice.

Vitamins and minerals

Supplements, including vitamins, should only be taken to restore an existing deficiency, usually identified through blood tests. Many vitamins and minerals are good for us, some essential, but we only need sufficient amounts – more is not necessarily better and can be very much worse. Current research suggests that, as long as you follow a varied healthy diet, all your vitamin and mineral requirements should be met through food. There are three possible exceptions to this rule: vitamin D, vitamin B12 and iron.

Vitamin D

Vitamin D helps regulate the amount of calcium and phosphate in the body, essential for a range of metabolic processes including healthy bones, teeth and muscles, as well as immune function. It is produced naturally in the body as a result of skin exposure to UV light from the sun. In the UK and other countries with similar light levels, we make all the vitamin D we need from exposure to sunlight between the months of April and September. However, between October and March, sunlight is unlikely to have sufficient UV of the right wavelength for vitamin D synthesis. Current recommendations, therefore, are that everyone should take a vitamin D supplement of 10 micrograms between October and March. People who cover their skin, have darker skin, or don't spend much time outdoors should consider taking a supplement all year round. Overdosing on vitamin D can be detrimental to health.

Vitamin B12

B vitamins are essential for numerous processes throughout the body, and the majority are relatively easily obtained through a healthy diet. However, vitamin B12 is only available from animal-derived sources and some fortified products. Vegans and some vegetarians are usually advised to take a vitamin B12 supplement.

Iron

Iron is essential for haemoglobin, the oxygen-carrying component of red blood cells. Insufficient iron can lead to iron deficiency anaemia, with symptoms including fatigue, breathlessness and heart palpitations. For most people, a healthy, varied diet will provide sufficient iron; however, vegetarians and vegans, menstruating females, and those who have suffered recent blood loss may be at risk of deficiency. Spending time at altitude also increases iron requirements, and insufficient iron may reduce an individual's ability to acclimatise. If you're someone who ticks more than one of these boxes, for example a menstruating female following a vegan diet who's planning to undertake a mountain race at altitude, it would be wise to get your iron levels checked to avoid detrimental effects on both health and performance.

Iron deficiency is identified through blood tests and treated accordingly, so visit your GP if you're concerned. Too much iron is also detrimental, so any iron supplementation should be carefully monitored.

Hydration

Water is essential for our bodies to function. We are around 65 per cent water, and water is necessary for everything from blood volume and heat regulation to the digestion and absorption of the food we eat. We lose fluid all the time – as water vapour in our breath, through our skin as sweat and through excretion. And, as we exercise, especially at high intensities and in warm conditions, those fluid losses increase rapidly.

Drinking to replace our fluid losses is something we do instinctively throughout our lives. But when it comes to sport and exercise, the messages around how much we should drink, and the content and composition of that liquid, can seem pretty complicated. So what, and how much, should we be drinking?

Until relatively recently we were told we should all be drinking as much water as possible, and that our sensation of thirst is an unreliable indicator of our hydration status. Drinking a magic eight glasses of water each day would improve our concentration and complexion, 'flush out toxins' and keep us energised. Drinking more when exercising and competing would also prevent a catastrophic decline in performance. Suddenly, plastic bottles and pee colour charts were everywhere.

In the UK, according to the British Soft Drinks Association, sales of bottled water peaked in 2018 at 2,986 million litres per year. While this is now thankfully declining due to better awareness around many related issues, purchases of sports and energy drinks are showing no signs of slowing down.

Based on claims from sports hydration companies and their sponsored athletes, it's easy to imagine that the moment we start doing any kind of physical activity, we need a personally customised electrolyte- and carbohydrate-balanced drink to avoid the perils of salt, fluid and energy loss. But in reality, we're finely tuned to know what we need, due to our body's mechanisms for detecting and rectifying imbalances. What we need to drink on any given run depends on a number of variables, including how far we're going, the intensity of the run, the weather conditions and the food and drink we had consumed before we set off. In cool conditions, setting off well hydrated, you probably won't feel particularly thirsty on a two-hour, low- or moderate-intensity run. Hot weather, higher-intensity running, and setting out slightly dehydrated all add to your body's need to take on fluids, so on some days you may find you have a raging thirst after only an hour.

No predetermined hydration plan can take all of these interacting factors into account, and drinking too much or too little can both be detrimental to our performance, enjoyment and even our health. So learn to listen to and trust your body's cues and, if you think it might be a thirsty day – because it's hot, you're running hill repeats or it's an early morning run and you haven't had time to fully replace your night-time fluid losses – have some hydration options available, whether that's carrying water with you or running a route with available drinking water.

Remember that most of the time, not taking on fluids on a run of up to about two hours – or finishing a run longer than this in a mild state of dehydration – isn't going to hurt you or your performance. In fact, regularly training in a state of mild dehydration may actually improve your body's ability to conserve and utilise stored water.

On race day, while it's important to start out optimally hydrated, drinking too much can lead to discomfort from a sloshing stomach, needing to stop to pee en route, and even potentially deadly hyponatraemia (see pages 53–54). Even over a marathon distance, faster runners in particular may not need to drink much along the way, especially in cooler conditions. In fact, studies have found that the best marathon runners are often the most dehydrated at the finish of a race. Most marathons have numerous aid stations along the route, so judge your need to drink by thirst, and sip rather than gulp.

If you're keen to avoid needing a pit stop halfway around a race, a good approach is to drink little and often up until two hours before the race starts, then stop drinking. Just before you start, drink enough to quench your thirst, then top up on the way round if you need it.

Most of the time, listening to our cues for thirst is the best way to determine how much we need to drink, whether we're on a run or just getting on with our day. A review of the literature found that when participants drank to thirst rather than to a plan, they lost an average of 2.1 per cent of their starting weight, whereas participants who drank to a hydration plan lost 1 per cent, but most importantly neither group showed any significant difference in performance (Goulet and Hoffman, 2019). The researchers concluded that this fact, combined with 'individual responses to the heat and the plethora of factors associated with the planning and logistics of training or competition', means there's no reason to pre-plan a hydration strategy so long as there's sufficient fluid available.

While drinking to thirst is a perfectly acceptable and effective approach, there are some situations when it isn't practical. The first is when water supplies are limited, for example if there aren't many aid stations in a race or if you're running a route where you can only refill at certain points. On these occasions, you may need to fit your hydration around what's available and, unless you're carrying it with you, it might be worth a quick drink even if you're not particularly thirsty if you know it'll be a while before you have the opportunity to drink again.

The second is during ultramarathons or other very long runs, when our cues for thirst might get confused. After several hours of running, the mouth becomes dry from breathing, which can mimic the sensation of thirst. This can present a problem in longer challenges, when excessive fluid intake is likely to be far more of a danger than dehydration. Many hours into a run, trying to listen to any kind of thirst cues becomes difficult, and this is where even seasoned ultrarunners can get into trouble. In these cases, keeping food intake up at the same time as drinking, and being aware of discomfort from a bloated or sloshing stomach are important, as these are good indicators that you're taking too much fluid on board.

Not long ago, athletes at some big ultramarathons were weighed at aid stations, due to the belief that dehydration was a serious health risk. Athletes who had lost weight were required to restore at least some of that weight through fluid replacement before being allowed to continue. Nowadays, with a greater understanding of the much lower dangers of dehydration in most races compared with over-drinking, this practice is thankfully rare. Remember, while true dehydration undoubtedly does impair performance, the first and most powerful symptom is a raging thirst – it's not something that can happen without you knowing about it.

All about electrolytes

There can't be many runners who haven't heard of electrolytes – look at any running retailer and electrolyte-containing powders, tablets and drinks are everywhere. But what are they, how do they work, and should we all be drinking them?

Chemically, electrolytes are substances that have a natural positive or negative electrical charge when dissolved in water. In the human body they have many important functions, including regulating chemical reactions and blood pressure, nerve conduction and muscle contraction, and maintaining the balance between the fluids inside and outside our cells.

The primary electrolytes we need to worry about during extreme or very prolonged exercise are, in order of importance, sodium, potassium and magnesium. It's rare for potassium and magnesium to be lacking without underlying health conditions or an extreme diet; however, blood plasma sodium concentrations vary greatly during exercise, depending on diet, sweat rate and concentration, hydration status and climatic conditions.

Drinking fluids with added electrolytes may help absorption of fluids from the gut into the bloodstream and can also help slow down the onset of *hyponatraemia*. However, due to the fact that electrolyte drinks are still more dilute than blood plasma, they will not prevent hyponatraemia if you continue to overconsume fluids.

What is hyponatraemia?

Hyponatraemia is a potentially serious condition that occurs when blood plasma sodium concentration falls below normal levels. When this happens, fluid is drawn into the cells in an attempt to re-establish an electrolyte balance across the cell membrane. Eventually, this influx of fluid causes dangerous swelling throughout the body, including in the brain. While thankfully rare, hyponatraemia can result in hospitalisation and, in the worst cases, be fatal.

Hyponatraemia can occur either due to insufficient intake of sodium or over-drinking, which dilutes blood sodium levels. The former is rare for most people, as our diets contain much higher levels of sodium (in the form of salt) than we need for optimal functioning. Within endurance sports, in an effort to avoid the 'perils' of dehydration, over-drinking is a far more likely cause.

Top tips for preventing hyponatraemia

* Drink according to thirst.
* If you're planning to drink to a set schedule, take into account factors that will affect your fluid and sodium losses, including ambient heat and intensity of exercise, along with the availability of water along the route.
* During longer races – those of five hours or more – take on sodium in the form of electrolyte drinks or real food (crisps, salty potatoes, sandwiches etc.).
* Be aware that during longer duration runs drinking electrolyte drinks may slow down the development of hyponatraemia, but won't prevent it.

Sweating

Sweating is one of our evolved responses that helps maintain homeostasis (see pages 8–9) by keeping us cool when our core temperature rises due to exertion or hot conditions. As well as thermoregulation, some researchers suggest that sweating may also play a role in eliminating unwanted or excess substances from the body, including the excretion of excess dietary salt.

Humans usually sweat for one of two reasons – either because our muscles are working hard and generating a lot of heat, which needs to be removed from the body for optimal functioning, or because of overstimulated nerves – the unwelcome sweaty palms and armpits we get before a job interview or a date.

Sweat is mostly water, with high concentrations of sodium and chloride and a low concentration of potassium. The fluid that makes up sweat comes from the spaces between cells, where it collects from blood plasma. When a sweat gland is stimulated, fluid travels through the sweat duct to the opening on to the skin. We sweat all the time, but what happens to the fluid on its way from the cells to our skin differs, depending on how much we're sweating – our sweat rate.

During times of low sweat production (rest; cool temperature) most of the sodium and chloride and much of the water from the fluid is reabsorbed by the duct as it travels slowly through the duct, so very little fluid or salt reaches the outside. During times of high sweat production (exercise; hot temperature), fluid moves rapidly through the duct meaning there's less time for sodium and chloride reabsorption. This then forms the powdery residue you'll often find on your skin after a long run in warm conditions.

Sedentary individuals who are not heat adapted are generally able produce about one litre of sweat per hour. With a combination of training and heat adaptation over a period of a few weeks, however, this can increase to between two and three litres per hour.

Keeping cool

Our bodies lose heat through several different mechanisms, including through radiation to the surrounding air and through evaporative cooling via our sweat. When sweat evaporates from the skin's surface, energy, in the form of heat, is used for the process of turning liquid water into gas. This energy loss results in cooling.

Humans' evolved high sweat rates and relative hairlessness compared with other mammals makes evaporating sweat a highly effective means of cooling. But what happens when we cover up our sweaty, hairless bodies? Sweating also makes our clothing wet, which then works to cool us down by conduction, as water is a much better conductor of heat than air. That's why wet clothing is highly effective as a cooling mechanism – a great thing in a warm weather ultra, but potentially deadly up a mountain in cold conditions.

A major factor that influences the rate of evaporation is the humidity of the surrounding air. Humid air is already saturated with water vapour, so sweat does not evaporate and cool your body as efficiently as when the air is dry.

Salty sweat

Many people believe they are either salty sweaters or not, giving rise to the theory that the saltier your sweat, the more 'lost salts' need to be replaced. But the amount of salt in your sweat doesn't necessarily reflect the salt content of your blood plasma – which is the important thing – and is related to how much salt is present in your diet. Salty sweaters may just be those who ingest the most salt, with the salty sweat being the body's homeostatic mechanism for restoring optimal salt levels. In fact, some researchers have suggested that one of the health benefits of exercise is to offset the negative effects of excess salt in the diet through sweat.

During extended periods of exercise, such as an ultramarathon, large amounts of salt are lost in sweat over time, and these do need replacing once exercise duration exceeds around five hours. Sports drinks contain some salts (electrolytes) but, especially during really long runs – ultramarathons lasting a day or more – you'll need to balance out your fluid intake and sweat sodium losses by ingesting more sodium. You'll probably find you start craving salt and savoury foods over sweet gels and chews at this point – the reason why ultramarathons tend to provide salty foods at aid stations later on in the race.

Do I need a sweat test?

Sweat testing, like much other testing, is big business. While sweat tests can be useful in understanding the rate and composition of sweat, particularly for researchers, there are some major caveats when it comes to private testing, especially if you're planning a hydration strategy based on the results.

Sweat tests are only accurate when carried out meticulously. Poorly conducted tests will collect and therefore measure salts from the skin and pores as well as salts being lost through sweat, giving an artificially high reading. Researchers generally discard the first two samples and use subsequent samples for analysis to reduce the likelihood of contamination.

Sweat rates and content vary hugely depending on multiple factors. It's easy to miss these nuances and assume that the numbers you're given after a sweat test are 'your' numbers. In reality, they're a snapshot of your sweating at a specific time on a specific day under specific conditions.

Balancing hydration and sodium levels should be fairly straightforward, left to the body's homeostatic mechanisms and our well-developed thirst and salt-craving responses. As we run a long way, we'll naturally gravitate towards the food and drink that appeals most. During the course of a long run or race we'll sweat a lot, eat a lot (including sodium) and drink a lot, and as long as this continues, we'll be fine. Add in gastrointestinal issues such as nausea, vomiting and impaired absorption due to gut damage, though, and the potential dangers of hyponatraemia are well worth keeping in mind (see pages 53–54).

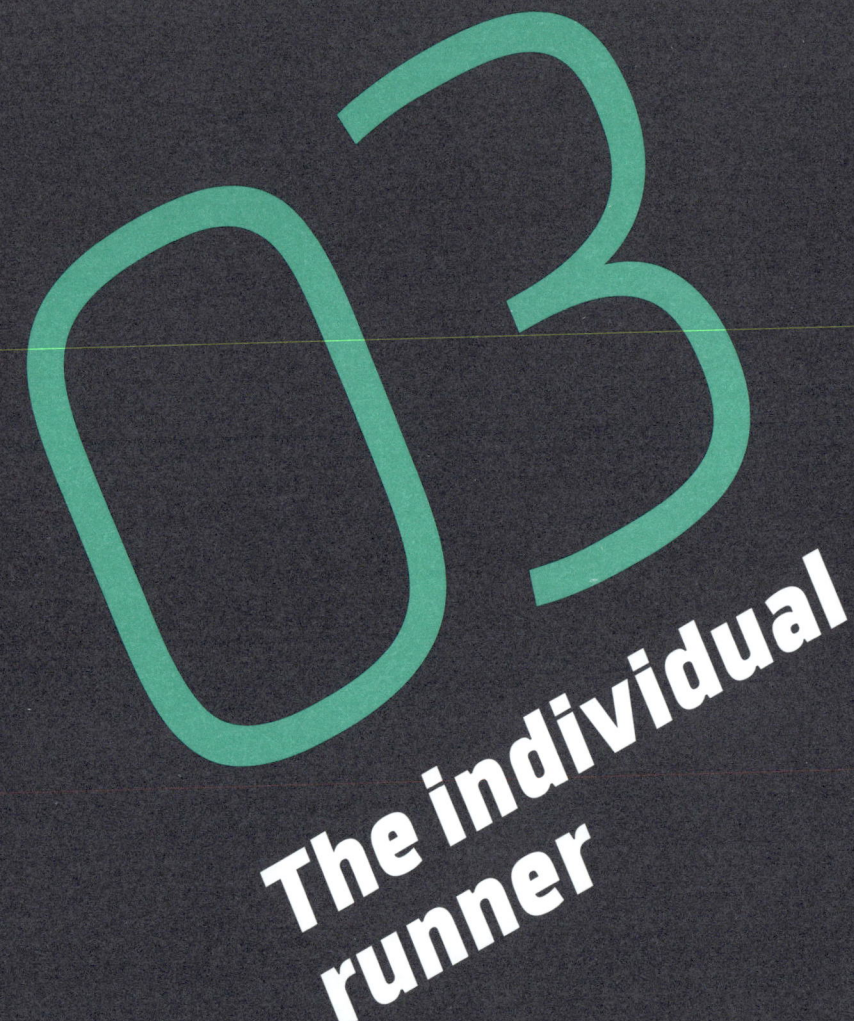

The individual runner

As individual human beings, our bodies and brains, passions and preferences, experiences and eccentricities are all absolutely unique to us. One of the challenges of writing a how-to book (like this one) is that it somehow needs to offer up the best available evidence-based guidance, while acknowledging that no two people experience running – or anything else in life – in exactly the same way. An important part of this process is addressing the big differences between the experiences of different groups of people based on often-interacting factors such as ethnicity, socio-economic status, sex, gender and age. In this chapter, we take a closer look at some of these factors and how they specifically apply to running.

Diversity and inclusion in running

Looked at objectively, running as a sport should be one of the most inclusive out there. But the culture around running isn't always as inclusive and accepting as it could be. As we explored earlier on in this book, becoming and being a runner isn't just about having the physical and psychological assets of a runner. It's also about everything we bring to running – our sex, gender, ethnicity, socio-economic and personal history, and the complex interactions of those with the others we meet during our running experiences.

Taking up any new pastime, whether it's running, lacemaking or morris dancing, the experience is far from just being about coordinating the required physical movements. If we're to truly experience that pastime, to understand it from within, it's about *becoming* a runner (or a lacemaker or morris dancer) and everything that entails, from learning the right words to use, what the leading influences are, the history, what to wear and so on. It's all these things that make our interests both intriguing and terrifying when we're new to them, and so involving and all-encompassing once we're in the know – once we are a part of them and they are, in turn, a part of us.

Running clubs can be daunting when you're new, especially if you don't see yourself represented in the club's existing members. If you're already a member of a running club, never underestimate the value of stepping forwards and welcoming newbies, introducing yourself and taking them under your wing for the first couple of club nights, until they've settled in. Jen says:

'As someone who finds big groups and social situations hard, but also loves running and the many friendships I've made through running, those who have shown warmth and welcomed me when I've been new and terrified hold a special place in my heart. When you're busy catching up with your club mates and you see someone new loitering nervously at the door, go and welcome them. It might be a hard thing to do, but honestly it means the world.'

It's also worth looking around more widely at the running cultures we inhabit, both in person and online, and those we watch or read about in the media. Runners from east African countries such as Kenya, Ethiopia and Uganda have dominated international distance running for years, inspiring numerous fantastic books and articles written by those trying to work out what makes runners from these countries so good. Take a look at the typical line-up at the start of an ultramarathon, though, and the picture couldn't be more different, although it is slowly starting to change. Most ultramarathons don't yet offer the kind of prize money it's worth dedicating the kind of infrastructure some countries have built around marathon running to. They're costly to enter, to buy the required kit for, and in terms of time away from work and caring commitments. Those who can afford both the time and money to dedicate themselves to ultrarunning are few and far between, and it's therefore necessarily a small pool from a diversity perspective.

What's our point here? Perhaps it's that enthusiasm and encouragement about a sport are great. That, yes, representation of under-represented groups of people is essential. But it's also worth considering *why* these groups are under-represented. If you're regularly putting out messages that anyone can do anything if they put their mind to it, consider that this isn't always the case for everyone – perhaps even for the majority of people. For those who would love to take on more big challenges but have caring duties they can't absent themselves from; for those struggling to make ends meet who couldn't conceive of spending hundreds of pounds on race entries; for those with any number of reasons for not being able to do the things you're able to do, however much they'd love to, be considerate that what's available to some isn't necessarily available to all. Yes, you're awesome for running an ultramarathon a few months after giving birth, but that's also an immense privilege, bringing together the necessary time, money and support in order to be able to do so. If you're just getting out at the weekends because you spend the rest of the week juggling childcare and work with financial struggles, then you're bloody awesome too.

In their excellent book, *Running, Identity and Meaning*, Neil Baxter and Helen Jefferson Lenskyj take a long, hard look at running and runners. They explore the roles of social variables in running, including how gender, age, ethnicity, occupation, wealth and education affect people's engagement – or lack thereof – in the sport. They highlight deep class inequalities in running culture, noting:

'**Running's status as a potent medium for the performance of a range of middle-class identities, tastes and virtues.**'

A fascinating deeper dive into the culture of fell running specifically illustrates how, over recent decades and in reaction to changes in the social make-up of the wider sport:

'**Fell running has evolved from an obscure rural tradition into a bastion of gendered, classed and ethnic privilege.**'

So, what can we do to help make running more accepting and inclusive? First by accepting that, as runners, we may be part of the problem. Many of us are also negatively affected by it. Increasingly, those from less well-represented sections of society are standing up and raising awareness of the inequalities in running, creating groups and safe, inclusive spaces for runners who don't conform to the affluent, white, male majority. Things are changing, but not fast enough, and change won't persist without continued action to make it happen. As runners – and as humans – we must all have our eyes open to inequality and do everything in our power to counter it.

Female runners

'**When I go to the Boston Marathon now, I have wet shoulders – women fall into my arms crying. They're weeping for joy because running has changed their lives. They feel they can do anything.**'
– KATHRINE SWITZER (the first woman to run in the Boston Marathon as an officially registered competitor, 1967)

Equity in sport is something women have always had to fight for. Over and over again we've been told we're not capable enough, not strong enough, not interesting enough to warrant inclusion on the international sporting stage. And yet, given half a chance, we've

proved that we are indeed capable and strong enough to compete at every distance and that women's sport is able to draw large crowds as long as it's given the airtime it deserves.

The inaugural Tour de France Femmes took place in 2022 and was widely pronounced a huge success. The London Marathon and Ultra-Tour du Mont-Blanc have followed other big races in announcing that pregnant women can now defer their race places. Women's football and rugby is being shown on TV, which is just as well as the UK teams are doing a far better job of winning major tournaments than our men's teams. Across the board it's being proven that, given the chance, women's sport is as exciting, competitive and highly skilled as men's sport and it's a joy to share the experience of women's sporting successes with our daughter – something that was still a very long way off when we were her age and the first women's Olympic marathon had only recently taken place.

And yet we find ourselves conflicted: yes, it's a fantastic time for women's sport and we're so happy our daughter has such a depth and breadth of female role models from which to draw inspiration. But why has it all taken so long? And we're still nowhere near equity: when it comes to participation in sport, from school onwards, and when it comes to inclusion in scientific research, there's still a long way to go.

Differences and similarities between male and female runners

Alongside factors such as our individuality, training and psychology, sex-related differences between male and female bodies, from anatomy and biomechanics to the influences of hormones, shape the runners we become. When it comes to running performance, some factors have more of an effect than others, and this effect can change depending on the conditions and distance of the run.

The fastest men have always been faster than the fastest women over every Olympic running distance. Analysis of existing data suggests that males have something in the region of a 10 per cent advantage over females due to a wealth of factors including larger hearts and lungs, more powerful muscles, biomechanical differences in the bony alignment of the pelvis and lower limbs, and even, on average, the effect of having larger feet adding just that bit of extra leverage through every step. But as the distances get longer, and particularly into extreme ultradistances of 100 miles and more, something interesting happens – the male advantage reduces markedly, and may even disappear altogether.

Women and ultrarunning

Women finishing high up on the overall finishers' boards at ultramarathons is becoming a regular occurrence. At the Western States Endurance Run, one of the best-known 100-milers in the world, women made up half of the top 30 finishers in 2021, including British paediatrician, Beth Pascall, who finished top woman and seventh overall. The same summer, US ultrarunning legend Courtney Dauwalter also finished seventh overall, this time at UTMB (Ultra-Trail du Mont-Blanc), the world championships of mountain ultrarunning, setting a new women's record on the course in the process.

Multiple-record-holding US ultrarunner Camille Herron only seems to be improving now she's in her 40s. In interviews she has talked about the wealth of running experience she now has behind her, how this has enabled her to hone and develop her training after years of running more than 100 miles each week in training. Instead of doing weekly long runs and regular speedwork, she now only runs long once a month and has reduced her fast running considerably. Listening to Camille talking about this process of discovery, of breaking her own trail as a woman in ultrarunning, it's clear how new women still are to the sport, how much they are still feeling their way, and how this is a legacy of having so few role models to follow.

In 2019, Jasmin Paris, a vet and mum of two, shot to global fame after she became the first woman to claim the overall win at the Montane Winter Spine. Widely regarded as amongst the world's toughest ultras, it covers 268 miles between Edale in the English Peak District and Kirk Yetholm in the Scottish Borders. Running through the cold, dark and mud of the British winter, runners cross the Yorkshire Dales, Hadrian's Wall and the Cheviot Hills, carrying their own kit for the entirety of the race. Jasmin crossed the finish line in 83 hours 12 minutes and 23 seconds, beating the course record and the previous women's record, all while expressing milk for her 14-month-old daughter along the way. Incredibly, Jasmin had gone home, showered, slept and appeared on BBC Breakfast before the second-placed runner, Eoin Keith, finished fifteen hours later.

When we recently interviewed Jasmin, she talked modestly about her achievements, about how fitting training in around a full-time job and being a mum of two young children means getting up at 5 a.m. every morning. We shared stories of running and breastfeeding and how, for ultrarunning mums, it's just another part of the logistical puzzle of running and racing that we need to fit in. For both Jasmin and Sophie Power, who also found the world discussing her breasts after a photo of her feeding her baby and expressing milk simultaneously at the UTMB went viral, the platform they're afforded by this unexpected publicity is an important one for showing other mums what is possible, as well as demanding more specific support for women at such events.

While male muscles are, on average, able to generate larger forces more quickly, female muscles have been found to be more fatigue-resistant, which may be an advantage when the distances get longer. Bring in the multifactorial aspects that come together to create ultrarunning success: good self-management, problem-solving, dealing with sleep deprivation, on-the-go food tolerance, fat metabolism and a wealth of psychological skills, and it's easy to see how the traditional male advantage in sport, gained by greater muscle strength and power, larger heart and lungs, and biomechanics can be reduced – or even overcome.

A recent study explored sex-specific physiological responses in male and female athletes running the UTMB (Tiller *et al.*, 2022). The findings investigated the overall impact of ultrarunning, and in particular ultrarunning at altitude, on runners, but found that these effects were less pronounced in female athletes than in males. These results, along with the growing number of high-placing females in ultramarathon races globally, suggest that over longer distances, and especially those that also involve numerous other challenges including everything from altitude to sleep-deprivation, the sex-specific advantages of male athletes may be drastically reduced, or even eliminated altogether.

The question of *if*, *when* and *how* female athletes might be able to consistently outperform males over ultradistances is one that fascinates sport physiologists. A detailed review of the literature (Tiller *et al.*, 2021) came to the following conclusions:

> **'The literature indicates that while females exhibit numerous pheno-types that would be expected to confer an advantage in ultra-endurance competition (e.g. greater fatigue resistance, greater substrate efficiency, and lower energetic demands), they also exhibit several characteristics that unequivocally impinge on performance (e.g. lower O_2-carrying capacity, increased prevalence of gastrointestinal distress, and sex-hormone effects on cellular function/injury risk).'**

The review concludes with the important point that those traits that are most advantageous to female athletes may only come to the fore during extreme endurance events and, paradoxically, these are the events at which women's participation is lowest.

The answer is, of course, to increase support for women in ultrarunning, including fairer entry selection methods and more vocal support from influential men with established reputations in the sport.

Training, racing and the menstrual cycle

Every runner is unique, and every menstrual cycle is unique. If you're a menstruating female, getting to know what's normal for you is important. Tracking your menstrual cycle can help you to know when you're ovulating, when to expect menstruation (good for planning ahead and to avoid any unwelcome surprises), and to know how you feel at different times of the month both in yourself and in training. It also allows you to pick up on changes quickly, such as bleeding at unusual times, changes to the length of your cycle, duration or heaviness of bleeding, or if you miss a period.

WHAT IS THE MENSTRUAL CYCLE?

The menstrual cycle is counted from the first day of one period to the first day of the next. Menstruation (bleeding) usually occurs every 21 to 35 days, averaging around 28 days, and lasts between two and seven days.

The primary phases of the menstrual cycle are the **follicular phase** (which runs from the first day of a menstrual period to ovulation) and the **luteal phase** (from ovulation to the end of the cycle).

A menstrual cycle might be regular or irregular, and your periods might be light or heavy, painful or pain-free, long or short, and still be considered normal. Essentially, within a broad range, 'normal' is what's normal for you. Because changes in our menstrual cycle can reflect issues elsewhere in our bodies, any lasting deviations from *your* normal should be checked out by a GP. Hormonal contraception, such as birth control pills and intrauterine devices (IUDs), will alter your menstrual cycle.

The effects of the menstrual cycle on training and performance in sport has become a hot topic for research in recent years. A recent systematic review and meta-analysis of the existing literature looked at athletes' perceptions of the effects of their menstrual cycle on their levels of motivation, competitiveness, sleep quality, stress, muscle soreness, fatigue, perceived effort, mood, menstrual symptoms, perceived endurance, and readiness (Paludo *et al.*, 2022). Changes in athletes' perceived effort during different stages of their cycle were assessed. The main findings were as follows:

* Level of perceived exertion does not differ between the two primary phases of the menstrual cycle.
* Motivation and competitiveness may vary during the cycle, with better outcomes in the ovulatory phase, compared to follicular and luteal.
* Mood disturbances may occur in the pre-menstrual phase; decreased vigour in the menstrual phase; increased menstrual symptoms in the follicular phase; and increased fatigue and decreased sleep quality in the luteal phase.

Another study (Garcia *et al.*, 2023) found that, compared with the mid-follicular phase, anger, anxiety, behaviour change, pain and negative affect (emotional experience) were significantly greater during menstruation, whereas fluid retention, anger and behaviour change were greater during the late luteal phase compared with the mid-follicular phase. It was also noted that participants felt less motivated to start exercise during menstruation compared with other phases.

> While it's clear that there are a number of effects of the menstrual cycle on the perception of effort and other factors during sport, the good news is that these effects aren't necessarily detrimental to performance. Researchers asked women to self-select their running speed on a treadmill and, regardless of where they were in their cycle, and the fact that they experienced symptoms, they settled on the same running pace – their cycle didn't slow them down (Garcia *et al.*, 2023).

Pregnancy

Running during pregnancy can be a good way to hang on to a notion of your former self when everything seems to be changing. As long as your pregnancy is uncomplicated and you ran before you were pregnant, there's no reason not to carry on.

> Your body will very quickly tell you if you're over-doing it – **always** be limited by discomfort, pain or anything just not feeling right.

According to current NHS guidance, active pregnancies are related to lower rates of complications later on. Being fit and strong is a huge benefit during labour – especially the often-lengthy labours of first babies. The whole experience can be not unlike an ultramarathon! Staying active will also make returning to running after pregnancy easier.

If you can keep running regularly throughout pregnancy, this will allow your body to adapt most easily to its rapidly changing shape, physiology and biomechanics. Because change happens so quickly, if you have some time off it can feel like you're running in a completely different body when you start again. If you need some time off, ease back into running gradually rather than picking up where you left off. Many women find the second trimester is the most pleasant for running, after the fatigue and nausea of the first trimester is done but the extra size and weight of the

third trimester is yet to come. If you find running too uncomfortable later on, swimming is a great alternative, allowing you to continue exercising while your body is supported by the water.

> You will probably need to make some adjustments to your running kit, including a new running bra to accommodate the larger breasts that typically accompany pregnancy, as well as clothing that accommodates your growing bump. A bump band, providing coverage and a little support to your bump, can be a useful addition.

The hormone relaxin, which is released during pregnancy to provide the 'stretch' required to accommodate and give birth to a new human, makes our tendons and ligaments more stretchy, so it's a good idea to avoid technical terrain as twisting an ankle is likely and the consequences of falling can be serious. Going to high altitude is also not recommended due to its potential effects on both mother and baby.

Postnatal running

After pregnancy, running can provide a valuable way to take time out for yourself, as well as helping your body heal and strengthen after the demands of pregnancy and birth. Current advice in the UK is to wait until after your six-week postnatal check with your GP before restarting running, but this should be combined with how you feel your body is recovering and how ready you are.

> In an ideal world, working with a specialist physiotherapist would be a standard part of postnatal care for everyone – then many of the more common longer-term problems associated with pregnancy and birth, such as incontinence, pelvic floor dysfunction and abdominal muscle separation, could be treated earlier and should become less severe. If you can, seek out a pelvic health specialist physiotherapist to oversee your postnatal rehabilitation.

While the specifics are highly individual and depend on many factors including the mode of delivery, most women will have some weakness and damage to their pelvic floor after pregnancy. Even fairly slow running generates high forces through the body – often two or three times your body weight with each footstrike. This is associated with a rise in intra-abdominal pressure, which pushes down on the pelvic floor. Unless the pelvic floor is sufficiently recovered and strengthened, it is at a high risk of further damage and even prolapse – for more on this and suggested exercises for pelvic floor health, see pages 107–108.

If you're suffering from incontinence, pain, heaviness or decreased strength/ function, go and see your GP and get a referral to a specialist. These symptoms are all indicative of pelvic floor and/or abdominal muscle dysfunction.

It can be tempting to rush back into running after pregnancy for many reasons, and sometimes running is the one thing that keeps us going through the physically and emotionally stressful months of new motherhood. You're the expert on your body, so listen to its cues. Doing too much too soon and ending up injured, especially easy to do when you're not sleeping well, will only add to the stress. Be prepared for a full return to feeling like you have full control over your running body to take a year or more, especially with second and subsequent pregnancies.

If you choose to breastfeed, you will be burning up to an extra 500 calories a day. Ensure your energy intake covers this as well as your training and other energy expenditure. Having (mostly) healthy snacks within easy reach of your favourite breastfeeding spot is definitely a top tip.

Running through the menopause

Female runners experience many hormone-related changes throughout life, some of which can have an impact on running. Going through the menopause, and the years leading up to it – the perimenopause – can change how we feel about our bodies and our relationship with running. But the good news is there's no need to stop, and running can even help with some of the more challenging menopausal symptoms.

WHAT IS THE MENOPAUSE?

The menopause occurs when females stop ovulating, and therefore having a menstrual cycle and periods. In the UK, this normally occurs between the ages of 45 and 55, although it can happen earlier or later due to a variety of factors. There are three distinct phases:

* **Perimenopause**, which can last anywhere from a few months to several years, is when oestrogen levels are reducing but may fluctuate.
* **Menopause** is the point when periods have been absent for 12 months.
* **Post-menopause** is simply the time after menopause.

In the same way as every female experiences their menstrual cycle differently, each journey through the menopause is individual.

Perimenopause and menopause symptoms are experienced by around 75 per cent of females and can include hot flushes, night sweats, poor sleep, irregular or heavy periods, breast pain, urinary incontinence, fatigue, joint and muscle aches, reduced motivation, weight gain, changes in body composition, headaches and emotional effects such as anxiety and low mood. But not everyone experiences all of these symptoms, and the good news is that running can help reduce or manage them.

Running has been found to improve mood, reduce stress and anxiety, and maintain familiarity with a changing body. It can also improve sleep and control weight gain. Including strength and mobility work and speed sessions in your training plan can also help mitigate against both the symptoms of menopause and age-related declines in muscle strength, bone density and joint range of motion.

While many women continue to race throughout menopause, if you're finding it's slowing you down this might be a good time to switch to the trails or choose longer, slower races that can be great adventures without as much time pressure.

Carbohydrate metabolism changes during menopause, in particular insulin sensitivity. This means that following a balanced diet is particularly important during these years, reducing the likelihood of unpleasant blood sugar spikes and dips. Including plenty of good quality protein in your diet will also help to support strength training, stimulating more muscle protein synthesis.

Some research suggests that plant foods that are a source of phytoestrogens (compounds that mimic the effects of oestrogen) can be helpful during menopause (Abdi *et al.*, 2021). These include chickpeas, ground flaxseeds and unprocessed soy.

Older runners

The world's population is ageing. While the accepted narrative is a steady decline in all aspects of our performance as we age, many older runners are nonetheless continuing to flourish – athletically and otherwise – well into old age. Staying active throughout our lives is a key way to lay the foundations for healthy and active ageing, while life events like the kids leaving home or retirement can open up a whole world of opportunities for embracing having more time to take up a new sport.

Not everyone wants to shuffle along the well-worn path of decline into their later years, and age certainly doesn't have to be a barrier to sporting hopes and dreams. So don't be afraid to tackle those stereotypes – or, for that matter, your first parkrun, marathon or Ironman.

We are both into masters athlete territory and having to accept that our race performances won't continue to improve indefinitely, along with the speed of recovery between sessions. But we're lucky enough to have some brilliant role models in our lives, showing us by example that ageing doesn't need to slow us down. Our parents run and rock climb, go camping and cycling, and spend their days tramping over mountains and moorland. Freed from work commitments, they appear to be embracing retirement for all it's worth. We hope we can do the same when the time comes – we've certainly got a lengthy list of projects lined up.

Understanding the specifics of training and fuelling to optimise our approach to running as we age helps us understand our own bodies over the course of our lifetimes, and support our older relatives to remain active, too.

Where the line we cross that identifies us as 'older' runners lies is an uncertain one. In competitive athletics, masters athletes include anyone over the age of 35, but in recreational running, and indeed physiologically, the true point at which age makes a substantial difference to our approach to running is usually somewhat later.

Many people take up running later on in life, and for many reasons. This is even the case with some top runners; legendary ultrarunner Nicky Spinks (who is currently in her fifties) didn't take up running until she was in her thirties. She regularly beats men and women less than half her age, even after dealing with breast cancer and a mastectomy. The number of older runners out there being incredible role models and proving that age is just a number – especially over the longer distances – gives us hope and dreams for our own running futures.

Jen says:

'I'm so fascinated by what happens when people take up running later on in life that I decided to do a PhD in it. I always think with these runners there's this enormous sense of potential – perhaps they were put off running at school and so never discovered it before

– but who knows what they could go on to achieve now? Even if it's rediscovering themselves in a new way: discovering a new identify – that of being a runner – that they never thought they'd have. As I learn more about these runners, I find their stories are a wonderful counter to the traditional narrative of decline that's so entrenched in our culture – life (as a runner) really can begin at 40 or 50 or 60 ... '

What happens to runners as we age?

In a recent study, researchers analysed the finishing times for 40 runners (39 male and one female) who had run a sub-three-hour marathon for five consecutive decades (Lepers *et al.*, 2021). The runners peaked at an average age of 28.6 years, with an average time of 2 hours 23 minutes, after which times increased by an average of 1 minute 4 seconds per year. The study concludes that:

'With consistent training and racing regimens, it is possible to limit the age-related decline in marathon performance to less than 7 per cent per decade at least until 60 years of age.'

For those of us whom these marathon times are beyond our wildest dreams, it's very probable that, through optimising our training and everything else that goes along with a healthy, active life, these declines could be even less. And there's no need to stop at 60, either. The researchers add a final note that:

'Further studies are required to verify if such a low rate of age-related decline in endurance performance could be maintained after 60 years of age.'

Marathon times tend to peak for both elite and non-elite runners between the ages of 25 and 35, with previous studies suggesting a linear decline from here to our 70s, and then a steep drop-off in performance as we reach 80. For longer distances, the effect of age may be even lower. In fact, the age at which elite athletes reach their peak endurance performance in both ultrarunning and Ironman triathlon has steadily increased over the past few decades for both males and females. Could this be, in part, due to a better understanding of the ageing body, and how to modify training to optimally suit its specific requirements? Or could it be a general turn against the entrenched narrative of decline – the 'it's all downhill from here' message that's so pervasive once we head into middle age?

As we age, our body composition changes, our VO_2 max starts to decline, our bones become more porous, and fitness becomes just a little harder to hang on to. One of the primary influencers of our ability to keep active, including running competitively should we wish to, is muscle strength.

> As we age, our rate of muscle protein synthesis – the building and repair of muscle – slows, meaning that without regular stimulus, muscle atrophy happens far more rapidly than it does when we're younger. To combat this, it's important for older athletes to ensure a combination of regular resistance training and sufficient dietary protein in order to keep muscles strong and functioning optimally.

As well as producing movement – from large movements to fine motor control – and the power and force required for activity, our muscles provide strength and support to our bones and joints, allow us to move more effectively and efficiently, and protect us from both acute and chronic injury. Without sufficient musculature, we can't cope with the stresses required to maintain and improve cardiovascular fitness. This means that keeping our muscles in top condition is therefore one of the most important things we can do in order to keep running and racing as we age.

If you've always lifted weights, there may be no reason not to carry on doing so. But for those new to weightlifting, or anyone with joint issues such as osteoarthritis, lifting heavy weights may cause more problems than it solves by putting large amounts of stress through our joints. For these people, therefore, rather than high-weight, low-rep weight training, keeping the weights low and doing more reps will get many of the same results without endangering your joints.

Younger runners

Given the freedom to do so from an early age, children run for the joy of movement, exhilarating in the thrill of speed. Unfortunately, once they reach school age, many children – and especially girls – become far more sedentary. Running is a great form of exercise for children of all ages. However, particularly if a child or young person is very keen on training and running in a more structured, competitive way, it's important to be aware of how the stresses of running can impact the growing, changing body. England Athletics currently recommends that children under 10 years old shouldn't run more than 2,000 metres, rising to 5,000 metres by age 13 or 14, and 10,000 metres by age 16 or 17. Supporting training with appropriate energy and nutrient intake, as well as strength, conditioning and mobility exercises is also important.

Becoming a resilient runner

04

Planning your training

One of the key developments in running in recent decades is *training theory* – the idea that how you train – including the volume, intensity and structure of that training – impacts your performance. But what's the best combination? Coaches, athletes and scientists alike strive for the answers to this complex and multi-faceted riddle, and recent research is finally shining some light on what works best, and why. In this chapter we go through the theory; later on, in chapter 17, you can learn how to apply this and build your perfect training plan.

The core principles of training

At its most basic, training is the process by which we become better runners. Regular, long-term, appropriate training strengthens and conditions our bodies and builds technique, confidence and experience. Regardless of our individual starting point or goals, training for running – or any other sport for that matter – comes down to the following key principles.

Individuality

Each of us brings our own, unique combination of physical and psychological characteristics to our running. What we want from our running depends on many things, including our running history, age, sex, health, goals and motivation. As a result, no single off-the-peg training programme will work for everyone. And for this reason, we encourage you to use the tools that follow to construct a training programme that is right for you, and update it regularly as you continue onwards through your running journey. See chapter 17 for full guidance on how to do this.

Consistency

It takes many years to work out what kind of runner you are, from what you like and what you don't to what works for your body and what doesn't. Both physical and psychological adaptations happen slowly. Allow yourself the time to build both fitness and experience in running, taking each success as an indication that the process is working, and each failure as a valuable learning opportunity for the future. Meaningful improvements in running should be viewed over a period of years, not months. Taking the long view, building up gradually, and prioritising consistency over big peaks and troughs in training will turn you into a resilient runner, ready to run at your best for many years to come.

Specificity

As well as taking time, adaptations are specific. Our bodies will adapt to the specific stresses exerted upon them, including the specifics of the pace, distance and terrain we run on. If you're training for a fast 5K fell race, you need to practise running fast over rough terrain, perhaps navigating as you go. If you're training for a road marathon, you need to include long runs, marathon-pace runs, and do much of your training on roads in order to condition your body to its stresses. If you're training for a mountain ultra, you need to be spending long hours on your feet in the mountains.

Specific training does a number of things. It stimulates physiological adaptations right through your body that will help you perform at your best on race day. It conditions bones, joints, muscles and tendons to the specific demands of the distance and terrain you'll be competing on, stressing them in the short-term in the way you want them to adapt longer-term. It also allows you to figure out where your weak points are, so you can work harder on them well in advance of race day.

Practising your nutrition strategy during training not only helps you to work out what you need and what you can tolerate, but also trains your gut to work with foods, drinks and other products you're using. Being specific in your training also pays dividends psychologically. Standing on the start line of your 'A' race, knowing you've put in months of training on ground that closely matches what you're about to encounter means you can feel relaxed and confident, rather than terrified.

Base training – undertaken several months out from a key race – can be fairly generic, but the closer you get to your race the more specific you need your training to be to prepare you for the specific conditions you'll encounter on race day. This includes everything from the pace you're aiming for, to the terrain, weather conditions, altitude, nutrition and hydration.

Specificity also extends to training appropriately for your age, biological sex and personal history – injuries, illnesses and long-term conditions, biomechanical anomalies and so on. Good training is specific both to an event, and an individual.

Balance

A successful approach to running balances hard days with easy days, training stress with life stress, enjoyment of the good things in life with enough moderation to support both health and performance. The best way to achieve balance is to listen to yourself. Be aware of your body's cues, and your mind's triggers. If you're feeling like you're constantly depriving yourself of something for the sake of your running – whether that's time with friends or family, a lie-in at the weekend, or ice cream – consider why you're depriving yourself. If the sacrifices aren't really worth the gains it might be worth reassessing your approach. If you're experiencing longer-term problems with motivation, fatigue, mood, or hormonal disturbances such as reduced libido or a missed period, these are sure signs the balance is out, and a professional medical opinion should be sought.

Progression

Once you begin a focused and structured approach to training, you should start to see improvements fairly rapidly. Our perceived effort (how hard it feels like we're working) during harder sessions improves after as little as a week. Meaningful improvements in VO_2 max, lactate threshold and running economy – and therefore time trial performance – can happen in a month. Body composition changes may be noticeable after six to eight weeks. If you're not seeing improvements in performance, along with tangible markers of increasing fitness such as a reduction in resting heart rate, it may be that your training isn't hard enough to stimulate adaption; your training is too hard for your level of fitness and conditioning; or that you're not fuelling and recovering appropriately.

It's important to bear in mind, though, that improvements in running are far from linear. When we start out as runners, improvements come quickly. Shaving half an hour off your time between your first and second marathons is perfectly plausible, but with each marathon run the improvements keep getting smaller. In the same way, if you're a relaxed and uncompetitive now-and-then runner and you decide to start following a plan, by increasing your mileage and including some harder sessions, you'll notice improvements relatively quickly, but these will gradually start to plateau over time. This is the law of diminishing returns: initial gains happen quickly and easily, but with time improvements get smaller and harder to achieve.

As we discussed on pages 13–14, using a progressive overload approach to structure your training over the longer term will result in optimal adaptations, provided both the rate of progression and the amount of overload are optimal. Remember, training should create sufficient stress and therefore damage to stimulate repair and adaptation (supercompensation) without overloading to the point of injury or excessive fatigue. Both progression and overload should be increased gradually, allowing sufficient recovery time between sessions. Progression doesn't happen linearly and won't continue indefinitely, so factor in recovery weeks during heavier training blocks and 'off season' periods during your training and racing year.

Self-efficacy

Self-efficacy is a psychological concept, which describes a person's belief in their ability to carry out the task at hand. It's a little like confidence, only it's highly specific to a task – someone who has high self-efficacy for football, for example, won't necessarily feel the same about knitting.

A good training plan is great for improving self-efficacy, as it means you know what you're doing and why you're doing it. You have confidence in your ability to reach your running goals through the daily training you're undertaking. Without this, training can feel directionless, and goals can feel daunting and unachievable. If you're struggling with low self-efficacy, reassessing your goals, talking to knowledgeable friends, joining a club, listening to podcasts with runners and running experts, and reading books like this one all help.

Enjoyment

Fun means different things to different people. But whatever your particular definition, running is meant to be enjoyable. Some runs will, of course, be hard work. But if you love running you can find joy even in the slogs. If you're stuck in a rut, it's always worth trying something new: explore a new route; leave the watch behind if you usually run with one; do a timed session with a watch if you normally don't; meet a friend; or listen to an audiobook. There are countless ways to inject a bit of enjoyment in a running routine that's gone stale, you just need to be a bit creative.

Self-care and resilience

Being a resilient runner throughout our lives requires paying careful attention to ourselves. It's easy to neglect when life's busy and so many other people have so many demands on our time and our physical and emotional resources. But having a solid foundation of good self-care practices that underpin everything else makes us more effective and more resilient as runners and human beings. Practising good self-care isn't selfish, in fact it's the opposite: making self-care a habit means you'll look after yourself first and then be more able to be there for others.

Key areas for developing good self-care habits

* **Expectation management/being kind to yourself:** part of being a resilient runner is being realistic about the time and effort you *can* and *want to* put into running. If you're constantly failing to reach your goals, whether that's in training or racing, it's not you that's at fault – it's the goals. It's easy to get caught in a cycle of guilt and failure, thinking you're not spending enough time with significant others because you need to train, thinking you're not training enough because of other demands on your time, with the result that you either find yourself struggling in every area or only meeting your expectations in one. There are times when life will demand that the balance is out – a new baby, a big work project, a once-in-a-lifetime race – but, if possible, this should be the exception rather than the rule. Accept that sometimes you can't do everything perfectly, aim for the best possible balance and, if you're repeatedly failing to live up to your own expectations, change the expectations.
* **Rest and recovery:** pay attention to your body's cues that it needs more time off or is ready to go; be flexible in your approach to training; prioritise evidence-based recovery modalities over expensive quick fixes (see chapter 5).
* **Sleep:** develop effective 'winding down' practices before bedtime; go to bed at around the same time each night; aim for a cool, dark and quiet sleeping space.
* **Good nutrition and hydration:** make food choices rationally rather than emotionally; pre-plan and pre-prepare meals and snacks; have good fuelling practices before, during and after training/racing.
* **Good sources of knowledge, motivation and support:** be open-minded yet sceptical about health and performance claims; check credentials; ask: why is this person telling me this and is it for my benefit or theirs? Know what motivates you – audiobooks, podcasts, films, meeting a friend to run, a coach, a favourite route, rewards. Surround yourself with people who champion you and genuinely want you to flourish and who you, in turn, do the same for.
* **Good strength, conditioning, mobility and cross-training:** physically support your running body by paying regular attention to keeping it strong and mobile. Use cross-training regularly to support your running as a way to increase cardiovascular workouts with less impact (e.g. cycling, swimming, StairMaster, etc.) or when injured to maintain fitness during recovery.

Why use a training plan?

A training plan provides a useful structure to work to, incorporating all the essential aspects of training while removing some of the decision-making process that can easily lead to missed or sub-optimal training. While it's difficult to scientifically assess the efficacy of different training plans, there are several reasons why you may want to consider following a structured plan, rather than simply running when and how you feel – although this latter approach can work very well for some.

Whatever level of running you're at, the essentials of a good training plan are the same, just with different emphases and volumes. All runners should begin by building a good, strong endurance base with plenty of easy running to condition the body to the stresses of running, along with regular, running-specific strength and mobility work.

> Spending time building a solid foundation will pay dividends as your running experience increases, helping your body to be resilient and efficient, decreasing injury risk, increasing running-specific strength, and improving running economy which, in the longer term, is the best way to improve your times if that's your aim.

This strong base also helps guard against those frustrating non-running injuries, including back and neck pain and other niggles that plague many of us, especially when we need to spend long periods of time sitting at desks or in cars. Even if you can't (or don't want to) go to a gym, incorporating a regular session of carefully selected, running specific, home-based strength training is a valuable investment for everyone, and particularly important when you start increasing your running mileage and intensity.

We think of the key aspects of a training plan a little like ingredients in a recipe. They're all essential for the best possible final result, but you can play around a little with the exact mix according to taste, including the relative amount of each element you want to include. Some ingredients, like speedwork, are more powerful than others and need to be used with care. Think of these a bit like spices, which can make or break a recipe depending on how you use them. We're not going to tell you exactly what to do on each day of the week – everyone's week is different. Everyone's days are different. Everyone is different! So, spend a bit of time working out which ingredient fits best where and you're far more likely to stick with a training plan, and get the most benefit from it.

Some runners like to use a training plan because it means they don't need to think about their running, instead they just follow the plan. While this might be helpful on those days when you're struggling for motivation, it also removes your ownership of the plan, and therefore of your running.

If a plan is to be effective long-term, it's essential you are fully invested in it. Our method provides the basic structure and guidance, but the specifics of the day should be decided based on a more subjective approach. If you've had a bad night's sleep, you've woken up with a sore throat, or you have a big work presentation coming up, it's perfectly fine to postpone that long or hard run to another day. You'll enjoy it more and get far greater benefit from it that way. Some days you won't feel great when you're out but have a hard run planned, so listen to your body and perhaps give yourself a bit more warm-up time before making the decision whether to go for it or not. By the same token, it's worth maximising those days when you're feeling unexpectedly strong and awesome, seizing the opportunity while you have it – this might be a great time to add in an impromptu interval or hill session, or add a couple of extra miles to your long run.

> Being both organised *and* flexible about your training is the best way to make sure you maximise each session, even if that's by turning off the alarm and going back to sleep.

Building a training plan

Building a plan that works for you is about bringing everything together – what you want from running, how much time and energy you can devote to it, and your running history and current level of fitness. Before working out a detailed training plan, it's worth asking yourself the following three questions.

Question 1: what are my running goals?
The first consideration when it comes to planning training is to think about what you're aiming for. While elite athletes work with a team and coach to target specific primary – or 'A' – and secondary – or 'B' – races over the forthcoming season, or structure years of training and racing around an event like the Olympic Games, most recreational runners find running is dictated by life, rather than the other way around. As a recreational runner, planning training should begin with considering what your running goals and aspirations are over the coming months and even years, with flexibility built in to allow for any unforeseen bumps in the road. Depending on everything else that's going on in your life, what you want from your running changes from year to year, and your approach to training should mirror this.

Broadly, most runners' plans over the course of any given year fall into one of the following categories.

One or two key races

The eggs-in-one-basket approach allows for very specific preparation and peaking for a specific 'A' race. In this case, training should be carefully planned and periodised around your key race(s), starting from a solid base, moving to a build phase to maximise cardiovascular fitness and increase volume, a peak phase to maximise race-specific adaptations, and a taper to allow optimal recovery prior to the race. Depending on how planned races are spaced, for a single big summer race this could look something like a winter of base endurance and strength training, building up speed through the spring and then focusing on race-specific preparation 8 to 12 weeks out from the race. 'B' races, such as a half marathon about five weeks before a key marathon, can also be used to fine-tune training and test out race fitness. Key races are followed by a couple of weeks of rest and easy running to allow full recovery before embarking on the next training cycle. For two key races in spring and autumn, this splits the year into two distinct cycles.

Regular racing

For some runners, racing is the main reason to run. Races offer an addictive buzz, motivation to push hard in a competitive environment, an enjoyable social occasion and (as long as everything goes to plan) a tangible feeling of success. Not to mention the all-important #medalmonday.

Racing is a lot of fun, but racing too often can lead to a continuous cycle of stress and recovery without much room for anything in between. While this might work for a while (and for some super resilient runners seemingly indefinitely), it can also be a rapid route to injury and frustration. If you're racing regularly, it's a good idea to take at least some time out in the year for a physical and psychological reset, reconnecting with the simple joys of running for pleasure rather than for competition.

Maintenance running

When other things in life need to take priority, it can be a good idea to switch your running to maintenance mode. The purpose of this approach is to keep the health and well-being benefits of regular running and to minimise any loss of fitness, while removing the pressure to improve or perform.

Jen says:

> 'I've switched to this mode in the past at times when life events such as pregnancy, huge work projects or caring for significant others have been my priority. At these times, running three times a week for half an hour offers just enough of an escape and a reconnection to my running self to keep me happy, without adding extra demands to an already stressful life.'

Good to go

While at times in the past we've found ourselves adopting each of the above approaches to running, the 'good to go' approach is the one we favour these days. We're busy and need to split our time and energy between family, work and training. But we also love running long and hard, having the fitness to run in the mountains when we're away on trips, and taking on the occasional race. At these times we'll train by feel, by perceived exertion, aiming to run most days but basing the specifics of each run on how we're feeling in body and mind, as well as the time we have available. When everything's going well, our weekly mileage can sit happily between 40 and 60 miles (60 to 100 kilometres), without feeling like it's negatively impacting anything else. This means we're not stressing about upcoming races but, if a race comes up we like the look of, regardless of its length, we're never too far away from being able to run it with just a little specific training in the run-up.

Question 2: what has worked in the past?

A good plan should draw on what's worked for you in the past, and what hasn't. Experienced runners get to know how their body reacts and adapts to the stresses of training, and a training diary is helpful in identifying general trends in training and life decisions that have led to better performance outcomes. However, what's worked before won't always work in the future as you change and evolve throughout your life.

Question 3: where is my running right now?

Now it's time for an honest assessment of your current running. Are you coming to it new or after a long time off? Have you built a good base of fitness and now you want to take the next step in improving your running? Are you an experienced runner who's hit a plateau and now wants to maximise your potential? Think about the level of fitness, health and well-being you're at today. This might not be the same, or even similar to a place you've been in the past, especially if you're returning from illness, injury, extended time away from running or childbirth. In this case, it's important to be kind to your body, not to expect it to jump straight in where you left off, and to rebuild training load – the combination of volume and intensity – gradually.

Do I need a coach?

While it's perfectly possible to plan and execute a great training plan that enables you to fulfil your running and racing potential, it's not an easy thing to do, especially if you're juggling training with other aspects of a busy life. A good coach will create a personalised, structured training plan that factors in everything from your current level of fitness and time availability to your race plans and ultimate goals. They'll also offer regular feedback on your running, answer your running-related questions, adapt your programme as you go and incorporate flexibility into your schedule, rather than keeping it fixed. When choosing a coach, ask trusted friends for recommendations, do your research into their experience and qualifications, and decide whether they're affordable for you. Most importantly, once you've identified a coach you like the look of, book in for a chat, so you can see whether you'd like to work with them. Coaching is often a close relationship, based on mutual trust, understanding and respect. You need to feel you 'click' with a coach in order for the relationship to work well.

If you're not ready, or able, to take on a coach, coaching apps are available, which offer more generic guidance on training, but can be motivating and helpful with structuring your approach. Again, look for recommendations from friends, and read reviews carefully before signing up.

Should I plan my runs based on distance or time?

Whether you plan your runs based on distance or time is a personal choice. Any running watch will record both, along with the vertical gain and loss of each run, which can also be planned alongside distance or time. This is particularly useful if you're training for a hilly race and want to replicate race-day conditions. In general, if you're training for a fairly flat road race such as a 10K, half marathon or marathon, distance works well as your primary metric. If you're training for a longer, hillier, more off-road race, however, paying too much attention to the distance you're running can be disheartening. Especially if you're used to running flat miles and you've recently switched to more adventurous terrain. In this case it's often a good idea to plan the number of hours you want to run for each week instead.

Jen says:

'In the spring of 2023, Sim and I were training for very different events. After decades of off-road running, Sim had spent the winter training hard for a new road marathon PB. I, on the other hand, was training for my first 100-miler – a tough, mountainous race with more than 6,500 metres of vertical gain.'

In this scenario, Sim's primary metric was distance, with each session undertaken at a specific pace. His long runs were designed to closely replicate race day, covering 20–22 miles in 2 hours and 30 minutes or 2 hours and 45 minutes. After a few runs where I covered about half his distance in the same time, albeit on rough, off-road terrain and with a considerable amount of ascent along the way, I decided to switch to using time as my primary metric, planning the number of hours I would run each week instead to avoid unhelpful comparisons!

Training load and training effect

The frequency, duration and intensity of training are collectively known as *training load*, and result in an outcome – the *training effect*. If training load is too high or too low, it won't result in the desired training effect. An appropriate training load promotes favourable physical and physiological adaptations, reduces the likelihood of illness and injury, and produces optimal performance. As adaptations and tolerance to training load are highly individual, trying out different combinations of training types and building training load gradually are essential.

> A good rule is to increase either **volume** (i.e. frequency or duration) or **intensity** (i.e. speedwork or hills) in any given week, but never both.

Training volume: how much should I run each week?

Your training volume is the distance (in miles or kilometres) or duration (in hours) that you run each week. This should be dictated by a combination of your running goals and your available time, and spread across the different types of training session. Be realistic about how much time you can dedicate to running, especially if you have lots of other commitments. It's good to have goals to aim for and achieve, but goals also give us opportunities to fail, which is unhelpful.

There are no fixed rules about how much you need to run each week in order to get the results you're after, and everyone's responses and adaptations to training will be highly individual; however, elite runners tend to run fairly high mileage consistently, regardless of their race distance. There is more on this later when we discuss creating your own training plan – table 2 on page 212 provides some different options for training volume (measured in either distance or time) you might expect to run in training based on how far your goal race is.

Training intensity

The pace you train at should broadly reflect the event you're training for. Those training for shorter, faster races should include more shorter, faster running in training, whereas those training for an ultramarathon need to prioritise time on feet, and probably some much slower training including hiking. However, even if you are training for a longer, slower race, it's a good idea to include some regular speedwork as it's a highly effective way of stimulating improvements in cardiovascular fitness – essential whatever distance you're planning to run. Even at ultramarathon distances, VO_2 max has been found to be a significant predictor of running performance, so there's no excuse to skip the faster sessions regardless of how long or slow your goal race is. Running at speed is also really enjoyable, offering some nice respite from plugging away at the slower miles.

On the downside, as running speed increases, so too do the forces experienced through your body, meaning an increased risk of certain injuries, so it's wise to approach speedwork with caution and, like everything else, build up gradually. Making sure you're fully warmed up and choosing a slightly uphill stretch on which to undertake faster running will both reduce the likelihood of injury.

It's important not to forget that many studies have found higher-intensity exercise elicits greater levels of enjoyment in both athletic and non-athletic populations. As well as stimulating different physio-logical responses, incorporating harder or faster sessions into your training once or twice a week shakes things up, stimulates adrenaline release and affords hard effort that you don't have to put up with for long. It lets you feel the wind in your hair and the thrilling sensation of moving at speed, reconnecting you with your inner child – running fast is fun!

Faster running sessions are usually divided into one of the following:

* **Strides** – short bursts of faster running, usually within a longer run.
* **Fartlek** – faster stretches of running that vary in speed and distance.
* **Intervals** – faster running with a set distance and pace. Intervals can be longer or shorter, on flat ground or hills.
* **Tempo** – sustained faster running, usually for between 30 and 60 minutes.

How fast do I need to run?

What feels like fast running is highly individual, dependent on a vast number of factors from genetics and training to how far you've run already and the mood you're in. But we can all feel the difference in our bodies between a slow and easy conversational jog, a pace that's hard but comfortable, and an all-out sprint. These are the three broad regions within which any given running pace will sit, with each relying on a different mode of functioning by the body's energy and neuromuscular systems – see chapter 1 for more detail on muscle fibre types and energetics. As a result, running at slow, moderate and hard paces will stimulate different responses and adaptations within your body.

How easy is easy?

Humans are extremely good at knowing their most efficient pace over a given terrain. Interestingly, if you ask runners to run at an easy pace, it isn't necessarily their slowest pace and doesn't vary much as distance changes, with the obvious exceptions of very short and very long runs. Lab-based studies suggest that we may have an energy-optimal running speed that we self-select if we're simply told to run. A recent study backed this up (Selinger *et al.*, 2022).

It's easy to think of times when we've run with a friend or training partner and discovered a mismatch between our 'easy' pace and theirs.

Jen says:

> 'When Sim and I run together, I find he's always pushing slightly ahead during the easy sections of our runs, even when we're at a similar level of fitness and expected finishing times. It's not that I can't keep up, just that if I do, I'm not feeling as comfortable as I'd like to at an easy pace. I'd always put this down to ego in the past, but perhaps I should give him the benefit of the doubt and assume that it's simply that his most economical pace is just a little faster than mine is ... '

It's important to bear this individuality in mind when planning training, especially if you're working to an external measurement of effort, rather than your perceived effort. Running a long run at, say, 10 minutes per mile pace, might sound like a good plan, but if running at 9:45 pace is more efficient – and costs less energy – for your individual body then it would seem like a good idea to allow this flexibility in your training rather than sticking rigidly to a pace that's just a little too fast or slow for comfort.

Intensity zones

While in reality running intensity is best thought of as a continuum – slow, easy jogging through to all-out sprinting – in order to make things clearer for the purposes of planning training, many athletes, coaches and researchers separate out different running intensities into *zones*.

There are a number of different models that allow you to divide your training intensity up into numbered zones but, for the vast majority of people, three zones are sufficient. These can be measured by:

* **how you feel** – this can either be measured by judging your rate of perceived exertion (RPE) or by observing your breathing rate or a talk test; or
* **using a heart rate monitor** – to ascertain what percentage of your maximum heart rate you're working at (see right).

The three intensity zones are summarised in table 1.

Intensity zone	RPE	Breathing rate	Talk test	Heart rate	Typical pace
Low	3–4	Breathing feels easy	Can comfortably carry on a full conversation	50–60 per cent of maximum heart rate	Roughly 2–3 minutes per mile slower than your 5K race pace
Moderate	5–7	Breathing feels steady	Can speak in single sentences	60–70 per cent of maximum heart rate	Roughly 1–2 minutes per mile slower than your 5K race pace
High	8–10	Breathing hard	Can only say a couple of words at a time	80–90 per cent of maximum heart rate	Between 1 minute per mile slower than your 5K race pace and your maximum pace

Table 1 – the three intensity zones

Judging your intensity zone by 'feel' – rate of perceived exertion (RPE) and talk test

How hard we feel like we're working at any given moment is called our *rate of perceived exertion*. Developed by Swedish researcher Gunnar Borg, the Borg Rating of Perceived Exertion (RPE) scale originally ran from 6 (no exertion at all) to 20 (maximal exertion). The numbers correspond approximately to your heart rate divided by 10. Today, many people use a modified version of the Borg Scale, with 0 representing no exertion and 10 maximal exertion.

Using RPE, studies have found that we humans are incredibly good at accurately gauging our effort level, even when compared to more objective measures of effort such as heart rate or lactate threshold. Unlike these physiological measures, RPE takes in a much wider range of factors that contribute to our feeling of effort, including our training and recovery status, illness and injury, and our psychological state.

The talk test is a quick and easy way to determine how hard you're working while running. At low intensity you should be able to carry out a full conversation comfortably, whereas during high-intensity running you'll be limited to a couple of words at a time.

Judging your intensity zone using your heart rate

If you're someone who likes to see the numbers on a screen, rather than pluck them out of your head, you can use a heart rate monitor to judge how hard you should be working in each intensity zone. First you need to work out your maximum heart rate (see below), then each zone falls within a particular range of this.

If you're training by heart rate make sure you use an arm- or chest-mounted heart rate monitor rather than relying on wrist-based measurements from your watch. While they may be suitable for measuring resting heart rate values, and technology is improving all the time, wrist-based heart rate measurements, even on the best watches, are still often inaccurate during exercise and especially at higher intensities.

MEASURING YOUR MAXIMUM HEART RATE

There are various ways of determining your maximum heart rate, including the much-overused formula of 220 minus your age, which has little evidence to back it up.

If you have an arm- or chest-mounted heart rate monitor, you can use this simple protocol to get a good idea of your maximum heart rate. Bear in mind that this may change depending on your age, health and conditions during testing, so it's well worth redoing every few months to check your zones are still where you think they are.

1 Warm up with 15 minutes of easy running.
2 Run one mile on a track or measured section of flat road or trail at a comfortably hard (tempo) pace.
3 With 400 metres to go, build up to an all-out effort, running the final 100 metres as hard as you can.
4 Review your heart rate data from the last 400 metres. The highest number recorded is a good indicator of your maximum heart rate.

Which is the best way of judging your intensity zone?

Heart rate provides a convenient, numerical representation of effort. But it's worth bearing in mind that heart rate data, especially if used during a session, has its limitations.

The first point to consider is whether most recreational runners really *need* to have a number on a heart rate monitor to tell them how hard they're working during a run. Research has solidly demonstrated our ability to determine how hard we're working by using an RPE scale. Unless there's a very good reason why you need to know your heart rate at any given time during a run, it may be far more effective to run to RPE and then view your heart rate data afterwards. Not only does this approach leave you free to focus on your actual running, but it helps you learn to be better in tune with your body, listening to its cues about how hard it's working, and therefore how much stress it's under.

It's also extremely unlikely you'd ever be able to discover your true maximum heart rate. Because we have many physiological and psychological controls in place to ensure we never exercise hard enough to cause lasting damage to our bodies, it's extremely unlikely we'd be able to exceed our own safe limits of exertion. Note that those with a pre-existing heart condition should always seek advice from a cardiac specialist before embarking on a new or updated training programme.

How are intensity zones typically used?

* **Low-intensity sessions** are used for active recovery between harder runs, or for your longer, slower runs, especially those in preparation for an event of five or more hours' duration. They should be at a conversational pace, minimising energy usage, and you should even be able to eat at the lower end of this zone – something it's definitely good to practise if you are training for an ultra.
* **Moderate-intensity sessions** are designed to condition your body and mind to the specific stresses of running at a comfortably hard pace. They should feel far more focused than low-intensity runs but not all-out like high-intensity runs. You should be able to have a conversation, but not talk continuously.
* **High-intensity sessions** work on improving your oxygen utilisation – your VO_2 max – as well as areas such as power and leg turnover. Running faster intervals broken up by periods of recovery allows you to accumulate time at intensity without becoming too fatigued to maintain good running form and make the most noticeable difference to your overall fitness.

Summary: intensity zones

* The great thing about using just three different intensity zones is that it's fairly simple and easier to get your head around than using more zones.
* Remember that the point of having different zones is to avoid falling into the all-too-common trap of doing all your training at a single intensity, and thereby not stimulating the range of training adaptions necessary for optimum fitness and performance.
* Don't sweat the small stuff: make sure that the majority of your training is easy, some hard, and some in the middle. Exactly how you go about fitting this puzzle together is known as *training intensity distribution*.

Training intensity distribution

Over the years, as training theory has developed, several different models of training intensity distribution have been proposed. As well as what the optimal number of intensity zones might be, the amount of training that should be done in each zone has long been debated.

80:20 running

Identified by sports physiologist Stephen Seiler and popularised in Matt Fitzgerald's 2014 book, *80/20 Running*, 80:20 training presents a simplified version of the way in which elite endurance athletes train. Since its launch as a training approach, it has changed the way many recreational athletes train.

Based on the premise that many recreational athletes do too much of their training at a single mid-paced effort – i.e. running their easy runs too hard and their hard runs too easy – this approach suggests carrying out 80 per cent of training at an easy effort and 20 per cent at a hard effort.

Taking this a step further, it doesn't necessarily mean that 80 per cent of running should be super easy and 20 per cent super hard – there's plenty of room for variety in the in-between effort levels too. Also, the exact structure of a training programme should reflect the specific demands of the event you're training for.

Researchers realised that, when they analysed the training structure of elite endurance athletes – whether they were cyclists, cross-country skiers, triathletes or runners – a relatively large amount (around 80 per cent) of their training was done at a low intensity. This is a factor that's easy to miss when you're relatively new to running and think every run should be as hard as you can go. Easier miles help to build an efficient and natural running gait, and they condition your body for the harder stuff. They should be your bread and butter, and the base upon which everything else is built – not just at the start of a training block, but all the way through it.

Whatever level you're currently at, separating your training out into effort levels, whether that's two, three, five, seven or more, offers an evidence-based and structured model around which to build more specific sessions. It ensures you're including a variety of easy, mid-paced and hard runs in order to optimise your body's adaptations to training, while minimising risk of injury. It keeps things interesting, bringing purpose to each training session, and, when there's a big race on the horizon that you want to do your best for, helps you trust the process.

Pyramidal and polarised models

Coaches and off-the-shelf training plans tend to utilise a couple of standard approaches to training intensity distribution:

* **Pyramidal** – the majority of training is at low intensity; some at moderate intensity; very little at high intensity.
* **Polarised** – the majority of training is at low intensity; very little at moderate intensity; some at high intensity.

A further piece to the puzzle is that it can be helpful to vary your training intensity distribution at different stages when you're preparing for a race. Many standardised programmes start out with a pyramidal approach and then move to a polarised approach in order to peak for a competition. Cross-country skiers often use a block-style approach, chunking longer or harder training sessions together to allow for more recovery between them, while keeping the same volume and intensity. But which approach works best?

Research on training intensity distribution

Until relatively recently, there's been precious little good quality research done to compare one method of training with another. But one recent study took a big step forwards in answering this question.

Researchers put 60 well-trained male runners through a 16-week training programme (Filipas *et al.*, 2022). Training load was kept constant; training intensity distribution was varied by splitting the runners into the following four groups:

* group 1 undertook 16 weeks of pyramidal training;
* group 2 undertook 16 weeks of polarised training;
* group 3 undertook 8 weeks of pyramidal training followed by 8 weeks of polarised training;
* group 4 undertook 8 weeks of polarised training followed by 8 weeks of pyramidal training.

All groups improved over the 16 weeks (this was measured by variables including 5K time trial and VO_2 max), but it was group 3 that improved the most.

While it's only the beginning of the work that needs to be done on systematically testing out the various training approaches that have developed over the years, this study is helpful in two primary ways when thinking about putting together a structured training programme.

* *All* athletes improved, showing that regardless of its specifics, a structured plan based on sound principles of training is likely to improve fitness and performance, even in athletes who are already highly trained.
* Structuring a programme with the least specific training furthest out from your target race and the most specific training closest to the race is the most effective approach – at least among those used in this particular study – providing a good rationale for structuring your training this way.

Testing fitness

In chapter 1 we looked at some of the different physiological thresholds that can be measured in the lab, and also 'felt' during running, including lactate threshold, critical speed and VO_2 max. But unless you have regular access to a lab, it's useful to have some more easily measurable means of seeing how your training is translating into fitness.

Time trials

As is so often the case, one of the simplest ways to measure fitness is probably also the best, and the most reliable: the time trial. Whether it's a local parkrun or a loop from your door, the first key point of a time trial is that it's on a course you have regular access to. It needs to be minimally affected by weather (no knee-deep muddy sections over the winter months) and as free as possible from potential hazards such as bikes, cars, dogs and pedestrians – you may need to choose your time of day carefully to ensure this.

If you're training for a specific race, the length of your time trial should be dictated by your chosen race distance. About five kilometres (three miles) is sufficient for races of up to half marathon, but if you're marathon training then 16 kilometres (10 miles) or slightly over is about right. These time trial distances have been found to be predictive of race performance.

Resting heart rate

As your fitness improves, your resting heart rate (RHR), measured first thing in the morning, will decrease. A smartwatch may give you this data, but this may be averaged from a full 24-hour period, so it's often more reliable to measure RHR manually. Simply locate your pulse (wrist or neck pulse is usually easiest to find) and count your heart beats for a timed minute before you get up. Note the value down in your training diary and watch the effects of your hard work in training. RHR does vary for other reasons, for example if you're coming down with a bug, particularly stressed, or, for females, over the course of the menstrual cycle, so it's important to take this as a long-term measure, establishing a baseline value

and overall trend, as well as considering whether an increased value might signal the need for more sleep rather than more training.

What are our wearables really tracking?

In a 2021 article in the *Guardian*, journalist Simon Usborne asked whether a person who tracks their steps, sleep and food can ever truly be free. It's a great question, and one worth considering carefully as we happily upload our most intimate data to Big Tech, strapping monitors to ourselves day and night, disclosing everything from the variability of our heart rates and route choices, and our menstrual and sleep cycles, to our activity and glucose levels. Apps track our whereabouts, building heat maps of where we choose to go, like millions of ants. 'How much privacy have we lost to the promise of self improvement,' Usborne asks, 'and is it time to stop?'

The more we use wearable tech and allow the inner workings of our bodies to be uploaded to companies to use for their own ends, the more we grow accustomed to doing so, and the less we find it uncomfortable – or even worth our time to consider. After all, it's only data, right? It's a bit like how it feels to share personal stories on social media – the first few times it feels a bit weird, but after that you get used to it and it becomes harder and harder to assess what's appropriate to put out there and what isn't. Especially when everyone else seems to be doing it.

While the hardwear to measure our various metrics has advanced massively over the past decade (anyone remember the size of early GPS watches?), the software to go with it is still very much in its infancy, particularly in some of the newer areas. Many of the metrics we see aren't direct measurements but composites of several measurements. Our raw data, which may or may not be able to be accurately measured in the first place, is put through algorithms in an attempt to make it applicable to everyone, building layers of potential error that multiply into larger errors. Algorithms for the same metrics differ between brands, and may be changed at any point without the user knowing.

Placing too much value on these scores undermines our ability to listen to our bodies. What happens if, after months of training and preparation for your big race, and a perfectly executed taper at the end, the readiness score on your watch isn't optimal come race morning? Is this something it's helpful to be told, given it's very likely to be highly inaccurate anyway?

> While some metrics, when measured properly – heart rate, heart rate variability, body temperature – may offer a useful extra insight into what's going on for us psychologically and physiologically, the very best, most sophisticated and fantastically complex yet accurate gauge of how we're feeling – from our fitness and sleep quality to our recovery and readiness for training or racing – is right between our ears.

Recording your training

If you use a watch or other wearable device to record your training, you'll have access to a wide range of numbers that sum up various aspects of your physical performance. These range from distance, duration and elevation to average pace and splits. You'll also be given scores for things like training load – often as a running training stress score – a recovery or 'readiness to train' score, your overall fitness trajectory, and an estimation of your current VO$_2$ max.

While distance, duration and elevation data are likely to be an accurate representation of reality, and therefore a useful means of tracking your training and progress, other measures, usually composites created by algorithms, may not be. Race or time trial performances are a far more reliable indicator of your progression, while a subjective measure of how you're feeling, which takes in far more variables than an algorithm ever could, is likely to give you a much clearer picture of how recovered and ready to train you are.

A training diary can be a useful tool in helping you to track your training, allowing you to draw meaningful conclusions about what works for you (and what doesn't). Record details digitally or with pen and paper, so it's easy to refer to later – especially useful in identifying combinations of training and other factors which might have contributed to particularly good or bad race performances. Important details to record include the distance, duration, elevation and specific details of your run; the time of day, weather and terrain; and how you felt before, during and afterwards.

Treadmills

Aided in recent years by the COVID-19 pandemic and increases in home-based working, having a treadmill at home has become more popular. We've been lucky enough to have the use of a NoblePro treadmill at home while writing this book, and the way it has fitted into our regular training and enabled us to train when we'd have otherwise not been able to – mostly due to childcare and parcel deliveries – has been interesting to explore.

Whether you love them or hate them, or simply see them as a way to get some miles in when the weather's bad, there's little doubt that treadmills have a place in the future of running. Enabling runners to keep training through lockdowns, times of high air pollution, extreme weather events and personal safety anxiety, they are a workaround – though clearly not a solution – to many of today's major obstacles to regular running. But how do they compare to 'overground' running and are they helpful for those of us training for the roads, trails and even mountains?

Search 'treadmill running' in academic literature and it's clear to see that the differences and similarities between running on a treadmill and 'overground' running are something that's been keeping scientists busy for many years. Coinciding with the wider understanding of running (or 'jogging') as a beneficial and time-efficient form of aerobic activity, scientific papers began to emerge in the early 1970s which analysed treadmill running and compared it with overground running, and many papers have been written on the topic since. As with many areas of research, the findings have often been conflicting. Fortunately, a recent review paper provides an excellent overview of the findings from the best studies (Van Hooren *et al.*, 2020).

DIFFERENCES BETWEEN TREADMILL AND OVERGROUND RUNNING

* There is a slightly longer contact time (i.e. the foot stays on the ground for slightly longer with each step) when running on a motorised treadmill compared with overground running.
* No differences were found in stride time, stride length or stride frequency.
* The main difference between the two types of running appears to be a reduction in the angle between the foot and ground at footstrike, along with greater knee flexion and less hip flexion when using a treadmill. As these are normal, natural modifications in running gait when running over harder surfaces, however, it isn't clear whether this factor, rather than the use of a treadmill, was more likely to be the cause.
* Runners tend to overestimate their speed when running on a treadmill, feeling as though they're running faster than they would do running at the same speed overground.
* It has been suggested that biomechanical differences in motorised treadmill and overground running might arise from a reduction in propulsion required when running on a treadmill as the belt moves the supporting foot under the body during the stance phase of running gait. However, this has been found not to be the case as long as belt speed is constant and air resistance low. When belt speed varies with each footstrike, though – which has been found to occur on some treadmills – this does have the potential to alter running biomechanics.
* Other factors that may affect running biomechanics during treadmill running compared with overground running include: familiarity or comfort with a specific treadmill (and treadmills in general), visual or perceptual abilities of the runner, belt dimensions, motor power and surface hardness of different treadmill models.

These characteristics of treadmill running seem logical, but are routinely ignored by those carrying out treadmill-based assessments of runners aimed at identifying biomechanical traits and prescribing the best shoes, insoles and orthotics. Be wary of shops offering this service, especially if you're unused to running on a treadmill and aren't given plenty of time to warm up and familiarise yourself with the specific treadmill being used – the running gait being assessed may be very different from your usual one.

Treadmills for prehabilitation and rehabilitation

Due to their consistent and controllable surface, gradient and environmental conditions, treadmills can be a highly useful tool when preparing for specific types of races, reducing the likelihood of injury, or recovering from previous injury. Runners training for warm-weather races can benefit from the lack of airflow and resulting heating effects of treadmill running, which can be further enhanced by purposefully increasing the room temperature (see pages 159–161 for more on running in the heat). Avoiding training in very cold temperatures by using an indoor treadmill may also reduce the need for a lengthy warm-up and cool-down, therefore maximising available training time, along with a reduction in the numerous increases in injury risk due to low temperatures – from cold muscles to slippery surfaces.

Doing speedwork on a treadmill may also have some advantages compared with overground running, allowing peak speeds to be reached with lower biomechanical stress. We find the added discipline that set interval training programmes brings to a session, and ensuring consistent effort throughout, makes for highly effective training, reducing the need to look at a watch and the likelihood of slowing towards the end of each interval, or as the intervals progress. Undertaking shorter, faster runs such as interval and tempo sessions on the treadmill, without dogs, cars and bikes to worry about, is something we've enjoyed about our treadmill, too.

When it comes to injury rehabilitation, data suggests treadmill use may be beneficial when rehabilitating from some injuries, but not others. Due to the slightly different stresses exerted on the body during treadmill running, it is recommended for those at risk of or recovering from bone injuries and plantar fascia strains, but not Achilles tendinopathy, Achilles ruptures or calf muscle strains. Stress on these posterior structures – i.e. those at the back of the leg – is increased as running gradient increases, so if you're prone to such injuries and choose to train on a treadmill, consider keeping the incline low.

Jen says:

'I've found that increasing the gradient on a treadmill increases the stress along the metatarsals of my feet, causing pain after a while. The mechanism by which this happens makes sense – there is increased bending at the forefoot as gradient increases – but it is much more noticeable during treadmill running than overground running so, particularly if you are prone to stress fractures, this is another area to pay attention to.'

Summary: treadmills

Motorised treadmills offer a suitable and effective alternative for those training for overground running, with the vast majority of biomechanical measures being similar between the two conditions, at least once a runner is familiar with the specific treadmill being used. They're great for training during extremes of weather, in the short days of winter and when you need to combine running with childcare.

05

Rest, recovery and adaptation

Every day, our email inbox fills up with promises of enhanced recovery. From protein powders and superfood shots to hot tubs, cold tubs, cryotherapy sprays and pneumatic boots, the amount it's possible to spend on recovery, something that, not so long ago, involved little more than putting your feet up, is truly mind-boggling. But does any of it really work?

As Dickens wrote in *Great Expectations*: 'Take nothing on its looks; take everything on evidence. There's no better rule.' In this chapter, we'll start out by looking in detail at the recovery methods that have been proven beyond any doubt to work. After that, we'll move on to a discussion around some of the less evidence-based ways to enhance your recovery. If you're getting everything else right and you're still looking for that extra edge, we'll give you an idea, based on current scientific knowledge, of whether or not they might be worth a try. Lastly, we'll move on to how we might be able to measure our recovery status, and whether technology can offer insights over and above waking up in the morning and asking ourselves how we feel.

If you're keen on learning more about the science and pseudoscience of recovery, we highly recommend reading *Good to Go* by Christie Aschwanden, who has tried, tested and evaluated a vast number of them with some surprising (and some entirely unsurprising) results.

Recovery methods

Sleep

Kicking off the best-evidenced of the recovery modalities, sleep is one of the key tools for being a healthy, happy human, as well as the best runner you can be. And yet research on athletes shows sleep is regularly affected by training and competitions, as well as life stress, with nearly three quarters of athletes reporting poor sleep going into a competition. Understanding more about sleep, and why it's so important, along with arming ourselves with some strategies to make sure our sleep is as optimal as possible for our health, happiness, and performance – both mental and physical – is therefore paramount for athletes, and everyone else, too.

WHAT IS SLEEP?

Across the animal kingdom, we all sleep, although particularly in humans some seem better at it than others. As it places us in a semi-unconscious and therefore potentially vulnerable state, we know sleep must be essential for our bodies and brains, and there's a vast amount of scientific literature on the topic, but scientists still debate the exact purposes of sleep.

Sleep is an essential part of our daily routine – something we spend around a third of our lives doing. Getting sufficient high-quality sleep at the right times is as necessary for our survival as food and water. Our brains need sleep in order to function, including neural communication and creating new neural pathways; we've all experienced the brain fog that accompanies sleep deprivation, rendering us less able to concentrate, focus or make good decisions – or any decisions at all. Our brains are remarkably active while we're asleep, performing 'housekeeping' tasks such as removing the toxic metabolites of brain function that build up while we're awake.

Sleep affects the maintenance and function of almost every type of tissue, organ and system in the body, including the brain, heart, lungs, metabolism, immune function and emotions. A chronic lack of sleep, or regular poor-quality sleep, has been found to increase the risk of a range of disorders including high blood pressure, cardiovascular disease, diabetes, depression and obesity. According to research findings, people who sleep poorly are five times more likely to catch a common cold than those who sleep well (Cohen *et al.*, 2009).

Sleep tracking

Being able to track the various sleep phases and plot how much time athletes spend in each one against their sporting performance might be interesting for sleep scientists working in labs with high-tech equipment. But how helpful is sleep tracking for the rest of us?

Wearable technology and apps offer the option of tracking your sleep, including sleep stages and cycles and the quality of your sleep. But, in reality, the only way to do this accurately with currently available technology is through the monitoring of brain waves via an electroencephalogram. But this hasn't stopped a rise in people reporting anxiety over the quality and quantity of their sleep, based on data from watches and smartphones. None of them is anywhere near as good as simply asking yourself how well rested you feel on waking. Anxiety is a primary cause of poor sleep, so being anxious *about* your sleep is extremely counterproductive. Losing sleep over losing sleep is a particularly special modern phenomenon.

Common causes of sleep problems

Sometimes, despite our best intentions and efforts, good sleep doesn't happen, and worrying about it can only make things worse. But being aware of the causes of bad sleep – and trying to focus on the areas we can actually do something about – is a good start. As parents of two young children, desperately trying to fit in work and training around childcare, being repeatedly told about the importance of getting enough sleep is a nightmare in its own right. Whether the baby needs feeding, the toddler's had a bad dream, the tween won't go to bed at a reasonable hour, or the teen doesn't get home until 2 a.m., parenting in general is not good for sleep. We don't know whether there is an answer to this, other than to prioritise sleep whenever you can (sneaky afternoon nap, anyone?) and try not to worry too much about it.

When our internal clock is synchronised to the external cycle of each 24-hour period, we will feel a strong drive to sleep at a similar time each evening, sleep onset will occur quickly and sleep quality is high. On waking after a good night's sleep, we feel alert, rested and ready to begin the day. If there is poor synchronisation between the internal and external clocks, such as when we're experiencing jet lag, or when sleep is chronically disturbed, sleepiness occurs outside appropriate times. In these situations, we may experience problems such as having trouble falling asleep, trouble staying asleep – i.e. waking regularly throughout the night and early waking – and waking up feeling tired and unrested.

Our psychological and physiological state can affect our sleep, in particular if it causes an elevated central nervous system response. Physical pain or unusual physical sensations – as well as excessive worry and anxiety – can activate areas of our brain that make it more difficult to fall or stay asleep. People who have existing physical injury, physical conditions that cause pain or psychological trauma commonly experience poor sleep. Personality and genetics also play a part in our propensity to experience sleep problems.

Other sleep-sappers are easier to deal with by ensuring good 'sleep hygiene'. Here are some tips:
* Establish (and stick to) a set time for going to bed and waking up.
* Reduce blue light before bedtime.
* Establish a relaxing pre-sleep routine, which should include a 30-minute winding down period intended to reduce central nervous system activity. This could involve reading, a warm bath, deep breathing, meditation or mindfulness practice.
* Avoid caffeine after lunchtime if you know you're a responder.
* Avoid alcohol – a glass of wine or two might help you fall asleep, but it is associated with poor sleep and frequent waking later on in the night.
* Keep your bedroom cool, dark, quiet and free from lights from electronic equipment.
* Write a to-do list before bed if you tend to lie awake worrying about everything you need to do the following day.
* Keep a pen and notebook next to your bed for jotting anything down in the night that might otherwise keep you awake.

Massage

Massage is the most prolific recovery tool out there. It is widely used amongst athletes from elite to recreational level, supporting a multi-million-pound industry of professional therapists and auto-massage devices such as percussive massage guns. But does it work? Here are the main suggested mechanisms by which massage may be effective – whether administered by a practitioner or through self-massage:

* **Mechanical:** massage may reduce adhesion and stiffness within the tissues.
* **Neurological:** massage may alter the way pain is interpreted and reduce the inhibitory control of the nerves that prevents injury by over-stretching of the tissues.
* **Physiological:** massage may increase blood flow and promote localised inflammatory responses.
* **Psychological:** massage may improve perceptions of well-being and recovery due to an increase in the release of endorphins, relaxation and/or the placebo effect.

When making the decision on whether or not the benefits of massage are sufficient justification to part with hard-earned cash or valuable time, it's also worth bearing in mind that massage does carry a small risk of harm to both our performance and, more worryingly, our health. Both massage by a therapist (Stankiewicz and Todd, 2020) and using a percussive massage gun (Chen *et al.*, 2021) have recently been implicated in cases of severe rhabdomyolysis. This serious and potentially life-threatening syndrome results from extensive damage and breakdown of skeletal muscle fibres and the release of their contents into the bloodstream.

Sports massage

The proposed benefits of sports massage include improvements in performance, recovery and injury prevention. But sports massage is both expensive and time-consuming so, especially for those at the non-elite end of the spectrum who may be juggling both time and financial pressures alongside training, is it time and money well spent? A recent systematic review and meta-analysis of the literature around sports massage (Davis *et al.*, 2020) aimed to answer this question.

After filtering the available studies for quality, the researchers analysed data from a total of 1,012 athletes, assessing outcomes following sports massage on variables including strength, jump, sprint, endurance, fatigue, flexibility and delayed onset muscle soreness (DOMS). Their conclusions support the use of massage for reducing the severity of DOMS, which may be particularly useful in cases of multi-day or consecutive day races when the pain and loss of function resulting from DOMS may impair performance. Some studies showed improvements in flexibility or range of motion following massage, which may be of benefit for some sports, but as greater flexibility may have a negative effect on running economy, running is unlikely to be one of them. Others reported a relaxing effect of massage, measured through self-reported scores and reductions in the stress hormone cortisol, but none of these were undertaken using sports massage techniques, some of which were found to increase markers of stress, probably due to the pain and pressure typically experienced during this type of massage. Importantly, though, the researchers did not find any positive direct effects of sports massage on performance.

These findings suggest that in some circumstances sports massage can be beneficial, particularly if rapid alleviation in the pain and loss of function resulting from DOMS is important. However, during regular training, when DOMS is typically not often experienced, and during preparation for competition, sports massage is unlikely to produce any significant benefits.

Self-massage

Recent years have seen an explosion in the number of self-massage devices and techniques on the market. During pandemic lockdowns, when in-person sports massage wasn't available, athletes sought alternative ways of reproducing the perceived benefits of massage at home. Self-massage devices range from low-tech foam rollers and tennis balls, used in combination with body weight to produce pressurised movement over specific areas of the body, to high-tech percussive massage guns.

Percussive massage guns: percussive massage – or neuromuscular vibration therapy – is delivered through a handheld massage 'gun' which looks like a cross between a power drill and a hairdryer. Many models feature interchangeable heads and varying speeds of vibration, which manufacturers claim send 'rapid, strong, and short-term pulsating strokes deep into muscle tissues ... to help stretch muscles and connective tissues, reduce soft tissue pain, improve blood circulation to the affected area, and enhance recovery and overall physical performance' (Chen *et al.*, 2021). However, to date there are few good clinical or evidence-based reports to back up these claims, despite their hefty price tags. A recent review of the admittedly sparse literature around percussive massage devices (Konrad *et al.*, 2020) suggests similar outcomes to the findings based on massage undertaken by a therapist. These included increases in flexibility or range of motion – again questionable in its effectiveness for runners – and a decrease in perceived muscle soreness after exercise, but no significant direct effects on performance.

Foam rollers: an affordable, easy-to-use means of self-massage, foam rollers appear to decrease pain from DOMS, and increase flexibility and range of motion, at least in the short term (Yoshimura *et al.*, 2022). It doesn't appear to matter whether you go for a smooth or ridged design (Adamczyk *et al.*, 2022). While increased flexibility in some muscles, such as the hamstrings and calf muscles, may not necessarily be beneficial to running, the ability to target and work on asymmetrical tightness of muscles such as those in the back and around the pelvis may be.

In a well conducted meta-analysis of the available literature around foam rolling (Wiewelhove *et al.*, 2019), researchers conclude that:

> **'The effects of foam rolling on performance and recovery are rather minor and partly negligible, but can be relevant in some cases (e.g. to increase sprint performance and flexibility or to reduce muscle pain sensation).'**

The analysis also found some evidence to justify the use of foam rolling as a warm-up activity.

Overall, any effects of self-massage are likely to be small and whether or not you choose to include self-massage as part of your recovery is down to personal choice.

Active recovery

Used by many athletes, active recovery simply involves undertaking light, low-impact exercise rather than complete rest. While there are no definitive answers in the scientific research as to whether active recovery speeds up recovery compared with complete rest, no adverse effects have been found, so there's certainly no harm in doing it if it suits you. It is important to ensure that active recovery is definitely *recovery*, though, rather than a premature return to training, which is detrimental to longer-term recovery and performance.

Cold-water immersion

Post-exercise cold-water immersion is popular with athletes across many sports, undertaken with the aim of speeding up muscle repair and recovery after training and competition. The procedure usually involves total or partial immersion in water at a temperature of 10–15 °C for 15–20 minutes immediately after exercise. It's easy, relatively cheap, and cold water after a hot, hard workout can even feel good. But how well does it work?

The rationale for cold-water immersion is that the constriction of blood vessels and increased hydrostatic pressure during immersion may decrease localised physiological responses to exercise, such as metabolic activity and blood flow, along with decreasing markers of exercise-induced muscle damage and inflammation. The theory is that this reduces DOMS, maintains muscle function and improves recovery. But in reality, this reduction in the body's natural inflammatory processes may actually slow down and impair recovery.

Over the past decades, evidence has built showing that cold-water immersion actually reduces adaptation to resistance and strength training, but many coaches and athletes still believe it is beneficial to endurance training adaptations. A recent meta-analysis looked at the overall effects of cold-water immersion on training-induced changes in both strength and endurance performance by combining the best quality currently available studies (Malta *et al.*, 2021). Their analysis showed clearly that cold-water immersion negatively impacted all reported measures for strength training. For endurance training, the effects were less sizeable but consistently showed either a small decrease in performance, or no effect at all.

Contrast therapy – alternate immersion in hot and cold water – may be more beneficial than cold water alone as it may increase overall blood flow compared with rest.

Like static stretching, cold-water immersion is a popular post-exercise pastime and it's unlikely that those who enjoy doing it because it makes them feel good after a workout are going to stop because its benefits haven't been proven. After all, scientists could simply be failing to measure some of these specific positive effects, which might include psychological positives such as an increase in feelings of relaxation. But if you're looking for those marginal gains to help get the edge in your recovery and subsequent performance, be aware that you might be hampering your efforts by actually slowing down your body's natural recovery and adaptation responses or, at best, wasting your time on something that has, as yet, no scientifically proven benefits.

Ice

From ice baths to the age-old practice of putting ice on injuries, the premise behind using ice is to 'reduce inflammation'. But, even more so than cold water, ice simply slows, or even stops, the body's natural healing process, preventing blood flow to the damaged tissues and slowing the transport of by-products of inflammation away from the injury. While ice may numb the area, thus providing short-term pain relief, the longer-term negative effects may not be worth it.

Heat

Hot tubs, saunas, heat packs and even the good old warm bath are all popular post-exercise recovery methods. They may feel good, but the evidence on their efficacy is sparse.

Saunas are perhaps the best evidenced of the heat-related recovery modalities, with 5–25 minutes spent in the sauna showing chronic adaptations of increased plasma and blood volume (Stanley *et al.*, 2015). They can also be a useful tool in a heat acclimation strategy when preparing for running or racing in hot places. Care should be taken if using a sauna immediately after exercise with an already elevated core temperature as this could lead to a dangerously high core temperature. Include a cool-down and recovery period between training and the sauna.

Compression

Compression garments can be worn during exercise, with the premise that they improve blood flow and reduce muscle oscillation, and after exercise as a recovery modality. Developed from medical compression garments, used with patients who have compromised blood flow, graduated compression garments apply the greatest pressure at the farthest away end of the limb, gradually decreasing as they move closer to the body in order to squeeze blood back towards the heart. This external pressure may also reduce the available space for swelling and associated tissue damage, and improve stability of muscle fibres, decreasing muscle soreness.

Compression clothing undoubtedly has the ability to improve comfort and reduce tissue stress during running – running bras and compression boxers are testament to this – but should also be used with caution so as to avoid restricting blood flow to hard-working muscles.

Measuring recovery

Heart rate

As discussed on page 83, heart rate is a familiar variable that can be measured relatively accurately using wearable technology and is a reflection of how hard we're working, amongst other things. It may, when used appropriately, also add to our awareness of our body's state of wellness and recovery. Heart rate – how many times our heart beats each minute – varies throughout each day, according to factors such as our circadian rhythm, physical and psychological stress, illness, fatigue, hydration and caffeination levels, and the menstrual cycle. It varies over the course of our lives, depending on our age, fitness and overall health.

Resting heart rate, which is quick and easy to take first thing in the morning for a minimum of a minute, can be a good indicator of our levels of exercise- and life-induced stress, and our general health. It is therefore a potentially useful metric, particularly if you're not sure whether that sore throat might be an impending viral infection or just that you slept with your mouth open. Measured regularly and consistently, once a baseline resting heart rate is established, any significant or persistent deviations from this baseline can be taken as an indication that we're poorly recovered or coming down with a bug. But even this is far from guaranteed in terms of efficacy. In a study tracking morning fatigue status in elite football players (Thorpe *et al.*, 2016), researchers concluded that morning-measured subjective ratings of fatigue, sleep quality and DOMS – i.e. simply how we feel – are far more sensitive than heart-rate-derived measures to our daily fluctuations in training load.

Heart rate variability

Our heart rate is influenced by our *autonomic nervous system*; this has two main branches: the *sympathetic nervous system* and the *parasympathetic nervous system*. These two systems influence:

* **heart rate** – the number of times our hearts beat per minute, and
* **heart rate variability (HRV)** – the amount of variation in the time between those beats.

Higher sympathetic nervous system activity increases heart rate – our fight or flight response – and decreases our heart rate variability, whereas higher parasympathetic nervous system activity slows down heart rate and increases heart rate variability.

> Having high heart rate variability reflects flexible, adaptable cardiovascular functioning and is seen as an indicator of good health, well-being and readiness for training.

There has been a fairly recent explosion in interest and technology around HRV, which our watches and smartphones use as a composite measure to approximate the overall life stress we're feeling at any given time. The higher the overall stress we're under, and therefore the greater the suppression of parasympathetic activity, the lower our HRV. During times of low stress, on the other hand, parasympathetic activity is high, and so is our HRV. Used carefully, with full knowledge of its strengths and limitations, HRV can be a potentially useful part of a range of tools to be used in assessing stress and recovery.

As we discussed when we first looked at the principle of homeostasis (see pages 8–9), acute (short-term) stress on the body results in short-term responses, whereas chronic (long-term) stress results in long-term adaptations. Following a similar pattern, acute stressors like exercise result in a short-term decrease in our HRV – during a hard training run our heart rate is high, with little variation between beats. Once that stressor is removed, however, such as once we've finished a training session, heart rate returns to normal which, in well-trained athletes, is typically low. Over the course of a 24-hour period, therefore, a healthy person combining periods of physical activity with periods of recovery would exhibit a high degree of HRV.

As soon as other stressors are introduced, though, those times when heart rate would be low start to be shortened. A stressful work meeting, family and relationship stresses, illness and anxiety can all reduce parasympathetic nervous system activity, therefore reducing HRV. The list of other potential confounding variables is long, with many points of interest and some surprises along the way.

A large-scale analysis of data from 28,175 people analysed the relationship between heart rate, HRV, age, sex, body mass index and physical activity levels, along with changes in heart rate and HRV in response to some of the most common acute stressors (Altini and Plews, 2021).

Interestingly, alcohol had the largest effect, with a high intake of alcohol associated with a subsequent 6 per cent increase in heart rate and a 12 per cent reduction in HRV. Illness had the next biggest impact, resulting in a 6 per cent increase in heart rate and 10 per cent reduction in HRV. Less dramatic but still significant were a 1.3 per cent change in heart rate and a 4.6 per cent change in HRV in response to training, and a 1.6 per cent change in heart rate and a 3.2 per cent change in HRV between the follicular and luteal phases of the menstrual cycle.

How to measure HRV

Given that HRV has some potentially useful applications for aiding our knowledge of how well recovered we are, not just from training but from the overall stress load in life, it's important to measure it accurately. Different devices measure HRV differently, producing vastly different levels of accuracy. In general, measurements taken during the daytime are not useful as there is a great deal of 'noise' caused by the various activities we undertake. Night-time measurements are only useful if they average the data from the whole night – some devices only take one reading, and the result from this can vary widely depending upon which point of your sleep cycle you're in.

Ideally, HRV should be taken first thing in the morning upon waking (go to the loo first if you need to). Some apps, such as HRV4training, which was developed by Marco Altini (co-author of the article we mentioned on the previous page), use your phone camera and light to take a one-minute HRV reading, alongside a short set of questions on your subjective assessment of your recovery state. Interestingly, Altini himself is the first to highlight the many limitations of HRV; his knowledgeable and balanced work is well worth a read.

Each person has their own baseline HRV – a range within which they will normally fall during healthy times. It's worth taking around a month of daily readings to establish this, and to understand your individual variations throughout that month, including changes that occur after a big night out, throughout the menstrual cycle, and those due to normal training, work and life in general. As HRV is a composite score, it's not possible to identify exactly which stressor is causing a change in HRV; however, daily monitoring alongside a training diary that records all the other factors can offer some useful insight into the physiological effects of your lifestyle.

Like many other emerging areas of exercise and fitness-related technology, HRV is interesting if you enjoy data, and the concept is based on sound science, but it must be used with the above caveats and should be understood as a small part in a range of assessments of fitness, recovery, health and well-being. Given that the best currently available HRV apps also require subjective feedback, it's well worth asking yourself whether your own, free, unbranded assessment of how you're feeling is, in the vast majority of cases, the only one you really need.

As well as being a potentially useful measure of recovery, health, well-being and readiness for training, HRV has some interesting uses in sport psychology. Because of its relationship to stress, HRV can be used to indicate how anxious someone is before, say, a big race and to assess the effectiveness of interventions. Recent work has found simple breathing exercises are able to increase HRV by activating the parasympathetic nervous system (Laborde *et al.*, 2022). This reduces heart rate, allows us to better regulate our emotions, and even to think more clearly, as parasympathetic activity is related to higher cognitive functions such as decision making. In this way, shorter-term measurements of HRV could be useful in indicating the effectiveness of interventions such as slow breathing, and give us tangible feedback that such interventions are working.

The importance of rest days

Rest days are when the microdamage we cause to our bodies through the stresses of training repairs and regenerates, creating the adaptations we need to get fitter and stronger. Bone, muscle, tendon and ligament that has been fatigued by running and other training needs rest, supported by good fuelling, to regenerate in a way that will resist those training stresses better next time. Without sufficient rest, you're more likely to suffer overuse-type injuries. Overtraining also suppresses your immune system, meaning you're more prone to picking up circulating viruses and other infections. While regular training is important, consistent training over years is the single most effective way to become the best runner you can be.

Rest days are also important for our mental health and well-being, giving us some time out from the demands of training. Scheduling rest days to coincide with quality time with family or friends is a great way to maximise their effectiveness.

Some runners like to have a set rest day – or rest days – each week, while others like the flexibility to take a rest day when they feel they need it or other life events require it. With time and experience, you'll learn which suits you best.

Rest days don't necessarily mean total rest, but just a rest from the repetitive, high-impact activity that is running. Active rest can be even more effective than complete rest, raising your metabolic rate a little to speed up the repair processes. Perhaps head out for a gentle walk with the dog, go for a swim or a bike ride, or head to the yoga studio or climbing wall. All of these move your body in very different ways to running, helping with strength, mobility and general fitness while varying the stresses on individual structures throughout your body.

Strength and mobility for runners

Being strong is beneficial for many things, from the general lifting and carrying tasks of everyday life to the specific stresses and demands of running. Building and maintaining muscle mass helps support and protect our bones and joints, keeps our metabolic rate high (muscle cells metabolise faster than fat cells) and means we can continue to move in a way that feels good and is less likely to cause us injury. Having good overall muscle tone and function helps us to maintain good posture whatever we're doing, and this, alongside the feeling of being strong, can contribute to our overall sense of confidence and how we carry ourselves.

Appropriate, regular, consistent strength training is hugely important throughout our lives, supporting our changing bodies as we go through life stages such as puberty, reproduction, varying athletic endeavours and work challenges, and into later life. Muscle becomes harder to build and maintain as we age, but with the right approach it's perfectly possible to do, even for the elderly.

Keeping our muscles functioning is one of the most important things we can do to protect our bodies, whatever age or stage we're at. A well-designed programme of resistance-based workouts that targets all the key muscle groups, from the stabilising muscles around our joints and trunk (core, back and pelvis) to the big, powerful muscles in our legs, will benefit running by protecting against injury and directly improving performance aspects such as force generation and stride efficiency.

Running injuries, especially those of the 'overuse' variety, are almost always caused by muscle weakness creating too much or too little mobility somewhere in the body. While many traditional approaches focus on treating the source of the pain – for example treating the knee in patellofemoral pain syndrome or the foot in plantar fasciitis – in reality the source of the problem is likely to be far wider-reaching. An effective, long-term approach to treating and preventing injuries should address weaknesses along with stability and mobility issues throughout the body.

The main aims of including strength and mobility work in a training programme for runners are:
* To target the primary muscles involved in running in order to directly improve running performance.
* To target the ancillary muscles around joints and larger muscles in order to provide support, stability and decrease injury risk.
* To improve overall strength and mobility for daily living, an aspect that is especially important as we age.

What does the research say?

Current evidence suggests that combining aerobic training, such as running, with strength and mobility training is really good for our general health. Being strong and mobile, as well as being fit, protects us against injuries and enables us to live a full and engaged life, regardless of our age. Large-scale epidemiological studies (Lee *et al.*, 2022), suggest that regular aerobic exercise lowers the risk of premature death from any cause by 15 to 35 per cent, while strength training alone lowers risk by 10 to 25 per cent. If the two are combined, however, the risk is reduced by a remarkable 30 to 45 per cent.

As to whether strength training specifically helps our running performance, the evidence from research is mixed, but does generally show a positive effect. One of the major limitations of some studies comparing a running-only group with a concurrent strength and running group is that the strength training component is *added on* to the running. Runners in the strength group therefore add an extra training session each week which, regardless of whether this was done through weights or just an extra hour of running, would likely result in an improvement.

In real life, for most of us to fit in strength training we need to swap it for a run rather than adding an extra session on top of our running. As the most important and specific training for running is to run, the overall result may be a stronger body that's less well trained for running. Even with those studies that did keep the overall training volume of the comparative groups the same (Paavolainen *et al.*, 1999), (Rønnestad and Mujika, 2014), performance benefits were found, particularly for *explosive strength training* (see pages 108–109).

As with everything else, it's all about balance and priorities. If you do have the time to add some strength work each week without it negatively affecting the time you have to run, then it's likely there will be benefits to your running and beyond.

If you enjoy lifting heavy weights, and you're well-versed in good technique or have a good coach, then this can form a great accompaniment to your running. Alternatively, if you're someone who'd rather work out at home using body weight, resistance bands and perhaps some home weights, then that's equally effective. We've provided a comprehensive guide to home-based workouts specifically designed for runners in chapter 19. See page 215 for how to incorporate strength and mobility work into your training.

Core and pelvic stability for runners

The core and pelvis act as a coupling mechanism between the upper and lower body, simultaneously controlling upper body rotation while providing a strong, stable foundation from which the large, powerful muscles in the glutes and upper legs can work effectively.

Running on its own doesn't necessarily build the core and pelvic strength and mobility required for optimal running. Incorporating regular core and pelvic work is, therefore, essential to becoming a better runner in terms of economy and the ability to produce power through the large muscles. It's also a good way to protect yourself from the frustrating overuse injuries that result from weakness, instability, malalignment and lack of mobility through this important area. Recent research suggests that the pelvis and its surrounding soft tissues may be implicated in several common running injuries, including patellofemoral pain syndrome (sometimes called runner's knee), plantar fasciitis and iliotibial band syndrome (Haghighat et al., 2021).

Many of the home-based exercises detailed in chapter 19 work to strengthen the supportive muscles around these areas, maintain or improve mobility through the various joints of the pelvis and lower back, and help to address any imbalances that might contribute to direct problems such as pain or stiffness through the lower back and pelvis, or further away problems such as at the hip, knee and even into the lower leg, ankle and foot.

Until relatively recently, strength training was considered to be counterproductive for endurance sports like distance running, where big muscles and large amounts of power aren't necessarily beneficial. But it's now clear that the benefits of weight training for runners go far beyond strength gains, while regular running itself prevents muscles from becoming bulky. Incorporating some strength work into your training schedule could also help protect against injury by improving stability around joints.

The pelvic floor

The pelvic floor is a group of muscles and ligaments that support the bladder and bowel in males and females, and also the uterus (womb) in females. The pelvic floor muscles attach to your pubic bone at the front and the coccyx (tail bone) at the back, forming the base of your pelvis.

The male pelvic floor has two openings – at the urethra and bowel – while the female pelvic floor has three – at the urethra, vagina and bowel. For this reason, it's often the female pelvic floor that gets the most attention as its structure means it's more prone to problems. However, good pelvic floor health is equally important for males and females as it helps to prevent incontinence from the bladder and bowel, and is also involved in sexual sensation and function. Sounds worth looking after.

Due to its repetitive, high-impact nature, running places high stresses on the pelvic floor, so knowing how to recognise any problems and what to do is essential. We're all caught short sometimes, and early morning runs can see any runner diving for the bushes, but if you're desperate for a pee every time you run, experiencing leakage, urgency or a sensation of being unable to hold on, it's time to seek advice. Pelvic health physios specialise in this area and have seen it all before, so if you've tried exercises and you're not finding things are improving, go and see one.

While weak pelvic floors are often the culprit in issues such as incontinence, the muscles in this area, like any muscles, can also become too tight and inflexible (hypertonic). Common causes of hypertonic pelvic floor muscles include stress, childbirth, and discomfort. Tightness can lead to pain throughout the pelvic, abdominal and lower back areas, as well as incontinence and sexual dysfunction.

Whether you're prone to mild symptoms, or you're simply keen to keep your pelvic floor in tip-top condition, pelvic floor exercises should be an essential part of your daily routine. They can help increase both the tone and strength of the muscles as well as improving sensation and flexibility.

Aside from running, other activities such as coughing, sneezing and straining on the loo can exert high levels of stress on your pelvic floor. Increasing evidence also suggests that some weightlifting practices may be particularly damaging longer term, especially for females using techniques developed by male weight-lifters. These include bracing, breath-holding and using a belt, all of which greatly increase internal pressure on the pelvic floor. More research is required, but current advice is to avoid using these techniques to avoid long-term damage and subsequent pelvic floor issues.

Pelvic floor exercises

Also known as kegels, pelvic floor exercises are simple and discreet to do, but must be done properly to achieve the desired effect. They involve tightening and then releasing the muscles in your pelvic floor.

* Done in a standing position, the squeeze should feel akin to holding in wind (rather than urine, as traditionally advised), in order to activate the full range of pelvic floor muscles.
* Contract and hold, including a mixture of longer holds (10–20 seconds) and shorter holds (2–3 seconds).
* In between holds, relax and breathe deeply into your abdomen to promote flexibility and relaxation in the muscles, an essential addition to building strength.
* Aim to build up to three sets of 10 reps daily and try to make it a habit. As no one is any the wiser, you can do them on the train, in the coffee queue or while you're brushing your teeth.

Heavy versus explosive strength training

The aim of *heavy strength training* (i.e. lifting heavy weights) is to increase or maintain a muscle's ability to generate maximum force. It usually refers to training with a load that allows for between one and 15 repetitions before failure. Unless you're an experienced weightlifter and have home-based equipment, heavy lifting is best undertaken in a gym and under expert supervision. If you don't have access to a gym, or you don't enjoy lifting heavy, the good news is that there are home-based exercises you can do that will provide many of the same benefits, harnessing body weight and gravity.

Explosive strength training involves exercises that concentrate effort on the concentric phase of lifting – for example, the pushing up part of a squat. These exercises can be undertaken with weights but, because of the explosive nature of the efforts, they are also effective body weight exercises, so great for those who don't have access to a gym or home weights.

A review of the literature (Rønnestad and Mujika, 2014) concluded that:
* Combining endurance training with either heavy or explosive strength training improved running performance, including running economy.
* Heavy strength training improved running speed at VO_2 max.

To summarise: unless you're trying to improve your running speed at VO_2 max, explosive strength training is just as, if not more, beneficial than heavy lifting for runners. And the good news is that this can be done very effectively at home, harnessing nothing more than gravity and body weight.

In fact, another study found that reducing heavy strength training improved running economy in trained runners (Taipale *et al.*, 2010).

Lifting heavy has its place, though, and if you enjoy the associated feelings, body changes and challenges involved, it can bring many benefits relatively quickly compared with lifting lighter weights. For running off-road, where running economy is slightly less important but the ability to power up and down steep inclines is essential, the higher loads involved in heavy lifting may also be beneficial.

The downsides, though, are the potential for injury, and the need for a gym and personal trainer. Lifting heavy weights requires instruction in the correct techniques, along with supervision during sessions, so, if you're keen, find a qualified coach or instructor who specialises in strength training for endurance sports.

Mobility for runners

When it comes to running, mobility shouldn't be confused with flexibility. Being overly bendy can actually be detrimental for runners, reducing the stiffness of our 'springs', which makes us less efficient, and increasing the likelihood of some injuries. However, lack of mobility is also detrimental, so spending some time keeping your body moving as it should is time well spent.

Stretching
Once a standard pre-run pastime, stretching when you're cold can make you more injury prone. A gentle warm-up, starting out with a very easy jog before moving into your main run, is the best way to get everything moving. Stretching specific structures, such as the bottom of the foot if you have plantar fasciitis, may be beneficial.

Yoga, pilates and similar movement-based activities can be great for supporting running. These promote working with the breath, mobility rather than flexibility (especially if you're able to attend a class aimed specifically at runners), stability and balance, and better body awareness.

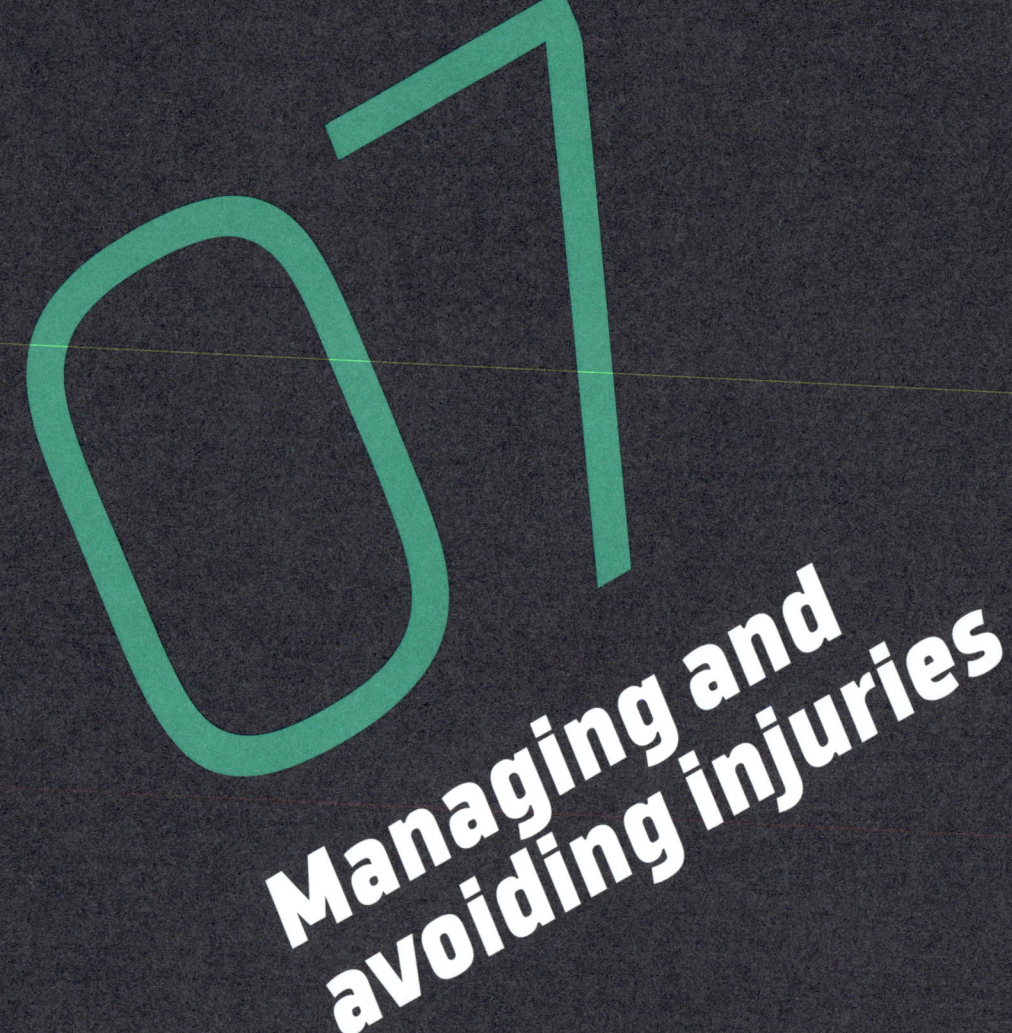

Managing and avoiding injuries

Running is a repetitive, high-impact activity that exerts a force of more than three times your body weight every time your foot hits the ground. It's therefore unsurprising that most of us experience the frustration of injury at some point along the way. When it comes to the prevalence and risk of injury, the science offers up some fairly unhelpful statistics. Between 20 and 80 per cent of regular runners experience an injury each year which, in terms of exposure, is between two and twelve injuries per 1,000 hours of running. The numbers are variable, but the message is clear: runners get injured.

Chronic or 'overuse' injuries

The majority of running injuries – around 70 per cent – are chronic in nature. These are often termed 'overuse' injuries, although this is something of a misnomer as new runners tend to be at a higher risk of injury, even though they may be doing fewer miles.

How to reduce your injury risk

Allow enough time for adaptation: whether you're new to running, upping your mileage for an ultra or aiming for a speedy new marathon PB, it's all too easy to get overenthusiastic and do too much before your body has had the chance to undergo the gradual process of adaptation to the specifics of these new stresses. It's sensible to follow the 10 per cent rule – don't increase your training load (volume and intensity) by more than 10 per cent each week. Generally, it's wise to err on the side of caution, especially if you're new to running, keeping increases low and increasing either the distance or the intensity of your running, rather than both at the same time.

Listen to your body: your individual injury risk will be down to a complex combination of factors including your sex, age, running experience, biomechanics, psychology and previous injuries. The best advice, therefore, is to listen to your body. A 'niggle' is a common warning sign that something, somewhere, is not happy with the way things are going. It's an *oooh* or a *hmm* that, if ignored, will soon turn into an *ouch*, but it's not quite there yet. The niggle signifies your moment to step in and do something differently – can you change your shoes, apply some tape or spend the rest of the week sleeping instead of running? If you can take note of a niggle and simply reduce or adapt your training for a few days, it might well prevent it from turning into a full-on annoying chronic injury.

Think carefully before making changes: a common cause of chronic injuries in more experienced runners is changing something about their regular running. In the same way as the body needs time to adapt to running in the first place, regular speedwork, off-road running, hills or weight training all contribute new and different stresses that need to be adapted to. Running off-road, for example, requires greater neuromotor control, balance and coordination than road running. Running on legs already fatigued from a new weights routine means your muscles and tendons may be less able to provide the required power, stability, shock absorption and control for your joints.

Pay attention to strength and mobility: perhaps counterintuitively, soft tissue tightness often results from muscular weakness or imbalance. In the absence of sufficient muscular control around a joint or series of joints, the soft tissues tighten up in an attempt to provide support and protection to these potentially vulnerable structures. While instinct might make us think we need to stretch tight muscles and tendons, the effects of stretching don't last long, and may even be counterproductive. As soon as we start running again, the underlying problem that caused the structures to tighten up in the first place means they'll simply revert to their former condition. The body's main priority is protecting hips and knees, not whether you can touch your toes. Doing regular strength and mobility work alongside your running will allow your muscles and tendons to function in a way that balances flexibility with economy. See chapter 19 for some of our favourite strength and mobility exercises for runners and see page 215 for how to incorporate them into your training plan.

Prioritise high-quality recovery: insufficient or poor-quality recovery – including overfocusing on gadgets and potions to the detriment of the tried-and-tested less technical or exciting things – can quickly lead to illness and injury. See chapter 5 for more on this.

Common running injuries

Running injuries can result from various factors, with the most common being:
* **Biomechanical issues**, which can be inherent or develop as a result of life events (accidents, childbirth, underlying conditions).
* **Training errors**, usually involving increasing training load (volume, intensity or both) too rapidly, without allowing sufficient time for recovery and adaptation.
* **Equipment**, often shoes, which have little evidence to back up their ability to cure or prevent injuries, but can certainly cause them. Shoes that are excessively worn can markedly change running biomechanics, so changing your shoes if they're well worn is a good first step.
* **Environmental conditions**, such as very cold weather, which means warming up takes longer and is even more important.

Here are some of the most common running injuries, along with their causes and treatments:

Patellofemoral pain syndrome (runner's knee)

Symptoms: an ache in the kneecap that worsens with prolonged sitting and eases when you straighten your leg.

Causes: while weakness of the inner quadriceps muscle has often been implicated in this injury, recent imaging studies suggest it is more likely a result of weakness in the hip muscles, resulting in excessive rotation of the femur. Tight quadriceps muscles can also aggravate the condition.

Prevention and treatment: reduction in running, or rest/cross-train until pain has subsided. Strengthening exercises for the hip and pelvic muscles. Stretching/mobilisation and massage of the quadriceps muscles, replacing footwear if overly worn. Over-the-counter orthotics may help to initially settle the pain.

Medial tibial stress syndrome (shin splints)

Symptoms: pain in the lower front portion of the shin, just above the ankle. May just be the soft tissue (tendons and surrounding structures), or the bone may also be involved.

Causes: building up training load too rapidly, footwear, overly tight lacing, shoes that are unsupportive/too large, unaccustomed running on hard surfaces.

Prevention and treatment: rest or reduction in running, more running on softer surfaces, address footwear issues including lacing and fit.

Plantar fasciitis

Symptoms: pain on the sole of the foot at the front of the heel bone. Worse first thing in the morning – 'first step pain'.

Causes: traction of the plantar fascia at its attachment to the heel bone causes inflammation and then degeneration and thickening of the plantar fascia. Tightness

and weakness of the calf and peroneal muscles, high arches, or improper footwear.

Prevention and treatment: reduction/cessation in running, stretching exercises for the foot – especially the big toe – and lower leg structures, strengthening of the intrinsic muscles of the foot, supportive footwear, taping – especially low-dye taping (see page 114), massage – self-massage of the bottom of the foot by rolling a bottle or ball can be helpful.

Achilles tendinopathy

Symptoms: pain, stiffness and crepitus (a creaking sensation when the tendon slides up and down) in the Achilles tendon. Most common in the mid-portion of the tendon, but can sometimes be at the insertion point of the tendon on to the heel bone.

Causes: wearing shoes with too little drop between the heel-and-forefoot; running uphill; biomechanical abnormalities.

Prevention and treatment: addressing any footwear problems, for example by wearing shoes with a greater heel-to-forefoot drop. Strengthening leg and pelvic muscles to reduce excess movement. Physical therapy as prescribed by a registered practitioner.

Iliotibial (IT) band syndrome

Symptoms: pain and a 'snapping' or 'burning' sensation over the outside of the knee.

Causes: once thought to be the iliotibial band snapping back and forth over the bony prominence on the outside of the knee and inflaming a bursa, recent research suggests the iliotibial band is actually compressed into the outer side of the femur during flexion of the knee. This is thought to be a result of poor muscular control and mobility in the pelvic muscles, especially the gluteals.

Prevention and treatment: strengthening the gluteal muscles and improving mobility through exercises and massage of the muscles (not the iliotibial band, which does not stretch).

Stress fractures

Symptoms: swelling and point tenderness, even with a light touch, on a bony area that gets worse with activity and is still present during resting. Hopping on the affected side will cause a sharp pain in the affected area.

Causes: while underlying systemic factors such as osteoporosis (low bone density) may predispose a person to stress fractures, it is more commonly due to overloading – either due to biomechanical abnormalities or increasing load too rapidly without adequate time for recovery and adaptation. Weakness in muscles that support bones can leave bones more susceptible to stress fractures.

Prevention and treatment: ensure both energy availability and overall nutrient intake are appropriate and supporting good bone health. Address training errors, ensuring build-up is gradual. Incorporate regular strength and mobility training to enable muscles to support bones.

Muscle strain

Symptoms: pain in the body of a muscle, which usually comes on suddenly during running – often when changing pace or direction rapidly. Common locations include the quadriceps (front of thigh), hamstrings (back of thigh) and calf muscles.

Causes: applying forces of a magnitude or direction that exceed the muscle fibres' ability to withstand those forces. Often due to rapid changes in speed or direction. Hamstring injuries are common in sprinters due to high acceleration and deceleration forces, whereas calf injuries are more common in older distance runners due to a lack of stretch through the muscle–tendon unit.

Prevention and treatment: muscle strengthening, avoiding rapid changes in pace and direction – for example using 'peak and fade' during interval training. Warm up thoroughly before undertaking faster or multi-directional running.

Taping and bracing

Used correctly, taping and bracing can be useful in helping to protect and support an injured area, as well as providing proprioceptive feedback when stretch receptors in the skin and underlying tissues have been damaged, for example during a sprain. Foot taping can also be highly effective in supporting the structures of the foot to allow injuries to heal. Low-dye taping for plantar fasciitis is an easy to learn technique that can be applied to your feet using non-stretchy zinc oxide tape; there are some useful videos online which can help you learn the technique.

JEN'S STORY – PLANTAR FASCIITIS

This debilitating condition is caused by traction on the plantar fascia, a fibrous band that forms the main arch of the foot. The results are inflammation, degeneration and thickening of the fascia. This was a whole new experience, haunting me through each and every day, right from the classic, sharp tearing sensation known as 'first step' pain as I got out of bed each morning to the dull, persistent ache that accompanied me everywhere. It felt as if I had a pebble in my shoe, just at the front of my heel, jabbing into my foot with each step.

I tried everything, starting with denial, moving on to orthotics and ending with a steroid injection, which only made things much worse. Eventually, I discovered a combination of low-dye taping and stiff-soled shoes helped, and I even managed to start running again without aggravating the injury. Fully supported, it appeared to be able to continue to heal while I, finally, got on with my life. Eventually, one day, after 18 months of pain, I realised it was no longer there, and it hasn't come back since.

One of the wisest comments I heard on the subject of plantar fasciitis was from a consultant podiatric surgeon during my master's degree. 'Plantar fasciitis lasts 12 to 18 months,' he said. 'Then it goes, and people attribute its disappearance to whatever treatment they happen to be using at the time.' My own experience certainly mirrored this, but I have had the chance to try out that magic combination of low-dye taping and stiff-soled shoes on many running patients since, and it does seem to offer relief. But what does the science say?

There have been hundreds of studies looking at the many and various proposed causes and treatments of plantar fasciitis, and many reviews trying to make sense of these individual studies. A summary of these reviews (Rhim *et al.*, 2021) came to the following conclusions:

* Athletic and non-athletic populations suffer from plantar fasciitis, but in athletic populations runners are at greatest risk.
* No definitive differences in gait, biomechanics, flexibility or strength were found between those who developed plantar fasciitis and those who didn't, except ...
* Those with plantar fasciitis have weaker foot muscles than those without.
* Low evidence for the use of corticosteroid injections, which also increase the risk of rupture.
* Some evidence for the use of platelet-rich plasma, which is harvested from the patient's own blood and injected into the plantar fascia with the intention of speeding up the healing process.
* Some evidence for the use of extracorporeal shockwave therapy.
* Low evidence for the use of insoles and custom orthotics.
* Some evidence for the use of taping, especially low-dye taping.
* Some evidence for plantar fascia-specific stretching, as opposed to calf muscle stretching.

This is just one example, but it illustrates the frustrating nature of chronic injuries and the difficulties involved in getting sound, evidence-based treatment advice.

Acute injuries

Acute injuries are usually the result of a trip or fall. Ankle sprains are by far the most common acute running injury, usually occurring while running downhill on uneven terrain, when the ankle is at its least stable.

If you do end up injured, it's not always the end of the world that it might appear to be at the time. You may still be able to continue running with some adaptations, such as sticking to flat, even terrain or reducing your usual running intensity and/or mileage to allow the injury to heal. Alternatively, it's a great opportunity to jump on the bike or in the pool for a week, a month, or however long it takes. Injuries are how many runners discover triathlon. It's also always worth consulting a professional, making sure you choose one with specific running expertise. Ask running friends for their recommendations – given the stats, they've almost certainly been there, too!

If you do experience a traumatic injury, such as a sprained ankle, thorough rehabilitation is essential to avoid re-injury. This includes regaining a full range of movement, working on balance and proprioception, and rebuilding strength in the injured area. Recovering full function of a sprained ankle can take many months but is well worth the time and effort as it will protect against future sprains.

Niggles, and when to seek help

The occasional niggle is a normal part of running life. When a niggle does crop up it's usually a signal that something's not right – perhaps it's time to replace those old shoes, reduce your running volume or intensity for a week, or increase your strength and mobility work. With speedy corrective action, many niggles resolve themselves quickly. Some need nothing more than a couple of rest days and they disappear completely.

When a niggle starts to become persistent, however, it edges towards being an injury. Without decisive action to change whatever it is that's causing the problem, there's a risk it will become chronic, leading to pain, misery and a lot of lost training. A good general plan of action is to drastically reduce your running for a couple of weeks, swapping run sessions for cross-training such as cycling, swimming, hiking or, ideally, a mixture. If the injury is one of those covered in this chapter, get going on the suggested interventions and exercises that should help to combat it. If it's not improving after a couple of weeks, it's a good idea to get an assessment and treatment plan from a qualified practitioner such as a physiotherapist or podiatrist, depending on what the injury is and where it is located.

Chafing

Chafing is another common running injury, particularly over longer distances and/or in warm and sweaty conditions. It's caused by the friction of repeated rubbing of skin against skin or skin against fabric; this gradually removes the top layers of skin and can cause some pretty spectacular-looking sores. Stepping into the shower with post-run chafing is a truly character-building moment.

Experience will tell you where your chafe-prone areas are, but common hotspots tend to be the underarms, between the thighs, feet in general but particularly between the toes and along the inside edges of the feet, waistbands, bras in general – especially if they're on the older side, and running packs – generally around the neck, shoulders and back.

To help prevent chafing, apply a good quality skin lubricant to chafe-prone areas. Popular choices include Squirrel's Nut Butter, petroleum jelly or pure shea butter. Try to avoid harsh fabrics, especially around waistbands and underwear. Moisture increases friction and therefore chafing, so more care needs to be paid in wet or hot and sweaty weather.

The longer you're running for, the more likely chafing is. If you're running for longer than you usually do, for example in an ultramarathon, it's a good idea to take some of your favourite skin lubricant with you so you can reapply as required.

Cramp

While we tend to put them under a single heading, there are actually many different types of cramp with many different causes. Most of us who participate in endurance sports like running are familiar with exercise-associated muscle cramps (EAMCs). These are commonly experienced by healthy individuals with no underlying conditions, and usually come on during the latter stages of an intense workout or race. EAMCs can strike out of the blue, bringing you down just when you thought everything was going well. They're intensely painful and debilitating and, unless you can stretch them out quickly and effectively, can easily be race-ending.

Contrary to popular belief, most cramps have nothing to do with electrolyte balance, although they're very likely to occur at times when this is something you need to be considering – such as on hot days, during harder or longer than usual bouts of exercise, or when you're in a fatigued state.

How to avoid cramp

Every runner gets cramp from time to time, usually when we're already in a fatigued state and then ask our muscles to do something a bit unusual. If you're regularly plagued with cramp, though, it's worth asking yourself whether it might be down to another factor or factors. Almost always, it's one or more of the usual suspects:

* Inadequate conditioning
* Lack of sleep
* Stress
* High caffeine intake
* Older age
* Underlying medical conditions

Delayed onset muscle soreness (DOMS)

Most people are familiar with DOMS – the pain and loss of function that happens after a bout of strenuous physical activity, especially if you're unaccustomed to that specific activity or more used to doing it at a lower intensity and it's an activity that involes high eccentric muscle loading, i.e. the muscle is working to resist lengthening. In running, long, fast downhills and hard road races are classic triggers for DOMS.

DOMS typically sets in 24–48 hours after the exercise session and gradually worsens before it gets better. It's characterised by muscle stiffness, tenderness and soreness, and can seriously impact both training and daily activities. It's thought to be caused by microscopic damage to muscle fibres, which triggers an inflammatory response, leading to the sensation of soreness and discomfort.

While DOMS can be uncomfortable, it is a normal part of the muscle adaptation process, and the muscles usually recover within a few days. Common methods to alleviate DOMS include rest or easy movement, gentle stretching and over-the-counter pain relief. It's important to note that DOMS is different from acute muscle soreness, which occurs during or immediately after exercise.

Running and immunity

Research suggests that running can be good for our immune systems, both in the short and long term. Like the rest of the body, the immune system adapts to the regular stresses of exercise, which over time makes it more effective at responding to, and dealing with, infections. However, during very hard training blocks or after a particularly long, hard workout, especially something like an ultramarathon that also includes a night or more of lost sleep, we may be more susceptible to infections. At these times it's worth paying particular attention to hygiene measures, including regular hand washing and even considering wearing a mask in crowded places.

I'm ill – should I train?

* As a general rule, if you feel up for training you're probably well enough. But running when you're under the weather is never the time to push the pace, run long or try racing. From extending the time you're ill to potentially serious long-term negative effects, the consequences of overdoing it are likely to be negative.
* Tracking your HRV or resting heart rate on waking each morning is a good way to add quantitative information to your subjective sense of how you're feeling. Taking your temperature to see if you have a fever is another one.
* If you have a cold, follow the old runners' rule that if it's above the neck it's fine to train, while if it's below the neck (i.e. on your chest) then it's time to rest and recover. You should feel better after a run rather than worse, so, if you go for a run one day and come back feeling terrible, it may be worth taking more time out before returning to running.
* Hard training and racing when ill with a virus can cause heart damage, so are well worth avoiding.
* If you're recovering from a mild respiratory illness during cold weather or if there's high air pollution, running indoors on a treadmill can be a good way to keep some gentle training going without stressing your airways even more.
* Being ill often disrupts good sleeping and eating habits, so be aware that your ability to recover from training and fight off other bugs will be compromised.
* If you're ill and due to run with a club or other group, don't. It's annoying having to miss training or an important race due to illness, so don't spread it about.

Mental
Mental
Menta
Men
Me
M

Mental skills for runners

08

Sport and exercise psychology

Psychology is the part of running science that's often forgotten about. But anyone who's ever run knows that running, from getting through the door in the first place to keeping going once you're out there, is at least as much a mental skill as it is a physical one.

The aim of using psychology in sport and exercise is to help us know and understand ourselves better, and to use this knowledge to better manage ourselves in navigating the many challenges that taking part in sport throws in our paths. Knowing how to recognise and manage anxiety before a race, a reduction in motivation to train, or the mounting desire to quit when things get tough is essential for getting the most out of our running. Understanding how our minds work can help us to support others in getting the most out of their running, too.

IS IT JUST A LACK OF MOTIVATION?

Knowing what motivates us and, on those occasions when we find ourselves struggling for motivation, knowing how to manage this, is an essential part of doing anything meaningful for any length of time. Especially when that thing is, like running, often hard work and not necessarily in-the-moment enjoyable. Everyone has off-days, so if your running mojo takes the occasional day off that's probably nothing to worry about. But if you're struggling to motivate yourself to run on a regular basis, or continually lacking enthusiasm once you're out, there are a few questions well worth asking yourself.

Motivational theories aside for a moment, a lack of enthusiasm for, or enjoyment of, running can be a sign that something else is up. If you also:
*   have signs of illness;
*   are experiencing weight loss; or
*   are generally feeling down
then get this checked out before looking at sources of motivation.

Other factors which might affect whether you feel like running include:
*   Chronic deficiencies of energy and/or essential nutrients (see chapter 2).
*   Lack of recovery (see chapter 5), and related conditions such as RED-S (see page 34).
*   General life stress.

Theories of sport and exercise psychology

A theory is a set of ideas intended to explain a phenomenon. In sport science, theories offer the most up-to-date explanation of how things work when they're difficult to study in real life, such as muscle contraction, the effects of the menstrual cycle on performance or why we experience fatigue in the way that we do. Theories are updated as knowledge around the subject increases.

Psychology is an area where theories abound, as it's much harder to carry out controlled experiments on our brains and our subjective experiences than it is on some of our physical aspects. But that doesn't mean this side of sport science is any less important or 'scientific' than the more easily measurable areas such as physiology and biomechanics. After all, if we're not enjoying running, and don't see it as meaningful, we won't do it in the first place.

Here's a brief overview of some of the main theories in sport and exercise psychology and how you can use each one to help improve your running.

Motivation and self-determination theory

Motivation is all about the reasons behind our decisions to do (or not do) things. In psychology, self-determination theory (SDT) aims to explore and explain the motivation behind the choices we make – the degree to which our behaviour is self-motivated and self-determined.

Originally proposed by psychology researchers Edward Deci and Richard Ryan in 1985, SDT suggests that sources of motivation can be broadly separated into two main categories: *intrinsic motivators* and *extrinsic motivators*. In reality, most of us have a mixture of the two going on at any one time, and the balance may well change at different points in our lives, but it's interesting to consider what it is that's really motivating us and, when we're struggling to find motivation, what we can do to help.

Intrinsic and extrinsic motivators

When we're purely intrinsically motivated, we exercise for the sheer enjoyment of it. We're still aware there are other benefits, of course – we'll be fitter, healthier, happier *and* faster in our next race – but the primary reason we're running is because we absolutely love running.

Having high levels of intrinsic motivation means we're more likely to exercise regularly and keep doing it for many years. But we all know running isn't always actually in-the-moment enjoyable. Sometimes it's only fun once it's done and we can fully appreciate the powerful extrinsic motivator of post-run cake.

For us, some days there's no doubt we run for the love of it. But on other days, when life gets in the way and intrinsic motivation feels a bit low, some extrinsic motivators can also be helpful. Good examples of helpful extrinsic motivators might be a race you're keen to run well and which therefore motivates you to train harder, or a Couch to 5K plan to complete. Sometimes running is only enjoyable once you're out there doing it, or even only retrospectively, so these kinds of extrinsic motivators can really help with that first mile, or the last one, or even every single mile from start to finish.

But certain kinds of extrinsic motivation can actually be harmful – if you're only running to please someone else, for example, or even to satisfy a demanding voice within that says you're somehow not good enough unless you've been for a run. At times it's certainly a fine line: a well-judged word of encouragement from someone whose opinion we respect can work wonders, but the feeling that we need to somehow 'earn' someone else's respect – or even self-respect – is a much less positive, and a potentially extremely detrimental form of extrinsic motivation.

Self-determination theory suggests that we have three basic psychological needs that must be fulfilled for us to be motivated to continue to participate in an activity such as running. These are:

Autonomy – the need to feel ownership of our behaviour, and that we're making fully informed, uncoerced decisions that reflect our beliefs, values and desires.

Competence – the need to feel we have the skills, experience and other necessary requirements (equipment, logistics etc.) to produce the outcomes we desire.

Relatedness – the need to feel connected to others, and that we're supported by others, supporting others and part of something bigger, rather than acting alone and in isolation.

If you, or someone you know, wants to run but is struggling with the motivation to do so, it's well worth considering these basic needs, whether they're being fulfilled and, if not, how to help.

Self-efficacy

When we believe we can do something, we pursue it with more energy and drive, we're more likely to stick with it through adversity, and we're less likely to be discouraged if things don't quite go as planned. If we're not sure we can do something, we're fearful and filled with doubt, we're more likely to try to avoid things we perceive as difficult, and more likely to be distracted and give up more easily.

In everyday life, we might refer to a belief in ourselves and our abilities as *confidence*. But confidence has both positive and negative connotations. Someone can be generally confident in their demeanour, willing to give anything a go as it usually works out for them. This kind of generalised confidence can be a good thing in moderation, but taken too far it becomes cockiness, and a lack of self-awareness that can hurt, rather than improve, performance – along with relationships with other people.

In sport psychology, confidence specific to our sport is often referred to as *self-efficacy*. A theory first developed by Albert Bandura in 1977, self-efficacy refers to our belief in our capabilities to organise and execute the courses of action required to get the results we desire. It's subtly different from confidence, in that it's not about having a belief in our ability to achieve an outcome, but about our ability to carry out the processes necessary to lead to that outcome.

Self-efficacy is a 'self-concept' that involves the cognitive process of making judgements about our ability to reach a particular goal. Our sense of self-efficacy is always goal-directed, whether that goal is a big race or simply getting through the door for that day's run.

As we train, go about our daily lives and build up to a key race, we're constantly assessing and reassessing how well we think we're doing in managing everything we need to manage to perform at our best. On race day, if we know we've nailed our preparation, we can then feel confident in our ability to undertake whatever is necessary to get to the finish line.

A lack of self-efficacy can result from many things, but the overall effect is likely to be a lack of confidence in our ability to meet our goals, along with anxiety, fear, helplessness and avoidance. Sources of poor self-efficacy might include:

*   Knowing we don't have the time to fit in the required training around everything else going on in our lives.
*   Lacking the ability to buy or use the kit we need.
*   Lacking the knowledge and skills we need to complete a particular event.

We can address these by reassessing our goals if they simply don't fit with the time and money we have available to spend on them, or practising with the specific kit and in the specific conditions we know we'll face on race day.

Our self-efficacy level reflects our confidence in succeeding at a task of a specific degree of difficulty. Someone might feel confident in their ability to run 5K in under 30 minutes, for example, but less confident in their ability to get under 20 minutes, or to run a 50K. The strength of our self-efficacy is the degree of confidence we have in our abilities, while self-efficacy generality reflects how wide the range of activities or conditions we feel confident in succeeding in is. Being generally good at sport, for example, might mean we're confident in trying pretty much any kind of sport – a high level of self-efficacy generality – but the better our opponent is, the less this might be the case.

If we're standing at the start line of a big race, flooded with nerves and feelings of impending failure, thinking back to the many hours of hard work we've put in can improve our *self-efficacy*, and therefore our *confidence* for the task at hand. Setting out with higher levels of self-efficacy, and therefore confidence, will allow us to fully and positively commit to the race, allowing us to perform at our best.

Helpfully, high levels of self-efficacy can also protect us from the negative effects of things going wrong, when we're more likely to blame an unlucky, isolated incident for our failings than our general rubbishness, leaving us more able to shrug off disappointment and move on rather than wallowing in self-pity and self-doubt.

How can we improve our self-efficacy?

Mastery experiences
The most powerful way to boost self-efficacy is through drawing on previous positive experiences. Looking back on times you've pushed through and succeeded in the past gives you confidence that you can do it again. When things get tough mid-race, think back to all the times it's been tough in training and how you've stuck with it. Think about previous races when you were on the edge of giving up but didn't, and how good it felt to cross the finish line. If your self-efficacy for a particular distance or event is low because it's the first time you've done it, consider it as a mastery experience that will improve your confidence next time around.

Vicarious experiences
Seeing other people who you consider to be similar to yourself achieving something important to them can help you feel more confident in your ability to achieve it too. That's why representation is so essential – seeing other people you identify as being like you doing the things you aspire to do is a powerful motivating and confidence-inspiring force. Always remember that you're out there inspiring others, too!

Verbal persuasion
Positive verbal persuasion – such as cheering and encouragement – works by strengthening our belief in our ability to succeed. If we're positively persuaded that we have the ability to complete a given task, we'll put more effort into doing so, as well as experiencing less self-doubt. It's important to remember, however, that negative verbal persuasion – even if it comes from a place of concern – can easily undermine self-belief, and also that no amount of positive verbal persuasion will help someone achieve something they're not ready to achieve.

Physiological and affective states
Our perceived physical and emotional state can also influence our belief in our ability to perform in a given situation. We take cues from our bodies that affect how we feel about our readiness to undertake the required actions to succeed in a task. Examples might be feeling tired after a poor night's sleep or experiencing pain from a niggle, both of which might reduce our self-efficacy for a race. Feeling stressed or unhappy because of life events unrelated to running can also negatively impact our confidence and motivation for running.

Goal setting

Developed in the 1990s, goal setting theory explains how the goals we set influence our motivation and behaviour (Locke and Latham, 1990). It suggests that goal characteristics, including how challenging and specific those goals are, the importance of the goal and how committed we are to it, our levels of self-efficacy, the feedback we receive and how complex we perceive the task to be, all play into our likelihood of success.

Using goal setting theory to improve your running
* Choose a goal that's challenging enough to push you to really try, without being so hard you've a high likelihood of failure.
* Be specific about your goals – goal setting theory suggests that challenging, specific goals are more likely to be motivating than easy, general goals.
* Tell people about your goal. Making goals public has been shown to increase commitment to them in some people.
* Work on ways to improve your self-efficacy around your goal (see page 125).
* Reduce task complexity by breaking bigger goals down into smaller, more manageable ones – this could be by following a training plan that guides you through gradual improvements towards your goal, or chunking up a long run into bite-size pieces according to time, distance or aid stations.

Habits

Are habits a good thing or a bad thing? Either way, they're something we're all familiar with, and which undoubtedly play an important part in our lives. Habits, our relationship to them, and their function as tool or torment, is also something that has intrigued many of history's greatest thinkers. Aristotle proclaimed that, 'We are what we repeatedly do ... Excellence, then, is not an act, but a habit.' Barack Obama is well known to cultivate good habits for the purposes of reducing the cognitive load of necessary everyday behaviours, saving his energy and focus for the important things.

Under the right circumstances, habits can be a great thing, reducing the effort and thinking time required to undertake actions that are beneficial to us but might possibly be viewed as a little too much like hard work, or at least inconvenience, for us to do purely because we want to do them. Like cleaning our teeth, doing the exercises prescribed by a physio, or even getting out for a regular run. These kinds of habits make us feel good *retrospectively*, adding to our sense of being effective, efficient and in control of our lives.

Some habits aren't so obviously good for us, but make us feel good at the time, stimulating our reward systems and filling us with that warm glow of well-being that makes the mundanity of daily life just that bit more special. In moderation, these kinds of habits probably do no long-lasting harm and add to our sense of structure and being who we are.

A glass of wine or a bar of chocolate after a stressful day, for example, carefully chosen and savoured in the moment, can be just the thing to help you relax and unwind. But if that behaviour becomes a daily – or even more regular – habit, that might end up damaging both your health and other possibilities in life, then it might be time to think about stopping. This is the dark side of habit formation. Bad habits, that serve us no positive purpose and can actually be harmful, but are nonetheless hard to break.

Habit forming and running

James Clear's multi-million-selling book, *Atomic Habits*, breaks habit formation down into four laws. Here's how you can apply them to forming, and keeping, a habit of regular running.

Make it obvious

This is the law that probably works best – leave your kit where you can see it, or even better, put it on. Not only does this act as a constant reminder that you need to go running, it means you're already ready to go.

Make it attractive

Different things work for different people here; have a think about what will work best for you. Good ideas include having a podcast or audiobook that you're looking forward to listening to, or arranging to meet a friend for a run. But this only works some of the time. Sometimes, the idea of running is about as unattractive as you can imagine, but if you really want to get better at running you have to force yourself through the door regardless.

Make it easy

Unfortunately this isn't really the point of running! Those starting out in running, or getting back into it after some time off, will likely find every single run is hard work. Marathon training is hard work whoever you are. More experienced runners might actually enjoy the challenge of making it deliberately difficult – unpleasant, even.

Make it satisfying

A good run, where you've achieved what you wanted to, made progress towards your training goals, or just enjoyed being out and about in the fresh air or with friends, will always feel satisfying. No one ever regretted a run, as the saying goes.

Psychological skills for runners

Psychological skills training is an approach widely used by athletes, coaches and psychologists as a way of enhancing performance and increasing enjoyment and self-satisfaction in sport. A systematic review of the literature around psychological skills training found that using the psychological skills of imagery, self-talk and goal setting improved endurance performance (McCormick *et al.*, 2015).

The review also concluded that mental fatigue plays a key role in undermining endurance performance, and that interventions that influence our perception of effort – a similar idea to the rate of perceived exertion (RPE) we discussed earlier (see page 82) – also affect endurance performance. In this chapter, we'll focus on these key skills, and some useful mind-mastering techniques, so you can harness them to get the best out of your running.

Imagery

Also called visualisation, imagery involves undertaking a detailed mental rehearsal of the sporting event you're preparing for. Done properly, imagery involves using all your senses to put yourself in a specific time and place, and really trying to 'feel' what it's like to be there, participating in that moment. Many professional sportspeople use imagery highly effectively, from racing drivers practising the turns on a course to climbers mentally rehearsing the moves on a route. Brain imaging studies show similar brain activity whether people are undertaking the actual activity, or simply visualising themselves doing it.

If you're visualising a race, you might imagine tackling a particularly technical stretch of trail, running strongly later on in a race, moving through an aid station quickly and efficiently, or crossing the finishing line. In training you might use imagery the night before an early morning training session to run through everything you need to do before you leave the house, including putting on your kit, having breakfast and so on.

Used effectively, imagery can reduce the mental load involved in carrying out actions; improve confidence, self-efficacy and a sense of mastery over the task at hand; and ultimately improve performance.

A downside of using imagery to prepare for a race is what might happen if you find yourself in a scenario you hadn't visualised. Perhaps you'd visualised meeting your crew at an aid station during a race and smoothly going through everything you needed to do – handing over water bottles to be refilled, swapping empty gel packets for full ones, changing your socks and so on – and then your crew gets caught in traffic and doesn't make it to the aid station. If the success of your race relies solely on one scenario playing out exactly as you'd imagined it, the slightest deviation can send you into a panic. That's when being flexible and adaptable and *if-then planning* can help.

Adaptability and if-then planning

Athletes are notoriously superstitious, attaching future success to numerous pre-race and race-day routines and requirements, from the obvious and logical such as food and clothing to the downright odd. Serena Williams famously wore the same socks, unwashed, for an entire tennis tournament, while Rafael Nadal is known for meticulously lining up his water bottles. Former 400-metre runner, Iwan Thomas, always put his left shoe on first before a race, and took his left shoe off first afterwards. He'd also only train in lane 2, and, towards the end of his career, would pull on his left ear just before going into the blocks.

Having specific goals and meticulous planning, along with any routines and superstitions that help you feel ready to go, both before and during a race, are important parts of achieving what you want as a runner. But, life being as it is, things don't always (perhaps even rarely) go exactly as planned. Perhaps that race you've spent six months working towards is cancelled, or the route is changed at the last minute, or your child is in a school play, or you pick up an illness or injury in race week. Maybe the hotel doesn't serve your usual porridge, the airline loses your lucky socks, or an aid station has run out of water – which isn't as unusual as it should be. What then?

Allowing some flexibility in your training schedule allows you to keep the consistency going even if you have to miss a day or switch sessions around. It also means you can maximise the productivity of each session, going longer and/or harder on the days when you feel fantastic, and taking it easy on days when you don't.

If-then planning is a psychological strategy for self-regulation based on the idea of implementation intentions. The idea is similar to habit stacking, where we tag a behaviour we want to begin on to a habit we already have, but it can be more specific. If-then planning can be helpful for all sorts of things, taking out the decision-making process that can, in some cases, be unhelpful.

IF-THEN PLANNING: RUNNING-RELATED EXAMPLES

* **If** I don't feel like running the six miles on my schedule today, **then** I'll just run the first mile and see how I feel after that.
* **If** I really want to stop at mile 60 of my 100-mile race, **then** I will eat some food, do some positive self-talk and not quit at an aid station.
* **If** I notice something's rubbing during a long run or race, **then** I will stop and sort it out straight away before it becomes a problem.

If-then planning can even be as simple as:
* **If** I see a race volunteer while I'm running, **then** I'll smile and say thank you to them as I pass.

While planning and preparation are undoubtedly key to good performance in running, incorporating the ability to be adaptable is also essential. Being adaptable and having if-then scenarios in place allows you to accept situations for what they are, even if they're not what you expected, and do the next best thing rather than letting unexpected events derail your day.

Self-talk

When harnessed in the right way, self-talk is one of the most powerful psychological tools in a runner's toolkit. Although it's seen a huge rise in popularity among sport psychologists in recent years, self-talk isn't new. We all talk to ourselves all the time; it's a basic human behaviour that must serve an important purpose to have endured. It's a strange phenomenon when you think about it – the idea that we can have one part of us that is able to talk to another, which is in turn able to receive those messages and create action around them. Sometimes there's more than one voice – conflicting, or even arguing, voices. The words can be helpful and encouraging, or they could be fiercely critical – we might even recognise them.

Self-talk for runners
Scientists divide the different types of self-talk we experience into two main categories: organic self-talk and cued self-talk.

Organic self-talk
This happens naturally as we go about our daily lives and meet various successes and challenges along the way. It is a natural, cognitive process that we do all the time, but we can also harness it to help us in running and everyday life. This type of self-talk is an important self-awareness and self-regulation strategy for everything we do.

It can be further broken down into **spontaneous self-talk** – the kind that just happens when we feel a swell of emotion – and **intentional self-talk**, which is the goal-directed,

problem-solving kind. Spontaneous self-talk is a reflection of who we are and what we're feeling at that moment. It's a verbal expression of a mental state, often a release of emotion, which helps that state come into our awareness. Once we're aware of that state, we can use intentional self-talk in order to understand and manage it – to self-regulate.

Cued self-talk
This is a behavioural form of self-talk which revolves around specific, learned, motivational and instructional words and phrases that have been pre-prepared for use in a situation. These are goal-directed and can be applied to anything from a race to a work presentation.

Researchers have found that when we're using cued self-talk, addressing ourselves in the second person is more effective than in the first person, so, 'You can do this, you're feeling great', instead of, 'I can do this, I'm feeling great.'

As well as being able to improve our mood state, self-talk is helpful for simply keeping the brain occupied so it doesn't start generating negative thoughts. Ultrarunner Courtney Dauwalter uses mantras for this purpose, repeating short phrases such as, 'Be patient, be brave, believe', or, 'You're fine, this is fine, everything's fine.'

Knowing your 'why'

It's almost become a cliché in sport psychology, but knowing your 'why' – why what you're doing really matters on a personal level – is another incredibly strong source of motivation, both for daily training and during the tough miles of a race. It's why running a big race for a charity that's close to your heart, or taking a message or memento with you to remind you of the meaning of what you're doing, can make the difference between quitting and carrying on when things get tough.

The idea isn't a new one. In his 1942 book *The Myth of Sisyphus*, philosopher Albert Camus wrote:

'It happens that the stage sets collapse. Rising, streetcar, four hours in the office or the factory, meal, streetcar, four hours of work, meal, sleep, and Monday Tuesday Wednesday Thursday Friday and Saturday according to the same rhythm – this path is easily followed most of the time. But one day the "why" arises and everything begins in that weariness tinged with amazement.'

Knowing your 'why', Camus is saying, not only makes weariness bearable, but actually *amazing*.

If you're struggling with motivation, it's well worth spending some time considering the meaning of what you're doing. Daily training can be tough to get done, but if you're training for a race that is really important to you, then that's your 'why' every time you need to step through that door, run that final interval or keep going to the top of that hill. Even when it's raining! Having a powerful 'why' to draw energy and motivation from during the tough miles of races is also invaluable. Perhaps a reminder of a loved one you're running for, a cause you're passionate about, friends and family waiting expectantly for you at the finish, a PB or qualifying time, or even a past failure you're keen to put behind you. One of the positives of having a bad race, or failing to finish, is the fire it gives you to do it better next time around.

Whatever you choose, make sure it's powerful enough to pull you through just about anything. If it helps, write a reminder of your *why* on your arm, or take something with you as a reminder. But if you're still not feeling the fire for your training or racing – or struggling to find a 'why' at all – you've got to ask yourself why you're doing it in the first place.

Voluntary slow breathing

On pages 100–102 we explored the concept of heart rate variability (HRV) as a measure of our recovery and readiness for training. We also touched on another interesting use of HRV as a measure of self-regulation, including its effectiveness as a visual aid to help athletes with strategies to reduce pre-race anxiety. Drawing from the use of slow breathing techniques as a means of calming anxiety and focusing the mind for thousands of years in meditative and relaxation practices (see right for more on mindfulness), researchers have recently explored the underlying mechanisms of slow breathing, how it has its effects on our bodies and our minds, and how we can harness this to reduce anxiety and improve performance.

Voluntary slow breathing involves breathing cycles of around six breaths per minute – normal breathing happens between 12 and 20 times per minute – with a deeper than normal breath and a slightly longer exhalation than inhalation. Past studies have associated the practice with a range of beneficial outcomes, including optimising autonomic nervous system function, decreasing anxiety and agitation, increasing relaxation and resilience, and lowering blood pressure.

A recent systematic review and meta-analysis of the literature around slow breathing and HRV suggests that voluntary slow breathing leads to an increase in the parasympathetic nervous control of the heart – and therefore an increase in HRV – and is effective as an intervention before, during and after stressful situations such as sporting competitions, presentations and performances (Laborde *et al.*, 2022).

It should be noted here that useful measurements of HRV during running are not possible due to the rapid and frequent fluctuations in heart rate, and slow breathing may well be counter-productive to running performance so runners should use slow breathing techniques to reduce anxiety and improve focus before the start of a race, and to relax afterwards.

Mindfulness

Based in ancient traditions of meditation, mindfulness is a generally non-spiritual approach to mind–body awareness. Applied to running, mindfulness techniques can help us deal more effectively with many aspects of training and racing, from stress and guilt to race-day nerves. Mindfulness works with our brain's interoceptive networks, helping us to notice and manage our emotional responses to stimuli both from inside and outside our bodies. Modern brain imaging techniques are able to demonstrate consistent changes in brain activity resulting from mindfulness training and regular practice.

JEN'S STORY – MINDFULNESS

While training for my first 100-mile race, I worked with Danielle Frake, an accredited mindfulness practitioner, to address some of the unhelpful sensations and emotions that were plaguing both my training and racing, particularly the negative automatic thoughts that invariably crept in during the middle hours of an ultramarathon. I'd successfully used techniques from sport psychology in shorter races, but found these hard to implement during the darkest hours of very long ultras. Mindfulness helped me to manage negative thoughts and emotions, learning to accept my situation during races, including any challenges that arose along the way, and to be patient and not overly goal focused when I still had many miles to go.

While I was working with Danielle, I had one of those moments where the way you think about something fundamentally flips on its head. If you think about it, completing a run or a race isn't actually about completing the time or distance you signed up for. Instead, it's about the experience of each and every moment leading up to that time or distance. For me, battling with the enormity of running 100 miles, I realised that each step, each snack, each decision I made at each moment along the way was how I would end up running 100 miles. Remembering this – and taking out the stress of striving for that finish line – was a pivotal moment. In fact, I found mindfulness so effective, for both running and everyday life, that I decided to train as an accredited mindfulness teacher myself and now offer training for athletes of all levels.

Many of the key principles of mindfulness have been incorporated into sports performance, with one of the more popular protocols being the Mindful Sport Performance Enhancement programme (MSPE; Kaufman *et al.*, 2009). Over a series of four to six sessions, athletes learn mindful breathing exercises, body scanning and sport-specific mindfulness exercises. For runners, mindfulness practice can help with staying present in the moment; overcoming distractions; accepting and even embracing sensations of pain, discomfort and fatigue; and letting negative thoughts pass without engaging with them.

Danielle's top tips for bringing mindfulness to your running, as well as to your everyday life

Understanding mindfulness

Mindfulness is about being aware of the present moment. This seems like an easy concept; however, our minds have a tendency to be drawn into both the past and future resulting in life happening without us really being fully involved.

Mindfulness is life changing but it is not magic. It does not prevent you from being a human being and experiencing all the emotions that humans feel. It's not about painting over difficult feelings with positive ones. It's about noticing and accepting how you feel so you can fully engage in being alive.

Starting with the breath

The breath provides the perfect anchor for your attention, and this doesn't just apply to meditation, you can do this at any time, even while you're running. Try noticing:
* the rise and fall of your abdomen;
* the cool air as it enters through your nostrils and how it is warmer on the exhale;
* the pace of your breath; or
* if you breathe deep into your tummy or up in your chest.

The importance of your senses

Tapping into your senses provides a way to connect to the present moment. If you're finding it hard to be in the moment, try noticing:
* five things you can see;
* four things you can hear;
* three things you can feel;
* two things you can smell; and
* one thing you can taste.

Connecting to your mind and body
Build mindful awareness by asking yourself, 'How do I feel in this moment?' Can you be okay with how you are feeling knowing that things are always unfolding and changing? Can you identify any physical sensations in your body?

Thoughts are not facts
The understanding that thoughts are not facts gives you a superpower. Even taking note of the fact that you are thinking can bring you back to the present moment and help place a little distance between you and your thoughts. Recognising this gives you a choice on how you interpret the world and how you react and respond.

2

Races, challenges and adventures

10
Racing

Racing is exciting. It's an event; a celebration of running; a chance to put all those training hours and miles to the test. Depending on how much you enjoy the thrill of a race, and on your personal circumstances, you might race every weekend, have one or two big goal races throughout the year, or be building up to your first race at a certain distance.

Racing enables us to dig deeper than we can in training, discovering exactly what we're capable of. It can be extremely rewarding, but it also brings with it pressure, expectation and the opportunity for both success and failure. At the end of the day, unless we're professional athletes, we only really race for fun. Racing isn't real life, so remember to keep your results in perspective and not let them dictate either your love for running or your sense of self-worth.

Not every runner feels the need to race, but, for those that do, races should be points of difference within a consistent, long-term running practice. Races can be a useful indicator of your fitness, and beating your previous PB time – or your running rival – can be a powerful motivator. But if you have a race that doesn't go as well as you'd hoped, bear in mind that this is one day out of many running days and its importance on a grander scale is negligible. You'll get over disappointments, and they often work well to inject a dose of extra motivation and drive into your training. Every race is a learning experience and often those that don't go to plan offer by far the biggest lessons.

When you're aiming for a specific time, whether that's to beat a PB, qualify for another race or dip under one of the arbitrary but no less important hour or half-hour targets, it's easy to become frustrated if you find yourself repeatedly just missing it.

Jen says:

'A few years ago, coming back to fitness after my daughter was born, I set myself the goal of breaking 90 minutes for the half marathon. I ran just a few seconds over on multiple occasions but just couldn't seem to find that tiny bit of extra speed over the course. I began to think I'd never manage it. Then one weekend I clocked 90:10 at a local half marathon held on the hilly lanes on the edge of Dartmoor. I knew this meant beyond any doubt that if I ran on a flat course, I could finally achieve my dream. The following weekend, fuelled by the frustration of so many near misses and the confidence of this recent performance, I ran a flatter half, finishing in 88:36 and finally smashing my goal. This experience really taught me the value of patience, alongside self-belief, when working towards an important personal goal.'

Regular racing, even if it's a weekly or fortnightly parkrun, gives us a useful indicator of our progression over time, and the confidence that we could go just that bit harder next time. Unless you're good at tracking variables such as resting heart rate over long periods of time, or undertake regular self-timed time trials, it's hard – without access to laboratory testing – to keep track of the impact your training is having on your fitness and speed. While minor variations in performance should be expected, incorporating regular races or timed sessions will give you a good indication of how effective your training is, and your longer-term improvements.

Choosing a race

We believe racing should be considered a privilege, not a right. Races are costly – both for those who put them on, those who race them, and in terms of their impact on communities, places and the wider environment. While things are slowly changing, thanks to campaigning and greater awareness, racing still involves many individuals driving long distances to run around a fragile natural landscape each weekend. There's often a heavy reliance on highly packaged sports nutrition and hydration products, vast amounts of logistics, and potential waste in terms of medals, T-shirts, goody bags and so on. None of this would be a particular problem if racing was done occasionally, but more and more runners are racing more and more frequently, and so the impact and the waste pile up. Perhaps instead of complaining at race organisers for providing T-shirts we should be looking at the culture around racing. A T-shirt that proudly displays the one big race we worked hard all year to complete is a wonderful thing, and something we'll probably wear regularly and with pride. A stack of unworn race T-shirts isn't necessarily a problem with the race organisers who offer them, but perhaps more with a culture that encourages racing too often.

With this in mind, we'd always recommend choosing your races carefully. Find those that really appeal, that truly challenge and excite you. Try to avoid getting drawn into the trap of ticking off lists like the world marathon majors, the world trail majors or as many 50-mile races you can run in a year. These approaches encourage unnecessary travel, as well as huge individual and wider costs. Instead, choose a few events because they're special. If you're keen to take on more regular challenges, there are plenty you can do in your own time, and even from your door (see chapter 15).

When you're choosing races, grouping them into an order of importance can be helpful, both in structuring your training and also in ensuring recovery from one race doesn't negatively impact the next one.

'A' races are your main goals. Depending on how far you're racing, these could make up between one and four races each year. If you're targeting a new 5K PB, you might get away with racing hard every couple of months; if you're running 100-milers, you probably only want to do one or, at a push, two each year.

'B' races are those that it would be nice to do if everything's going to plan but these aren't your main focus. Many runners plan in 'B' races as training events – a good time to get in a long, supported run when training for a marathon or ultra, when you can also test out your kit along with nutrition and hydration strategies. A half marathon or 20-miler a few weeks out from an 'A' race marathon can work really well in this respect, and is a great test of how your training is going too. Don't read too much into these races, though – remember you probably won't taper for them so won't be as rested, recovered and race-ready as you will be for your 'A' race.

'C' races are those races that you do purely for the enjoyment and/or challenge of racing. They don't serve any direct purpose in terms of preparation for your 'A' races. Often they're last-minute entries, making up team numbers or just trying something new.

Be aware that a race is a race, and it's hard to moderate your effort, even when you know a race isn't your main focus. 'B' and 'C' races can work well sometimes, but if you're not careful they can negatively impact your preparation for, or even race-day performance at, your 'A' race.

> **Common mistakes in race timing to avoid:**
> * Running a 'B' or 'C' race too close to an 'A' race and therefore not allowing yourself sufficient recovery time between them.
> * Having a poor performance at a 'B' race and knocking your confidence for your 'A' race.
> * Running too many 'B' and 'C' races, so you're never able to really focus on having your absolute best performance at an 'A' race.

Race-specific training

Once you've chosen your goal race(s), it's time to plan your training around them. This is where periodising your training (see chapter 17) is helpful, allowing you to build up gradually from your current level of race-specific fitness and preparedness to one that's highly specific to your goal race.

Planning out your year ahead – factoring in both racing goals and other life events – can be really helpful, especially if you're someone who juggles running with working and/or caring responsibilities. As an example, autumn marathons can work really well for many runners in the northern hemisphere, as the summer months offer longer hours of light and drier weather for training. But for parents, trying to fit in the mileage training weeks during the school summer holidays can be very difficult, in which case a spring or early summer marathon might be a better choice.

Once you have your 'A' races scheduled in, work your training around these. You'll need up to a two-week taper before each race, and some recovery time afterwards – depending on the distance of the race this could be anything from a couple of days for a 5K to a month or more for an ultra.

Plan in your training building up to the race, making sure the training that's most specific to the race is closest to race day, and the training that's least specific to the race is furthest away from race day. If you're planning a flat, 10K road race, your longer, slower conditioning runs should be furthest out from your race, whereas your flatter, faster-paced interval and tempo runs should be closest to it. In the same way, if you're training for a mountainous ultra, your fast interval sessions should be furthest out from race day and your steepest power-hiking sessions should be closest to it.

Tapering

Once all the hard work is done in the build-up to a race, a well-planned taper allows for maximum adaptation and recovery, meaning you're in the best possible shape you can be once you're standing on the starting line.

Tapering involves a gradual reduction and mani-pulation of training in order to recover as much as possible from training-related fatigue, without losing the specific adaptations that have resulted from that training. It is generally accepted that the optimal way of doing this is to reduce the volume of training, while maintaining its intensity. A meta-analysis of the effects of tapering on performance suggests that optimal race-day performance follows a taper that reduces training volume by 40–60 per cent of normal training volume (Bosquet *et al.*, 2007). The same study found that reducing training intensity too much negatively affects race performance.

In the same way as every athlete's response to training is individual, every athlete's response to tapering will be individual too.

> A well supported approach is to taper over the two-week period before race day, reducing training volume by 40 per cent in the first week and by 60 per cent in the second week.

Maintain the intensity of your harder runs, but reduce the number of reps in an interval session, or the duration of a tempo run. Try to keep the number of runs you do each week near to your normal frequency. Following this approach should mean you arrive on the start line feeling fresh and ready to go, having maximised adaptations to the months of training that have gone before, without detrimentally affecting things like muscle recruitment and running economy. Simply taking more rest days may mean you get to race day feeling sluggish – having been doing it for over 20 years, we're always amazed at the way a couple of days off can make us feel like we've forgotten how to run.

Race day plans

A lot of race-related stress and anxiety isn't even about the race itself, but about the logistics – from getting there with enough time to register and warm up to what to eat, drink and wear.

The night before

Depending on how far from home your race is, it's worth considering whether the pros of staying near the start (more time to sleep on race morning; quick and easy journey to the start; making the race into a mini-break) definitely outweigh the cons (sleeping in a strange bed; lack of control over variables such as heat, light and noise; eating unfamiliar food). Often this decision will be made for you – when the race start is obviously close enough to commute from home or obviously too far to do so – but it's well worth accepting a bit of extra travelling on race morning if it means you'll arrive feeling rested and confident that your pre-race meals and routines have gone to plan. As long as you won't lose sleep stressing about catching trains or getting stuck in traffic, that is.

'In 2021, Sim and I camped for the two nights before I was due to run a 100-kilometre race. I'd booked the campsite after spotting it was five minutes from the start and, with an 8 a.m. start time, thought this would make for an unusually relaxed race morning. The reality turned out to be somewhat different.

'After two sleepless nights thanks to being pitched on a slope added to an invasion of springtails – tiny, hopping bugs that are completely harmless but nonetheless very unpleasant in a tent – by race morning I was so tired I couldn't stomach breakfast, deciding I'd just try to eat regularly right from the start. I managed to absorb a copious amount of coffee though, which seemed to do the trick. In the end the race went pretty well and also taught me two valuable lessons. Firstly, that staying near the start wasn't necessarily a better choice than it would have been to make the 1-hour-and-40-minute drive from home on race morning. And secondly, that even when pre-race prep doesn't go to plan, it doesn't necessarily mean the race won't go well. After months of preparation, the final week of tapering and pre-race routines are important, and in an ideal world they'll go to plan. But, if they don't, it doesn't usually make the difference between race day triumph and disaster.'

The night before the race, lay all your kit out, pin your number on (check the race instructions so you know where your number should be attached) and run through everything you'll need to do and take with you in the morning. Writing a list to tick off as you go can be really helpful; use the list as somewhere to add those last-minute thoughts that slip out of your head seconds after they appear. Try to make your bedtime routine as normal as possible and try not to worry about the race – the best thing you can do at this point as far as your performance is concerned is have a good night's sleep.

Race day

Ideally, race morning should be as relaxed as possible, eating breakfast in plenty of time to allow it to be fully digested and ready to fuel your efforts by the time you reach the start line (two to three hours is usually about right). Make sure you're well hydrated but not overly so – you don't want to be sloshing uncomfortably or needing to pee within minutes of starting your race. If you struggle with nerves on race day, try the voluntary slow breathing technique (see page 134).

For races longer than 10K it's worth considering applying a lubricant such as Squirrel's Nut Butter, petroleum jelly or shea butter to any chafe-prone areas. These may include your feet, underarms, nipples for men, under your running bra for women and any other suspects – you'll *definitely* get to know your own personal selection before long.

Arrive at the start with plenty of time to register, warm-up and familiarise yourself with the start. If it's wet, it's a good idea to take a different pair of shoes and socks with you for wandering around at the start, so you can begin the race with dry feet. Warm up, but don't waste energy bouncing around at the start line. Use this time to focus on the race ahead, remember what a privilege it is to be on the start line and get your watch ready for the off. If the nerves are getting the better of you: *breathe*.

Pacing strategies

Depending on the distance you're racing, you might be aiming to run as fast as you can (or want to) for anything from 15 minutes to 24 hours or more.

> However far you're running, good pacing is key to good racing.

Surrounded by all the excitement and pre-race nerves of the start line, it's all too easy to set off too fast, fatigue your legs early on, forget to eat and drink in longer races, and then heavily pay the price in the second half.

This is when having a pre-planned race strategy can be invaluable. You can go old-school and wear a pace band around your wrist, set your watch to beep if you're running too fast, or simply focus on keeping your breathing easy over the opening stretch. Heart rate isn't a good measure at this point as it will be elevated due to race nerves, and you may therefore end up running too slowly to compensate.

Pacing strategies

These fall broadly into four camps, each with their own pros and cons.

Go out hard and try to hang on

This approach is a risk-it-all one that can work well in shorter races but, as the distances get longer, has more and more chance of letting you down. On the upside, setting out at an optimistically swift pace can set you free from your self-imposed limitations. If you're having an amazing day, feeling great, your training's gone perfectly, and the conditions are ideal, then this approach might be worth trying. Beyond 10K, or perhaps a half marathon if you're lucky, it's likely you'll need to slow down considerably in the second half. At which point, everyone else who paced more sensibly will come flying past ...

Even pacing

This strategy is the most reliable, particularly for those aiming for a new PB, or to finish a new distance. The pace you set out at should match the pace you've trained to run, with a finishing time that's challenging but achievable. Flexibility within your plan is still important though. If you've gone for an even pacing approach, but you're struggling to hit your set pace early on, it's well worth slowing down a little to avoid disaster later on in the race rather than grimly trying to keep hitting your splits when it's feeling unsustainable.

Negative split

You'll often see world records broken by the elites using this approach. A negative split involves speeding up in the latter half of the race, so that the second half is run slightly quicker than the first. The downsides of this approach can be taking it too conservatively in the first half, and then not achieving your potential overall, or going too hard in the first half and then not having enough left to increase your pace over the final miles.

Tactical racing

If you're racing for a position, rather than for a time, you'll need to be highly flexible in your approach. Sometimes the main pack will start out above goal pace, aiming to drop those with a fast finish well before the end of the race. At other times they'll keep it steady until the final mile or so, benefiting those with a turn of speed later on. If you're training for a race where you'll be running with a pack, it's important to train with these differences in mind. Add in harder efforts during the later stages of a long run, practise 'surging' during a run, so you're ready to cover any breakaways during the race, and, if you can, research your fellow competitors before race day, so you have an idea how things might pan out.

11

Ultramarathons, FKTs and multi-day adventures

'Most people never run far enough on their first wind to find out they've got a second.'
– WILLIAM JAMES, philosopher and psychologist

Ultramarathons

The term *ultramarathon* is used to describe any race longer than a marathon but, from a physical, psychological and logistical point of view, a 50K ultra isn't really that different to a marathon (42 kilometres). However, longer ultras – those when you'll be on your feet non-stop for many hours – are not simply long marathons, and it's therefore not possible to extrapolate findings from marathon running and apply them to the longer distances.

Ultras provide a whole new problem for researchers and those aiming to translate scientific findings into real-world advice that coaches and athletes can use to aid training and performance. The question of whether women can outperform men in ultras has attracted the attention of researchers over the last few years – we discuss this in detail on pages 60–61.

JEN'S STORY – ULTRAMARATHONS

I remember feeling pretty confident as I lined up at the start of my first ultra – the 32-mile Dartmoor Discovery, which takes in (what felt like) all the hills that Dartmoor has to offer. I'd run a few marathons – how different could it be? I set off at a little under my marathon pace, finding myself ascending the first hill with a tiny, grey-haired lady with a Cornish running vest and a big smile. As we slowed to a near-walk I wondered whether I was losing time too early on. Then runners started passing us, striding up the hill, quickly leaving us behind.

'Let them go,' my Cornish companion advised. 'It's a long day – they'll come back to us later on.'

It was sound advice. Later on, as I started going backwards, I wished I had heeded it. On the long, final hill up to the finish at Princetown, I passed the *1 mile to go* marker. That morning, when I'd passed it in the car, I'd imagined how wonderful it would feel to reach that point – only one single mile to go! But now, many miles and many hills later, it felt impossible that I could force my legs to move me another whole mile up the road. In the end that last mile felt like the longest of the entire race.

My second ultramarathon was the Boddington 50K, a looped course around the lanes of rural Gloucestershire. This was some time ago – the strong women's field was headed up by ultrarunning legend Lizzy Hawker. Yet again my pacing failed me, as I underestimated the distance, even though it was a mere five miles further than a marathon, and I started out much too fast. But everyone knows the marathon doesn't even really begin until mile 20, so perhaps it shouldn't have

11 ULTRAMARATHONS, FKTs AND MULTI-DAY ADVENTURES **149**

been such a surprise that adding on extra miles – even only a few – feels just so hard. Ten loops (out of fourteen) in, and I was barely walking, let alone running. Lizzy overtook me for the second time, and I watched her power past feeling a mixture of admiration, despondency and frustration. Why was I finding it so hard? How did she make it look so easy?

Ultramarathon number three went better. Taking on 45 miles of towpath on the outskirts of London, it was by far the furthest I'd run, and I was determined not to ruin it by setting out too fast. I let the lead runners go, settling into a comfortable, sustainable pace right from the start. A few miles on I spotted those same runners rejoining the route just ahead of me – they had all taken a wrong turn and done an annoying extra out-and-back as a result. It was an added bonus to my pacing strategy that seeing them meant I didn't do the same. I trundled on as the hours passed, ticking off runners who were slowing down as the race progressed. At 30 miles I still felt completely – almost weirdly – fresh. The final 10 miles were really tough, but manageably so, and I finished first woman and fourth overall.

Thinking about it on the train home I was, of course, pleased with the win. But most of all I was pleased with my strategy. I had, at long last, stuck to my pre-race plan and hadn't got carried away with the excitement of it all at the start. I had conserved energy as much as possible, set out at a pace I knew I could carry on running at for a long time, and surprised myself (and, I think, a few other people) with the result.

Top tips for ultramarathons

Start out as you mean to continue – pacing is key in ultras and starting out too fast is a common mistake that will see you grinding to a halt in the second half. Especially if you're fit and well-tapered when you line up, the first few miles can feel frustratingly slow. But remember all that pent-up energy must be rationed so it lasts the full distance. No one gets to the end of an ultra with energy to spare. If you know you struggle to keep it slow enough at the start, this can be a useful time to run to a set pace. Heart rate won't be a reliable guide, as you'll be fired up and buzzing with adrenaline at the start of a race and might end up taking it too easy if you try to run at a low heart rate (see page 83). Rate of perceived exertion (RPE – see page 82) might also be a poor guide at this time, as the excitement of the start line and the infectious energy of the surrounding runners can make it hard to judge your level of exertion. Knowing the pace you're aiming for, though, and trying to stick to this using your watch, is a reliable way to keep the brakes on early on – you'll be so glad you did when you're overtaking people in the second half.

Chunking – this well-known technique in sport psychology involves dividing the full distance up into manageable sections and focusing on running these. In longer ultras, especially if they're further than you've run before, the sheer size of the numbers can be overwhelming. Thinking about a race in terms of its aid stations can be really helpful – instead of thinking about running 100 kilometres all in one go, think about ticking off the number of aid stations and simply getting from one to the next.

Fuel little and often – start taking on food early and keep fuelling regularly throughout your race. Fuelling early on, when your stomach is most able to deal with processing food, means you're more likely to be able to carry on fuelling and it'll be less of a problem if you stop being able to eat much later on in the race. A good strategy is to set yourself a goal of eating something small every 20 or 30 minutes, right from the start, and stick to it. Variety can be helpful to avoid taste fatigue, so have both sweet and savoury options available and top these up at aid stations.

Have a plan for aid stations – when you stop at an aid station during an ultra, it can feel like a party. Suddenly, after hours on your own, there are lots of people, a buzzy atmosphere, music, food and oh so many tempting places to sit down. Unless your race is *really* long and you'll need to sleep or have some hot food, plan not to sit down at an aid station unless you absolutely have to. While it's important not to take longer than necessary at aid stations, rushing through them in a panic to get back out on the trail can mean you forget or neglect important things like topping up with enough food or water, or omitting to put a blister plaster on a sore foot. A good plan could be:
* refill bottles – one with water and one with electrolyte drink
* bin empty packets
* eat something that looks appealing and choose a couple of other things for the road
* visit the toilet
* say thanks to the volunteers
* get back out there!

Don't be afraid to walk – even top ultrarunners regularly throw in hiking, especially when the ground gets steep and technical. Power hiking up hills gives your muscles a break from the constant running action and is more efficient than running on steeper gradients (see page 4). Walking breaks are also useful if you're struggling to eat, as the slower pace reduces the joggling action on your stomach and allows more

blood to flow away from the working muscles and to the stomach for digestion. If you're crossing technical terrain and you're worried about tripping, walking can end up being far quicker than taking a tumble and dealing with the consequences.

Especially if you're training for a hillier ultra, get plenty of hiking into your training plan. Many runners only run while training for an ultra and then struggle with the amount of walking on race day. Walking places different stresses on the body, and a fast walk is a highly efficient way to cover rough or steep terrain safely.

Fix problems quickly – it's easy to think problems will go away if you ignore them, but, nine times out of ten, they'll just get worse. If your shoelace is too loose or too tight, stop as soon as you can and fix it. If something's chafing, apply some anti-chafe balm, tape or a plaster at the first opportunity. If you're getting cold, stop and get some extra clothing out of your pack. It only takes a couple of minutes to deal with most things straight away, but could cost you far more time – or even your race – if you ignore them and carry on regardless.

Never try anything new on race day – whether it's kit, nutrition or even a strategy, trying new things out on race day is a high-risk approach. It's essential that you train with your kit, including the pack, shoes, clothing, food and drink you'll be using on race day. While you don't need to do all your training with a heavy pack, getting a few runs done in full kit will mean your body becomes accustomed to running with the extra load, you'll notice any potential problems in advance, and overall you'll feel more prepared and therefore more confident on race day. Knowing every pocket on your pack and exactly where everything is will really help your race run smoothly.

Ride the roller coaster – ultras are well known for being physical and emotional roller coasters. At times you'll be sure you cannot take another step, only to push through and feel great half an hour later. Knowing in advance that this is a normal part of ultrarunning is important, so you don't read too much into it on race day. It's also useful to have some strategies in place beforehand to help you deal with the lows when (not if!) they arrive. These could include:

*   **Eating something** – remember the saying 'low mood eat food' and, as soon as you notice your mood deteriorating, eat something. It's often a better indicator of the need for fuel than hunger during a race, so learn to respond quickly with snacks rather than wallowing in self-pity.
*   **Think about why you're there** – remember it's your decision to be there, it's something you wanted to do and it's important to you. Think about the hours you've spent training, the people who have supported you, the time and money you've put in. Imagine yourself a week from now, when the pain has stopped – would you rather look back on a race where you stuck with it and finished, or one where you gave up and dropped out? As long as you keep going, giving up is always an option available to you. Once you give up, however, you can't change your mind.

Ultramarathon crewing and pacing

When you're preparing for an ultramarathon, one of the decisions you'll need to make is whether you want to recruit some helpers to support your run. The two main types of support to consider are:

*   **Crew**, who'll meet you out on the course to provide you with everything from food and water replenishment to spare clothing, massage and motivational talk.
*   **Pacers**, who'll meet you at a prearranged point on the course and run some – or all – of the remaining distance with you.

Some races allow pacers and crew, while others forbid any outside assistance during the race, so make sure you read the rules and regulations carefully. Even in races that do allow crew and pacers, many runners choose to run solo, preferring the challenge of completing the course purely under their own steam.

Pros of crew and pacers

*   Having a crew means you'll probably need to carry less, and you can make choices about nutrition, hydration and kit as you go, rather than having to stick with your pre-race choices. While your crew is refilling your bottles and reapplying lube to your feet, you can concentrate on relaxing, eating and drinking, ready to get going again. Your crew can also help get you out of an aid station if you're flagging, reminding you of all the reasons you really don't want to quit.
*   Pacers can help by doing any required navigation, offering motivational chat or empathetic silence, reminding you to eat and drink, or keeping you company on parts of the route that you're worried about, for example running in the dark, or running through city or mountain environments.

Cons of crew and pacers

* Crews can provide an easy way out, turning up with a warm, comfy car at an aid station that can be all too tempting when you're fatigued, nauseous and sleep deprived. Unless your crew is thoroughly briefed and on-the-ball, they can make things more complicated, offering you too many choices, forgetting items of kit, or even – often due to no fault of their own – not managing to get to an aid station in time to meet you.
* Poorly prepared pacers can easily break your race; in particular, if they get you lost or they're not happy with the pace, distance, terrain or conditions you're running in. Poorly judged conversation topics or observations can change your whole mindset deep into a race when you're highly suggestible. Pacers can also separate you from the camaraderie of the race, stopping you from running with other racers and sharing in the specialness of being a part of the event.

Remember – if you're successful at completing your ultra, you share the glory with your pacers and crew, but if you don't complete it, you share that with them, too. The fallout from a DNF can be a strain on a relationship, so choose your crew and pacers with care.

Top tips for if you're pacing or crewing for someone else

* **Research the course** – crews and pacers should have detailed knowledge of the course and any sections they're pacing, or be expert navigators.
* **Be prepared for the conditions** – runners spend months researching the right kit for their race, so don't scupper their chances by turning up to pace them in the wrong shoes, or without your running poles, or by not wearing enough kit.
* **Choose your words carefully** – regardless of what your runner looks like, or how bad you think the weather conditions are, unless you're genuinely concerned for their safety it's not worth commenting. Stick to cheerful, positive, proactive words and sentences, and ask simple questions with just a couple of options for answers – 'Would you like the lemon or the chocolate gel?' tends to work better than, 'What flavour gel would you like?'
* **Plan well, but be prepared to be flexible** – thorough pre-planning is essential for good crewing and pacing, with timings and food and kit preferences all arranged well in advance. However, it's the nature of ultrarunning that the unexpected happens, so if none of the food you've got is working, send someone off to get something else to try, be handy with lube and tape to fix chafing and foot issues, and be willing to try new things with the aim of keeping your runner going.

Food during ultramarathons

Often, over the course of a long run or ultramarathon, sports nutrition products just aren't appealing enough to encourage a tired, depleted and often nauseous runner to keep eating. And without food, it's only a matter of time before their race is over. Due to the lower intensity most people run longer races at, real food can be a great alternative, offering palatable, appealing and stomach-settling nutrition without the refined sugars, plastic packaging and dodgy additives.

Here are some of ours and our athletes' tried-and-tested favourite 'real food' options for ultras:
* Sandwiches – cheese, jam and peanut butter all work well.
* Hot cross buns – you can even make cheese sandwiches using hot cross buns, which sounds weird but can be just the thing midway through a long run.
* Savoury crackers.
* Sweet biscuits – ginger snaps, digestives or fig rolls.
* Flapjacks.
* Crystalised ginger – especially good if you're feeling nauseous.
* Sweets such as jelly babies/Haribo/jelly tots/Turkish delight.
* Crisps and other salty snacks.
* Rice balls/sushi.
* Cake – dense cakes work best as they're easy to eat on the go. Try pre-packaged madeleines, ginger cake, banana bread or even fruit cake, which rolls up into balls well.
* Energy balls made from dried fruit and nuts.
* Scones (sweet or savoury).
* Savoury snacks such as mini samosas, pasties and scotch eggs.
* Fruit – apples, watermelon, oranges.

Multi-day races and FKTs

From weekend mountain marathons to races of a week or more, multi-day races are a big adventure in their own right. As a consequence, they usually require more kit, more planning and more complex logistics. Depending on the specifics of your chosen event, multi-day races may require you to be entirely self-sufficient (where you'll be carrying everything you need including a tent and cooking equipment), entirely supported or somewhere in between.

While organised multi-day races offer a great way to explore somewhere new, test out your limits and meet a group of likeminded friends, self-devised challenges have a charm of their own. You can do them where and when you want, there's no entry fee and they're infinitely customisable. You could take on an existing trail or round and pit yourself against its current fastest known time (FKT), set out to put your mark on an obscure trail that, as yet, has no recorded FKT, or simply head through the door and keep going.

Kirsty Reade, a Lake-District-based ultrarunner, has completed many of the biggest UK multi-day ultras, including Cape Wrath, the Northern Traverse and the Dragon's Back. Here are her top tips for multi-day ultras:

* **No faffing** – a minute faffing is a minute better spent eating, or resting.
* **Leave early** – a lot of people get caught out when they leave late because they're tired, then they're up against the cut-offs all day. It's a vicious cycle – you get back late, you get less rest, you get up late and you make it harder for yourself.
* **Look after your feet** – deal with problems before they get too bad.
* **Get confident with a map and recce the route if you can** – it makes a huge difference.
* **Be a good tentmate** – leaving kit everywhere and making noise late at night or early in the morning won't foster good relationships with your tentmates. Their support might make or break the experience for you.
* **Spend time on similar terrain** – I met some people at Dragon's Back who hadn't really spent any time in the hills, but they thought that because they were really strong runners they'd be fine. There's no substitute for spending long days on really tough terrain – if your ankles and legs aren't conditioned to it, they won't hold up.
* **Take enough food** – I ran out of food at Cape Wrath; it's so hard to judge what you need for eight days of hill food and to get stuff that you'll feel like eating and won't go off. I took a lot more food to Dragon's Back!

12

Different environmental conditions

The best running adventures take us out of our comfort zones and into places and situations with which we're unfamiliar. Some visit places that are fairly challenging to humans – even hostile at times. This could be because of high altitude, extremes of temperature or long periods of running in the dark. Some runners are lucky enough to live in places with easy access to the more extreme training environments. But even for those of us who don't, there are many things we can do in training that will help our bodies become adapted to the conditions we'll experience during our adventures. Being prepared means they're more likely to be both successful and enjoyable.

Running in the dark

In many countries, over the winter months, there's often no alternative but to run in the dark. Whether you're heading out for a few early miles before work or have an evening run planned, there's always going to be a few weeks of the year when darkness is unavoidable. But, once you're happy running in the dark, it's a bit of a secret weapon, meaning running time isn't reduced just because the clocks have changed. It can also be a lot of fun – we've often spotted owls, foxes, bats and badgers on evening and night runs.

Scientists have unearthed some interesting findings on the ways in which our bodies and brains react and adapt to walking and running in the dark. A recent study (Eiken *et al.*, 2022) found that Swedish military recruits burned more energy (calculated by measuring oxygen usage) when walking with a blindfold on, compared with when they could see. The effect was almost as great as when they walked wearing a 25-kilogram pack. Under the blindfold condition, recruits changed their walking gait, shortening their step length, widening their base of gait (the width between their feet) and increasing their step height. As the tests were conducted on a treadmill, these modifications are automatic, rather than to avoid known hazards.

Another study looked at the effect of changing optic flow on perceived speed and rate of exertion (Parry and Micklewright, 2014). When objects are closer, they appear to move past faster, causing us to perceive that we are travelling at a greater speed that requires more effort. This effect is heightened at night, when objects suddenly appear out of the darkness.

While regular running in the dark will almost certainly reduce these adaptations, and therefore some of the extra energy expenditure required, they're worth bearing in mind if you're comparing a session you've done in the dark compared with the same session in the light. If it's slower and/or feels harder, there's a good scientific reason behind that. It's also a good reason to train in the dark if you'll be racing in the dark. Allowing your body and brain to adapt to low light conditions may well save you some energy on race day as well as ensure you go into the race confident in your ability to run at night.

Should I practise running overnight?

Many longer ultramarathons involve running through a whole night – and sometimes more than one night – often without sleep. Whether or not to run through the night in training is very much an individual decision, and the jury is out on whether sleep deprivation 'training' has any beneficial effects in helping people deal with future sleep deprivation. Many runners are afraid of running in the dark, and in this case the more you can do the better. But running through a full night, experiencing the disorientation of sleep deprivation and sometimes even hallucinations, is a unique experience. If you've never done it, it can be a very daunting prospect, in which case it may be beneficial to try it in training. But the downside is that sleep deprivation is highly detrimental to your ability to train and recover well – as well as function well in general. If you're someone who struggles to get enough sleep anyway, for example shift workers or parents of young children, for whom sleep is often at a premium, sleep deprivation training is unlikely to be of benefit. If, on the other hand, you find it easy to catch up on lost sleep and the overnight section of a race is really bothering you, the extra confidence you'll get from running through all of, or at least part of, a night may be well worth it.

Even if you choose not to use it all the time, a good headtorch is an essential bit of kit for running in the dark. As well as illuminating your route, including any potholes, low-hanging branches and other unseen hazards, a light indicates to other people that you're there. Whether that's increasing your visibility to drivers when you're running on roads and pavements, or as an emergency beacon if you find yourself injured or lost in some remote place, if you're running after dark, it's always worth wearing – or at least packing – a fully charged headtorch just in case.

The key points to consider when choosing a headtorch are that it fits comfortably on your head with minimal bounce while running, and that it provides the level and duration of illumination you require. Those that allow the beam strength to be adjusted quickly and easily are really handy for running on footpaths and pavements when you might meet other people who don't want to be blinded by your dazzlingly bright headtorch. While brighter is almost always better on rough terrain, when the ability to see the way ahead clearly makes a massive difference to your speed and comfort on the run, walkers, cyclists and other runners don't always take kindly to having 1,000 lumens straight in their faces.

Running in heat and cold

Earlier, we introduced the principle of homeostasis (see pages 8–9) – that our bodies work best within a relatively narrow set of internal conditions and, if we do something that causes a deviation from these optimal conditions, our bodies' regulatory systems will detect this change and act to return the system to normal, optimal functioning.

Exercise, and especially intensive exercise, is a disruptor of homeostasis in its own right. During a hard run, our bodies are working hard behind the scenes, keeping everything from sodium and glucose levels to core temperature within safe limits. It's easy to imagine, then, how much more stress we put our bodies under when we exercise in extreme environments.

Running in hot conditions

Exercise in the heat is necessary for most people who want to run all year round. Whether you're heading off to run a desert marathon, or simply want to keep running at your best over the summer months, knowing the multitude of effects heat has on the exercising body and how best to manage them are key. Even for those of us living in relatively cool places like the UK, summer heatwaves are becoming more frequent and more intense due to climate change.

The body's normal core temperature is around 36.6 °C. The many biochemical reactions in our bodies occur most effectively at around this temperature, so our homeostatic mechanisms work to keep our core temperature around this level. Venture too far either side and not only do conditions become suboptimal for performance, but health and eventually survival are threatened.

Body temperature varies between people and for individuals over the course of a day, peaking in the evening and dropping to its lowest point in the early hours of the morning. In healthy individuals, not including while exercising, this natural variation is around 0.5 °C. In menstruating females, the menstrual cycle affects core temperature, which increases by around 0.4 °C during the luteal phase compared with the follicular phase of the cycle (see pages 62–63 for more on training through the menstrual cycle).

When the surrounding temperature rises, both our behavioural and homeostatic mechanisms kick in to keep our core temperature within safe levels to avoid the potentially harmful, and even fatal, effects of hyperthermia (overheating). Behavioural changes include seeking shade, reducing activity, drinking cool drinks, wearing loose-fitting clothing and applying water, ice or cold air to facilitate skin cooling. During exercise we may also feel the need to reduce our intensity in response to increases in core temperature.

Our internal mechanisms are guided by the hypothalamus, a pea-sized area of the brain that acts as the key control centre for the body's temperature regulation. Signals from temperature receptors in the skin, bloodstream and organs combine with those from the hypothalamus. During exercise in hot environments, the cerebral temperature rises alongside core temperature – scientists believe that cerebral temperature may be a key factor in regulating activity and performance.

During extremes of hot or cold, our internal thermostat and the autonomic nervous and neurohormonal systems work together to maintain a safe core temperature. When core temperature rises, the blood vessels to our skin dilate, increasing blood flow to the skin in order to facilitate convective heat loss. The amount of blood flow diverted to the skin can vary from none at low core temperatures, to eight litres per minute at high core temperatures – around 60 per cent of cardiac output. Cooled blood from the skin is transferred back to the core, minimising temperature rises.

An interesting paradox occurs as a result of the combined effects of hot conditions and exercise. During exercise, more circulating blood is also diverted to the muscles which, in normal conditions, reduces the amount of blood flow to the skin. In the heat, however, both skin and muscles compete for blood flow. This results in higher oxygen and energy usage, increased lactate production – effectively a lowering of both VO_2 max and the lactate threshold – and a higher heart rate and perceived rate of exertion at a given pace than in cooler weather. Dehydration due to an increased sweat and breathing rate when exercising in the heat also plays its part in increasing stress on the body, resulting in a reduced blood volume (thicker blood), meaning the heart has to work harder to supply the working muscles and organs with sufficient blood. It's easy to see why, during a warm-weather ultra, all these factors – reduced blood flow to the skin for cooling, reduced blood flow to the muscles for running, reduced blood flow to the stomach for digesting food – add to the already significant task of running a long way and make it even tougher.

A number of recent studies have looked at the relationship between air temperature and performance in marathon running, finding that the optimal temperature range for most groups of runners seems to be between 7 °C and 15 °C. As temperatures deviate below and above this range, average marathon finish times tend to become slower.

If the accumulating effects of heat stress are not managed and mitigated, brain and core temperatures will continue to rise. Heat illness ensues, and covers a continuum of symptoms from severe discomfort, extreme lethargy and confusion to collapse, loss of consciousness and death. While this cascade of effects is unlikely for most runners, they do emphasise the dangers of becoming lost without access to water and shade when out running in hot places, of pushing on through severe discomfort during very hot races, and of insufficient heat acclimatisation.

Heat acclimation and acclimatisation

Scientists studying the effects of heat on the human body use *acclimation* to describe artificial means of inducing hot conditions, such as saunas, heat chambers or running on a treadmill with the heating on. *Acclimatisation*, on the other hand, refers to exposure to naturally hot climactic conditions – i.e. training outdoors in hot weather. Both can be done *passively*, for example by simply spending time in a hot environment, whether that's outdoors or in a sauna or hot bath, or *actively*, by training in heat thus raising core temperature from both outside and within the body. Passive methods work well if you're training for a high-intensity race, such as a marathon in warm conditions, as you can acclimate your body without negatively impacting your training. Training in hot conditions, whether artificial or natural, will result in lower quality training and recovery, at least until adaptations have occurred. However, they may be more specific and therefore applicable to your goal race.

Adaptations to heat happen:

* involuntarily – such as during a spell of hot weather; or
* deliberately – when you're based somewhere cooler but preparing to run or race somewhere hot.

Adaptations to unaccustomed heat begin within two days of regular exposure, while two weeks is recommended for full acclimatisation.

While it's clear that hot conditions negatively impact performance and increase the likelihood of heat-related illness, spending time in hot environments – while being active or inactive – helps to moderate these to a significant degree. Acclimatisation to heat develops through frequent exposure to hot environmental conditions, which repeatedly elicit homeostatic mechanisms to mitigate the results of heat stress. These adaptations are an increase in sweating and blood flow to the skin, better fluid balance and cardiovascular stability, decreased heart rate, lower internal body temperature and a lowered metabolic rate. Acclimatised individuals experience improved comfort in the heat, and are able to perform closer to normal levels, although even highly trained individuals retain a reduction in their VO_2 max in hot conditions.

Recent research has underpinned the use of a hot bath immediately after training as a highly effective means of heat acclimation, which is convenient and cost effective. A recent paper compared post-exercise hot water immersion with exercise in the heat and concludes that the hot baths actually 'conferred more complete heat acclimation than exercise heat acclimation without increasing over-reaching risk' (McIntyre *et al.*, 2022).

Running in cold conditions

Like running in hot conditions, running in cold conditions produces a number of behavioural and homeostatic changes in order to conserve body heat and reduce the potential risks of hypothermia (dangerously low body temperature). Unlike hot environments, however, we have limited ability to acclimatise to cold environments, instead relying more on behavioural changes. These include wearing more clothing, increasing activity levels, eating warm food and drinking hot drinks, and the direct application of heat through maintaining close proximity to heat sources. Homeostatic mechanisms include constriction of blood vessels to reduce heat lost through the skin by convection, the raising of the hairs all over our body in an attempt to trap a layer of warm air, and shivering – a result of involuntary contractions of the skeletal muscles.

Whether, and to what extent, cold affects running performance depends on the specifics of the conditions. As air temperature falls, the air itself contains less water vapour, so the water content of the air we breathe in is much lower. Cold, dry air causes the mucus that lines our trachea (windpipe) to thicken, and our airways to constrict, which can make breathing harder, especially when exercising at higher intensities. At lower intensities, breathing through the nose helps by warming and humidifying inhaled air.

As well as stimulating vasoconstriction of the blood vessels supplying the skin, a drop in core temperature reduces blood flow to the limb muscles in order to conserve body heat. Blood pressure, stroke volume (the amount of blood pumped by the heart in each stroke) and blood volume in the central part of the body all rise. Because of the initial restriction of blood flow to the limbs, warming up in cold weather is even more important in order to optimise blood flow to the working muscles.

If the limbs continue to cool, nerve conduction slows – the reason it's so hard to do laces and buttons up with cold hands. When local tissue temperatures fall below 10 °C, nerve transmissions cease, pressure and touch receptors in the skin stop reacting, and movements become increasingly hard to control and coordinate.

Systemic effects of cooling include a slowing of metabolic rate, a reduction in enzyme reactions that produce muscle contractions and the commencement of shivering, which requires a substantial amount of energy from glycogen and fat reserves. If exposure to cold continues, the effects can be disastrous, with severe hypothermia resulting in a wide range of impairments including loss of movement and cognitive function, loss of respiratory control, anginal pain, cold injury leading to frostbite, and eventually death.

While this might all sound a little dramatic, those who run in exposed and weather-affected environments need to be aware of the potential seriousness of hypothermia. Without sufficient emergency clothing and equipment, a broken ankle when running solo in the hills can rapidly lead to a warm, sweaty body cooling to dangerous levels.

Running at altitude

Scientists have studied the changes the human body undergoes at altitudes of over 8,000 metres – the highest places on the face of the earth. In terms of running, most training and racing is carried out at a somewhat lower altitude, but many mountain races exceed altitudes of 2,500 metres in places. Runners might acclimatise to altitude either in preparation for a race at higher altitudes than they are used to, or to take advantage of the chronic adaptations to altitude,

which may benefit performance at lower altitudes.

As we reach higher altitudes, the partial pressure of oxygen in the air around us decreases. That means that every lungful of air we breathe in contains fewer molecules of oxygen to fuel our working bodies than it would at sea level, resulting in a state of *hypoxia* – low oxygen saturation. The effects of altitude are usually not noticeable until above 1,500 metres. The reaction to hypoxia resulting from altitude is multi-systemic, involving the cardiovascular, pulmonary and endocrine systems. General physiological changes include increased heart rate, increased breathing rate, increased blood pressure and decreased VO_2 max. These changes result in increased oxygen transport to body tissues, and decreased exercise performance.

When first exposed to high-altitude conditions, athletes may develop a headache and dry cough, loss of appetite, insomnia and increased fatigue; these are symptoms of acute mountain sickness and should resolve within a few days of being at altitude. Failure of the body to adapt to hypoxic conditions sufficiently during this time may lead to the serious and potentially life-threatening conditions of high-altitude pulmonary oedema and high-altitude cerebral oedema.

Humans can effectively acclimatise to altitude (meaning heart rate decreases and VO_2 max improves back to nearer normal levels), but responses are highly individual, and may differ for individuals at different times. The ability to adapt to altitude is thought to be based on a number of factors including genetics, fitness and training status, physical and psychological stress levels, diet, and overall health. Acclimatisation for those who respond well takes about two weeks for altitudes up to 2,300 metres, during which time the body goes through an acute response and then chronic adaptation to the hypoxic environment, resulting in improved tolerance and ability to perform physical activity. Those who respond slowly may take several months to fully acclimatise.

It is these adaptations that entice many elite

endurance athletes to train at altitudes between 1,800 and 2,800 metres as part of their preparation for races, improving their body's ability to deliver oxygen to working muscles – the rationale behind EPO doping, which achieves a similar outcome without the need to travel to high altitude. However, the precise performance benefits of altitude training are much debated among sport scientists, while some 'non-responders' receive little benefit and only a reduction in their ability to train effectively.

Top tips for training at altitude
* For those who live at low altitude preparing to race at high altitude, allow a minimum of 10 days' acclimatisation prior to a race.
* Take it easy for the first few days, when the body is acutely responding to altitude. During this time training will feel much harder, sleep may be poor quality and immune function may be compromised.
* Responses to altitude are not guaranteed. Responders may not respond on subsequent visits to altitude, whereas non-responders may.
* How long the effects of training at altitude last on return to sea level is unclear. Some improvement may be seen initially but larger improvements may take several weeks.
* Diet is an important factor in the ability to acclimatise to high altitude. Low energy diets, and those low in carbohydrate, increase physiological stress and risk of illness and injury. Sufficient protein intake is also required to support an increase in protein synthesis.
* Sufficient blood iron levels are considered to be essential to adaptations to high altitude, and this may be particularly important to consider for plant-based and/or menstruating athletes. Should supplementation be required it is important to seek medical advice as excessive iron has many negative effects.

Running and air pollution

Air pollution is made up of a number of different elements, including solid and liquid particles, and gasses such as nitrogen dioxide, carbon monoxide and ozone. Each of these can have its own effect on both our health and our running, and it's likely that combinations interact to affect us, too. Pollution varies greatly in both amount and type depending on factors such as location, weather conditions, season and time of day. While we can't avoid pollution altogether, having an awareness of its habits and effect can help us to minimise or at least manage our exposure as much as is practically possible.

Top tips to minimise exposure to air pollution
* Try to schedule training times and places that avoid busy roads and the busiest times of day. If you need to train near to busy roads, early morning – before rush hour – tends to be the time when most pollutants are at their lowest.
* A diet high in antioxidants may help reduce the negative effects of ozone on lung function.

V

Practicalities

13

Running kit

'The best [insert relevant bit of kit] is the one you already own.'
We hear this a lot, and, although it's partly true, it's not that helpful.
Good kit not only has the power to make the difference between an
enjoyable run and an uncomfortable slog, it can also equip you to
avoid injury and run safely in any environment. If it's not right for the
conditions, the kit you already own might hinder, injure or endanger
you. Of course, it is important to stop and think whether you *really*
need another new running top, or the latest colourway in your favourite
trainers or any of the additional functions on the latest watch, but all this
assumes that you already have reasonably functional kit to start with.

If you're new to running then any clothing that's unrestrictive and breathable is fine to run in. Hopefully you have some trainers that are comfortable; if you don't, this is the first thing to buy. Once you start running more often – and start to love it – you can get more specific kit that will help you run further, faster and longer, and make the whole experience more enjoyable.

If you're a more experienced runner, then you are likely to already have a set of trainers and some running clothing that have worked well for you so far. Here we will expand on the function and specification of the different types of footwear, clothing and equipment available, from general road and trail running through to specific kit for more extreme terrain, weather and longer adventures.

In all cases, we've found that buying the best that you can tends to be the best investment. Cheaper kit often isn't as good functionally and won't last as long or be backed up by good after-sales service. Also think about who made your kit and what it's made from; if it's very cheap then it's unlikely that the person who made it was paid fairly and the construction may have harmed our planet. In most cases, it's much better to buy top-quality second-hand kit than lower quality new kit.

Running clothing has a demanding job: it needs to keep you warm enough, but not too warm. It must protect you from the wind or rain without trapping so much sweat inside that you get wet anyway. Running shoes have to cope with whatever surface you run on, giving you adequate traction and protection from both the impact of each footfall and the terrain underfoot. Packs need to carry everything you need without bouncing and rubbing. Tech needs to give you useful, helpful, accurate data without being confusing. Everything has to be light and comfortable enough to allow you to run without feeling weighed down or restricted. The fabrics need to be quick-drying, durable and easy to look after. It needs to be reasonably priced, and it would be nice if it looks good as well. Quite a big ask for the kit designers!

We've often heard it said – and probably said it too often ourselves – that one of the many joys of running lies in its simplicity. We all have far too much stuff, and brands – even those purporting to be environmentally friendly – really just want to sell you more *stuff*, whether you need it or not. We were born to run, after all, so all we really need is a pair of shoes and we're good to go – right?

Well, perhaps it's not quite that simple. Because which shoes you choose depends on where you're going running and what the underfoot conditions are like. If it's raining and muddy, you'll probably want a shoe with decent grip – and you'll also need a water-proof jacket that's lightweight and breathable, allowing full freedom of movement while also being protective enough to keep you warm and dry if the weather gets really bad. In exposed upland areas, a decent waterproof jacket can quite literally save your life.

But what if the weather turns out nice, instead? Then you'll need somewhere to stash your jacket, and probably a way to carry water, too – and food if you're staying out for longer. A good running pack or race vest does this brilliantly, but you'll want a decent top to wear it over – one that won't chafe, in a fabric that will manage your temperature and sweat to allow you to run in comfort. And if it gets really sunny, surely you'll also need a hat and some sunglasses ...

As you can probably tell, our relationship with running and other outdoor kit is complicated. We've been testing, reviewing and recommending gear for outdoor magazines for years, so we're pretty well acquainted with what's out there, and in particular what's really useful and what's just another fad. One thing we're sure of is that the right kit makes running safer, more comfortable and more enjoyable – and it can last for years, too. So, what – exactly – is the right kit?

Materials

Before we look at the specific types of clothing and equipment, it's useful to know the advantages and disadvantages of the various materials that most running kit is made from.

Polyester

Most polyester used in running kit is a synthetic petroleum-based fabric. It's light, strong, cheap and easy for manufacturers to use. The fibres don't hold moisture, so it dries very quickly. It's not breathable but can be constructed in a fine mesh to allow airflow between fibres. Polyester can also form a fluffy synthetic material which traps air and offers good insulation properties. It can be treated to make it water-resistant or anti-odour. Plastic bottles and used polyester fabrics can be recycled into high-quality polyester fabric which can be recycled again at the end of the garment's life. Bio-polyester can be made when renewable feedstocks or bio-waste replace some or all of the petroleum in the initial production. Polyester fabrics contribute to microplastic accumulation by shedding tiny fibres during use and in the wash. Polyester is not biodegradable, although some biode-gradable polyester fabrics are in development.

Polyamide (nylon)

Similar to polyester, nylon is usually a synthetic petro-leum-based fabric, although bio-based alternatives are on the rise. It's slightly stronger than polyester and slightly more expensive to construct but shares a lot of its other characteristics. This means that nylon is often used in higher-value outer layers of clothing like jackets, and in high-stress areas like footwear and packs. Recycled nylon is increasingly available, normally made from fabric offcuts produced during clothing production or from discarded fishing nets. Like polyester, nylon sheds microplastics.

Polypropylene

Another petroleum-based plastic fabric, polypropylene is similar to polyester but is used less frequently in running clothing. It has a lower thermal conductivity rating than polyester or nylon, so it is a warmer base layer fabric. Unfortunately, it holds body odour and usually becomes antisocial faster than other fabrics. Polypropylene can be recycled into new fabric, but demand is lower and we haven't yet seen this in outdoor clothing. Polypropylene also sheds micro-plastics with use.

Merino wool

Wool from the Merino breed of sheep can be finer and therefore less itchy than traditional wool. Fine grades of Merino wool are used in base layers and next-to-skin clothing, while coarser wool is used as an insulating material in jackets. Merino is very comfortable because it is soft, breathable and has good insulating properties. It's naturally odour-resistant so you can wear it several times without needing to wash it, making it particularly useful for multi-day adventures and generally keeping washing levels down. It is tough but not as durable as polyester or nylon and it takes longer to dry, however it does retain some of its insulating properties even when wet. For these reasons, Merino is often blended with other materials to improve the durability and reduce the drying time of the resulting fabric.

Wool is a natural, biodegradable fabric. Ethically it is a good choice if the sheep are farmed to a high standard of animal welfare. Always look for assurance that it is non-mulesed wool. Over-grazing can also be a problem. Look out for RWS (Responsible Wool Standard), ZQ Merino or Woolmark certification to be sure of ethical practice.

Cotton

Cotton is the fluffy fibres that surround the seeds of the cotton plant, which is harvested and then spun into a thread. Cotton is natural, strong and feels nice against the skin, but it soaks up water and takes a long time to dry so it's not necessarily suitable for running, especially in wet or very sweaty conditions. However, a cotton T-shirt can be nice to wear for a short run in dry weather. Non-organic cotton plants use a lot of chemicals and water to grow and are therefore bad for the people harvesting them and the local environment. Organic cotton production reduces these impacts significantly. Look out for GOTS (Global Organic Textile Standard) certification to ensure ethical production.

Down

The fluffy plumage under the outer feathers, down is the birds' mid layer. In outdoor kit it's collected and used as jacket or sleeping bag insulation. It's brilliant at this because it fluffs up, trapping a lot of air for its weight and pack size – a process known as 'lofting'. Down is almost always from ducks or geese and is a by-product of the meat industry. EU down can't be collected from live birds but down produced elsewhere can, so look out for RDS (Responsible Down Standard) accreditation particularly from non-EU down. Even better, choose recycled down, reclaimed from used clothing and bedding and washed and sorted for reuse. Down jackets can become saturated and lose their loft in wet conditions. Hydrophobic down is treated with a water repellent to reduce the loss of warmth when wet. Unless it's very cold and dry, down is best suited for warming up before your run or staying warm when you stop. The warmth-to-weight ratio is very good so a down jacket or sleeping bag can be a good option if you have to carry it for an event. The quality of down is rated with a fill power; this refers to the volume a set amount of down will take up when it lofts: the higher the number, the better the warmth-to-weight ratio.

Lyocell (Tencel)

Lyocell is a wood cellulose fabric made from pulped hardwood which is chemically treated and then spun into fibres. The resulting fabric is soft, breathable and durable, but won't dry as quickly as synthetic fabrics. It's sometimes added to Merino wool to increase the wool's durability or to polyester to reduce the petroleum content of the overall fabric and improve its feel. The production of lyocell should be a closed-loop system in terms of chemical use; the chemicals can be recovered and reused in the production of the next batch, but this isn't always the case. Lyocell is biodegradable but it can only be classed as environmentally sound if it is a closed-loop system and the forests felled for its production are well managed. Lyocell can be certified as organic – look out for GOTS certification.

Bamboo

A fast-growing grass, bamboo doesn't need much water or almost any chemical fertiliser to grow. It's cut rather than uprooted which protects the soil and allows it to regrow quickly so it's a good raw material to use. Almost all bamboo fabric in sports kit is bamboo viscose; this is made by cutting the bamboo plant and then crushing and softening it with chemicals before it can be turned into a fabric. Unfortunately, this isn't normally a closed-loop system, and the chemicals must be treated carefully to avoid them escaping into and damaging the environment. Bamboo fabric can be made using the lyocell closed-loop system or with a purely mechanical process which would be better environmentally, but we haven't come across this in running kit. It's therefore important to look at a supplier's green credentials and make sure that they are clear about the production methods before you take their word that what they are using is an environmentally sound fabric. Bamboo viscose feels soft and breathable. It dries faster than cotton, similar to lyocell but more slowly than the synthetic fabrics. It's often mixed with Merino, lyocell or cotton with added elastane for stretch. Bamboo running kit feels comfortable, but because of its slow drying time it is best for shorter runs and dry conditions.

The layering system

A good layering system is an essential part of safe and enjoyable running all year round. Layering utilises the unique properties of different fabrics in combination with the heat generated by our bodies during exercise to create optimal conditions for comfort and performance. Adding or removing layers as you go means you can quickly and easily adapt your clothing to keep you warm, dry and comfortable, even when the weather or your activity level changes.

While the specifics of a layering system vary, the principles remain the same. Here's how to get your layers right every time:

1: Base layer

Base layers are worn against the skin, so need to be comfortable and breathable. They also need to draw moisture away from the skin to avoid the discomfort and cooling associated with being wet. Synthetic base layers, made from polyester, nylon or polypropylene, 'wick' moisture away from the skin via capillary action. Natural fabrics absorb moisture but, whereas cotton will feel damp against the skin, Merino wool holds the moisture within its structure and still feels dry. Base layers should fit snugly but not be tight or restrictive. Go for a heavier-weight fabric for cold weather, or a light, breathable option for warmer weather.

2: Mid layer

Mid layers create a layer of warm, dry air between your base layer and jacket. They're commonly made from a natural or synthetic fleece with an open woven or knitted structure that traps a layer of warm air between your base layer and jacket.

3: Insulation layer

An insulating layer is important in colder weather, when your mid layer alone doesn't provide sufficient warmth. Insulating jackets usually feature a windproof outer shell, with an insulating material sandwiched within it to trap warm, dry air as it leaves your body. The most common insulation materials are down – the fluffy underfeathers from ducks and geese – and polyester wadding, but wool also works well.

4: Shell layer

An outer or 'shell' layer is made from a tightly woven fabric that protects you from wind and rain and traps warm air inside your layering system. In dry weather, a windproof is usually sufficient, while in wet weather you'll need a waterproof. Layering systems work most effectively if they're kept dry, so in wet weather all hoods, zips, cuffs and hems should be done up to avoid water getting in, and make sure your wicking and absorbent layers aren't protruding outside your waterproof as they'll soak up the rain water and take it inside.

Waterproof fabrics are usually treated with a durable water repellent (DWR) coating to help water 'bead' and run off. While many companies are now moving to more sustainable alternatives, some DWR treatments are still made using PFCs (perfluorinated compounds). Evidence is mounting that these chemicals are persistent, pervasive and toxic to life, so we'd recommend avoiding them whenever possible and opting for products labelled as PFC-free.

Lightweight waterproof fabrics are usually made using a three-layer construction bonded together as a single sheet of material:

* a tough nylon or polyester outer,
* a waterproof membrane glued to the inside of the outer fabric; and
* a very light nylon or polyester protective inner fabric.

Another option are 2.5-layer fabrics, which feature a printed or mesh layer bonded to the inside to protect the membrane.

HOW ARE WATERPROOF FABRICS TESTED?

Waterproof fabrics are rated with a laboratory-based test to measure the hydrostatic head (HH) or waterproofness. This is a pressure test where a column of water stands on a tight piece of fabric; the height of the water column that the fabric can withstand is the HH, measured in millimetres. To be classed as waterproof clothing the fabric must have a minimum HH rating of 1,500 millimetres. Most outdoor waterproof fabrics have a far greater rating with a HH of well over 10,000 millimetres.

Most running jackets claim to be breathable as well as waterproof, which is necessary because as you run you generate heat and sweat and if the jacket doesn't allow this to escape you will end up soaked and overheated. Fabrics are given a moisture vapor transmission rate (MVTR) which is measured in a laboratory under set conditions. The MVTR is the amount of moisture that passes through the fabric in 24 hours – the higher the MVTR the more breathable the fabric is.

So, in theory you can look at the HH and MVTR of a jacket to see how well it will protect you from the weather and how it will deal with moisture build-up inside. These are lab tests though and MVTR in particular is affected by the conditions. The best results come when it's cold and dry outside and warm and moist inside, but in these conditions, you wouldn't be running in a waterproof. If it's warm and wet outside MVTR would be much lower and even in cold wet conditions the fabric wouldn't be able to move moisture through it as much as it claims.

Although HH and MVTR are important, it's often the design and cut of the garment that make the most difference to how wet you get, either from the rain or from sweat. When a jacket fits well, has a good hood, well-placed zips and allows airflow using vents or zip openings, you are most likely to stay warm and comfortable.

Clothing

Running clothing comes in a wide variety of shapes, sizes and designs. It's essential that anything you're going to be running in fits perfectly, performs well and has all the features you'll need for the kind of running you do. It can take a while to find the brand or style of clothing that works best for you, so be sure to try on a few before committing.

When shopping for new kit, keep the **four Fs** in mind:

1 **Fit:** does it fit perfectly with no baggy excess fabric that might catch or blow about in the wind or restrictive areas that will soon become uncomfortable? Does it allow you full range of unrestricted motion, maintaining coverage throughout? Is it designed and cut in a way that means you'll enjoy wearing it and feel good in it?

2 **Function:** do you really need this item? Is it versatile enough that you'll use it a lot, or specialist enough that nothing else will do? Does it do the job it's designed to do as well as possible? And will it last for many years of adventures?

3 **Fabric:** is the fabric comfortable, durable and fit for purpose? Is it produced in a responsible way, that minimises potential harm to people, animals and the planet?

4 **Features:** check the garment has all the features you'll need, including pockets for secure storage, drawcords and adjustments to customise the fit, reflective details for after dark safety, and all the zips and vents you need.

Underwear

Sometimes neglected, this is not an area you want to get wrong – underwear-related discomfort and chafing is no fun. You may not need underwear as running shorts often have an inbuilt brief liner, so wearing another layer here can increase the likelihood of rubbing. If your shorts don't have a liner, or you prefer to double up, then go for close-fitting pants in either polyester or Merino fabrics. Cotton underwear is fine unless it's particularly wet or sweaty weather, when it won't dry, which is cold, uncomfortable and increases the likelihood of chafing ...

Sports bras

For those who need them, a well-fitting and appropriately supportive running bra is an essential item of kit and can without any doubt make or break a run. As well as being mightily uncomfortable, too much breast movement during running, especially if you have larger breasts, can lead to pain and damage in the surrounding structures.

The search for the perfect running bra is something that many runners will be all too familiar with. Generally, it's a case of trying a few and working out the style and fabric that works best for your specific anatomy and preferences. Unfortunately, running bras don't come cheap, and you never know what's going to chafe or be otherwise horribly uncomfortable until you've been wearing it for some time – and by then it's too late to return it. As a result, many of us end up running in a range of slightly imperfect bras a lot of the time.

The sports bra started out life as the 'jockbra', invented in 1977 by graduate student Lisa Lindahl and theatre costume designers Polly Smith and Hinda Miller. This was the height of the first jogging boom, and as yet there were no suitable bras available. Frustrated by running in discomfort, the prototype bra utilised two jockstraps – designed to reduce unhelpful movement in male anatomy – sewn together to create supportive cups. The subsequently renamed 'Jogbra' was purchased by Playtex in 1990 and brought into the mainstream.

Research on breast movement during running and how best to control this for optimal comfort, breast health and performance, is still ongoing. But what we now know, and the range of different bras available to fit every pair of breasts, is far more comprehensive.

Despite this, even in elite sport many women are still training and competing alongside breast discomfort. A recent study looking at elite athletes (Wakefield-Scurr, *et al.*, 2023) found that 51 per cent of the participants experienced breast pain, which affected performance for 29 per cent. Seven athletes used medication and one had undergone surgery to relieve symptoms. When assessed, most wore ill-fitting, unsupportive bras and were keen to receive better bra advice. Bespoke bra interventions were reported to eliminate breast pain, improve breast position and spine rotation, and improve performance. The researchers conclude that, for elite athletes, most breast and bra issues can be resolved through good education, advice and fitting.

Top tips for choosing the right running bra

Our bodies and our breasts change in shape and size throughout our lives. Puberty, hormonal contraception, weight change, pregnancy, breastfeeding, menopause and aging can all affect our breast morphology. The bra you were fitted with in your 20s may well not be right when you're in your 40, so it's well worth getting remeasured every decade and/or during or after life events that affect your breasts. Bra shapes and sizes vary between brands, so always buy a bra on fit rather than size.

The Research Group in Breast Health at the University of Portsmouth is responsible for many international scientific publications in the area of breast biomechanics, bra science and breast health. They have released the following five-step process to help you choose the perfect bra.

1 **The underband:** this should fit firmly, but should not be too tight or uncomfortable and should be level all the way around the ribs. The underband is where most of the support comes from.

2 **The cups:** the breast should be enclosed within the cup. There should be no bulging or gaping at the top or sides. If the material is puckering then the cup is probably too big.

3 **Underwires:** if there is an underwire, it should follow the natural crease of the breast. It should not rest on the breast tissue at any point.

4 **Centre front:** for most bras, the front of the bra between the breasts should sit flat against the body and not gape at any point. If the front of the bra is lifting away the cup may be too small.

5 **The straps:** the shoulder straps should be adjusted to provide comfortable breast support without being too tight. The main support should come from the underband, not from the straps.

What level of support do I need?

Sports bras offer different levels of support; the type you need depends on your cup size and the type of exercise you do. Bras designed for low- or medium-impact sports act like compression wear, flattening the breasts against the body to control movement. They typically don't have separate cups and often don't feature fastenings, meaning you pull them on and off over your head. Designed for activities such as walking, strength training, dancing and cycling, those with smaller breasts may also find this type of bra comfortable for running.

High-impact sports bras are designed for activities that create a lot of bounce, such as running, aerobics and mountain biking. They generally use an encapsulation method of support with a defined cup structure – more like regular bras – that enclose and support each breast separately. Some high-impact bras will use a combination of both encapsulation and compression methods to maximise support.

Legwear

Many people run in shorts in all weathers but there are advantages to wearing tights or trousers in some situations.

* **Basic running shorts** are usually made from polyester or nylon – they don't need any particular features, just a good fit. The length of shorts doesn't really affect the performance, so choose whatever you feel most comfortable wearing. Some shorts have a tighter liner short or liner briefs, but these are easily removed with some scissors if you don't like them.

* **Running tights or leggings** are available in various lengths from short through three-quarters and full length with several companies offering seven-eighths lengths and everything else in between. Tights offer more weather protection, support and coverage than shorts. They can be warmer than shorts but super-light fabrics are available that are just as cool so you can choose what you are happiest in. Running tights tend to be polyester, nylon or a mix of one of these with added Merino, lyocell or bamboo. Some full-length tights will have a short zip at the ankle to make them easier to put on.

* Some companies also offer **running trousers**; these tend to be made of lightweight polyester or nylon but sometimes have panels or linings made from mixtures of the synthetic fabrics and Merino, lyocell or bamboo. Some runners might find a looser-fit trouser more comfortable than tights, as well as offering a bit more protection from the weather as they aren't skintight.

Tights and trousers are available in windproof fabrics or with windproof panels to add protection for your legs in cold weather. The fronts of the thighs can become very cold in strong wind, so this is a good feature for winter-weight running tights.

Lightweight, waterproof, running-specific over-trousers are a useful bit of emergency kit; they are very light and take up hardly any room in your pack but can really help warm you up in bad weather. They don't normally have pockets or features, which helps keep the weight and pack size down, but they should have zips to allow you to put them on without taking off your shoes.

A waistband drawstring will allow you to keep any style of legwear up even with things in the pockets and after the waist elastic starts to lose its stretch.

Pockets on the waistband of legwear can be useful, allowing you to carry items without needing a pack. If you like the sound of this, check that your phone and anything else you need to carry fits in the pocket easily and doesn't make the legwear fall down. At least one zipped pocket is a good idea for your keys and a card. Stretch pockets on the outer thigh of tight inner shorts or tights can be used to carry a phone or soft flask without bounce.

Tops

Made from natural fabrics such as Merino wool, or synthetics such as polyester, running tops range from minimalist vests to cosy, long-sleeved base layers, and can be standalone garments or worn as part of a layering system.

Some tops feature a short front zip so that you can increase the ventilation; this also allows a higher collar for better sun protection or increased warmth.

Thumb loops or integrated mitts can help to make a top feel snug on a cold winter's morning and stop the sleeves riding up and exposing your wrists. Make sure the sleeves are cut long enough to comfortably use the thumb loops.

Jackets

It's nice to have two different running jackets – one which is weather resistant and another which is actually waterproof.

* A **weather-resistant jacket** will get most use because it will be much more breathable so you won't get as sweaty as you would in a waterproof jacket, but it will still drastically reduce cooling from wind chill. A weather-resistant jacket is lightweight and packs small so you can wear it for a bit of extra warmth but easily stash it in your pack or tie it around your waist once you warm up. It is also much cheaper than a good waterproof jacket.
* A **waterproof jacket** is also windproof so it's an important layer to have in bad conditions or in situations where the weather could deteriorate rapidly and keeping warm and protected is important for your safety. A waterproof jacket is the most common item of mandatory kit for races (see pages 184–185). Waterproof running jackets will have taped seams so that the rain can't come through the stitching holes and a hood to stop the rain going down your neck. Some hoodless waterproof jackets are available, but these won't pass a race kit check and don't offer the protection you really need in bad conditions. Waterproof jackets range from thin, superlight race or emergency jackets – which are waterproof and can weigh less than 100 grams but will have minimal features and won't be particularly durable – through to mountaineering-style jackets – with thicker and more durable fabric that will protect you from the worst conditions but weigh in at around 400 grams. For most runners, something between these extremes will be perfectly suitable for normal training and racing.
* Some running jackets are **insulated** – this can be nice in cold weather but makes the jacket less versatile as it has to be quite cold to need an insulated jacket when running. It's often better to wear two or three base or mid layers under a weather-resistant or waterproof jacket than to use a single warmer layer.
* **Hybrid-style jackets** use a combination of different fabrics to create a more versatile option. This is often a combination of more protective materials on the front and shoulders and more breathable materials on the back.

A small, zipped pocket is a useful addition to a jacket for keys and a card, but you can't normally carry anything heavy in a jacket pocket without it bouncing so large pockets are unnecessary. Hand-warmer-style pockets can be nice if you stop for any reason.

A good hood will make a jacket work much more effectively; a wired or stiffened peak is a nice addition to stop the rain running into your face. If a hood doesn't have a peak, you can wear a cap under the hood. Volume adjustment behind the head and the ability to cinch the sides of the hood around your face will improve the fit and stormproofing. We've found that some hoods are so well designed that they don't need these adjustments. Be careful of cords and toggles that hang around the sides of your face – they will whip you in strong winds.

Gilets or vests

Although less versatile than a full sleeved jacket, a gilet can be a nice thing to wear; it will give your core protection but will be more ventilated than a jacket. It's also smaller and lighter than a jacket so you could consider carrying a warm gilet as an emergency layer to reduce weight in your pack. Available in weather-resistant, waterproof and insulated or mid layer fabrics, they can add some extra options to your running wardrobe.

Hats and gloves

* In cold weather a simple **fleece hat and gloves** can make a lot of difference to your feeling of warmth; they are also easily removed and stashed in a pocket when you warm up. A warm hat and gloves are a standard item of compulsory kit for many races because of the increase in warmth they offer for the size and weight of the items.
* **Windproof or waterproof hats and gloves** offer more protection and warmth by reducing the breathability and windchill. In cold weather it's important to be able to use your hands for delicate things like navigation or using a phone to call for help so it's important that you keep them warm. Waterproof overmitts are a useful addition in cold conditions because they are easy to put on over normal gloves and have a tiny pack size; they will blow away easily though so consider attaching them to your wrists or jacket.
* **Caps or wide-brimmed hats** can protect your face and neck from the sun. Cotton fabrics work well in hot weather, and you can soak them in water to increase the cooling effect.
* A **neck tube/gaiter** (Buff) is a versatile item that can be worn as a hat or around the neck or face in cold weather.

Footwear

With running, our shoes are perhaps the most important item of kit to get right. They create the interface between our feet and the ground, giving us feel, grip and protection. Most runners are on a constant mission to find the right shoe, but with a little patience and experimentation it is possible.

All running shoes have a grippy *outsole*, usually made from a mixture of natural and synthetic rubber. The exact rubber compound gives a level of grip and durability appropriate for the shoe's specific use. The tread pattern is then created to work with the terrain the shoe is designed for: a shallow, even tread for use on roads, through to deep studs with wide gaps for the best grip in mud.

The *midsole* of the shoe offers cushioning and protection from the ground. It is normally made from ethylene-vinyl acetate (EVA) foam or similar and sometimes incorporates a rock plate to protect the foot from sharper ground or a sprung plate designed to improve energy return. The midsole creates the *stack height* of a shoe which is the distance between the ground and the base of the foot. A larger stack height can provide more cushioning and protection from hard ground, but this comes at the expense of stability and ground feel. The stack height can differ across the shoe – it is often listed in millimetres at the forefoot and under the heel. The difference between these heights is known as the *drop*.

* A standard road or trail running shoe will have a drop of somewhere between eight and twelve millimetres.
* Shoes designed for more technical terrain have lower drops, usually between four and eight millimetres.
* Minimalist or low-drop shoes usually have a drop between zero and three millimetres.

The *insole* is the removable foam layer that sits inside the shoe under your foot. This provides underfoot comfort and can allow fine tuning of fit by using a slightly thicker or thinner insole. Some runners use custom insoles or orthotics; if this applies to you, make sure that the insole can be removed and that the shoe fits with your preferred insole.

The *upper* of a running shoe protects the foot and holds it securely to the sole. It's normally made from a lightweight nylon mesh or fabric and more structural nylon webbing joining the lacing to the sole. A plastic heel counter provides the shape and structure of the heel. The rear of the shoe is normally lined with a polyester or nylon fabric with some thin foam padding to increase comfort. The rubber used on the outsole is sometimes curled around the front of the shoe to create a durable and protective toe bumper. Thermoplastic polyurethane (TPU) is often used to overlay the mesh or fabric to provide more structure and increase durability, protection and water resistance. The tongue is padded to protect the foot from the lacing.

Running shoes are normally fastened with *laces* that allow a variety of lacing patterns (see page 178) and good fit adjustment. Sometimes quick-lacing systems are used which fasten with the pull of a toggle or the turn of a dial.

How to choose the perfect running shoes

Here are the most important factors when choosing running shoes.

Fit

A perfect fit is essential for comfort and safety when you're running. Shoes come in a vast range of sizes and shapes, so it's a good idea to visit a specialist running shop where you can try on a variety of brands and models in a range of sizes to find the one that works for you. Try shoes on with your favourite running socks and take them for a short jog to test them out; most good shops will have a treadmill or an outdoor space where you can do this. If you use a specific insole or orthotic, make sure you take these along when you're trying out shoes.

Sizes

Running shoe sizes may not match your usual shoe size – it's quite normal to need go up a half size or so. Check there's a good thumb-width of space in the front so your toes don't hit the ends when you're running downhill. Your heel should fit comfortably and securely without lifting inside the shoe as you run. The shoe should feel like it flexes in the right place for your feet, and once laced up your foot shouldn't move about or feel painful or restrictive. If anything feels uncomfortable when you're trying a pair of running shoes on in a shop, it probably won't get better a few miles down the road. If you can, always try shoes on in the afternoon, ideally after a run, as this is when your feet will be at their largest. Sounds odd, but it's amazing how much difference it can make. Also, high-mileage training, pregnancy, weight gain and aging can all increase your shoe size, especially if you have higher arches.

Function

Alongside the perfect fit, your shoes should match the kind of running you're planning to do. For this reason, many runners have a fleet of shoes that they can switch between depending on the terrain and conditions. Particularly if you'll be heading off-road, the combination of the tread pattern and rubber compound will dictate the amount of grip and the terrain a shoe is best suited to. In general, a harder rubber compound with a shallower tread will be more durable on hard-packed trails; a harder rubber compound with a deeper tread will offer better grip on mud and grass; and a softer rubber compound will grip better on rock, but won't be as durable. Getting the grip right will make your run safer and more enjoyable.

If you're planning to run a long way, like in an ultramarathon, you may need to size up more than you would do for your normal running shoes. This is because your feet swell with the prolonged weightbearing and inflammation associated with hours of impact and friction. Jen says:

'Finding the perfect shoe and sock combination for a mountainous, potentially wet and boggy ultra was an interesting process of trial and error. In the end, Injinji toe-sock liners, Sealskinz waterproof oversocks, La Sportiva Mutant trail shoes and Kahtoola debris gaiters provided the perfect solution, alongside copious amounts of Squirrel's Nut Butter to lubricate my feet.'

Common shoe-fitting problems

Everyone's feet are unique, but some common problems can be tackled easily with a particular type of shoe or even a different lacing technique with your current shoes.

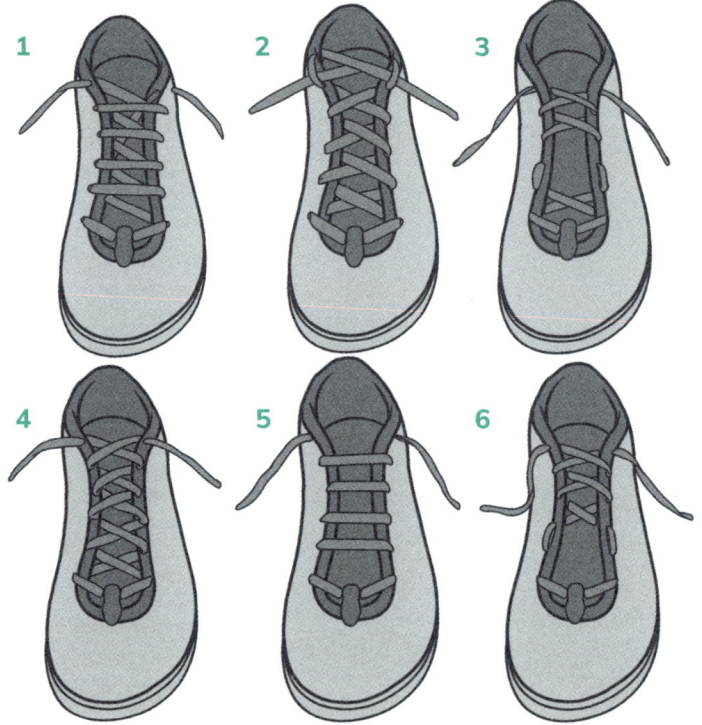

Lacing techniques: 1 Black toenails, **2** Heel slipping, **3** High arches, **4** Narrow feet, **5** Wide feet, **6** Wide forefeet.

Black toenails

Sore and black toenails are either caused by your shoes being too short – you need a good thumb-width of space in the toe box to make sure your toes don't hit the end when you're running fast downhill – or lacking enough volume so your nail repeatedly catches the fabric at the top of the shoe. Making sure your shoes are large enough is the first step, but if you're still finding your nails are taking a battering, the *black toenails lacing technique* pulls the fabric up and off the toes, giving them more breathing space.

Heel slipping

Getting the fit perfect around the bony heel area, where there's not a lot for the shoe to hold on to, can be tricky. Our calcaneus (heel) bones come in many shapes and sizes, making it hard to standardise fit. The *heel slipping lacing technique* utilises the extra lacing holes found below the top eyelet on most running shoes and is a surprisingly effective way of locking the heel in, making the whole shoe feel more secure.

High arches

High-arched feet tend to be fairly rigid, lacking the natural shock absorption of more flexible foot types. As a result, they are usually well suited to neutral, cushioning shoes. Runners with high arches often experience discomfort over the bony prominence at the top of the foot, so the *high arches lacing technique* misses out this central section, maintaining secure lacing at the top and bottom while avoiding uncomfortable pressure or irritation on the top of the foot. Pressure on the nerves at the top of the foot from overly tight lacing can cause shooting pains, tingling and numbness in the foot.

Narrow feet

Some brands make their shoes on a narrower side; others on a wider side. Very few offer different widths. If you have narrow feet, it's worth shopping around to find a brand and model that fits without bunching up over the top of the foot, which can quickly become uncomfortable. Once you've found the right shoe, the *narrow feet lacing technique* ensures a snug, foot-hugging fit through the length of the foot.

Wide feet

As with narrow feet, the starting point for those with wide feet is to find a brand and model of shoe that fits comfortably, allowing sufficient width through the length of the foot without the feet feeling loose. To add extra width, the *wide feet lacing technique* avoids the cross lacing that pulls the fabric of the shoe around the foot, resulting in a more relaxed fit.

Bunions, bony protuberances and wide forefeet

Those with wide feet and/or a deformity around the first metatarsophalangeal joint on the big toe (a bunion) or the fifth metatarsophalangeal joint on the little toe (also known as a tailor's bunion) need shoes with a wide-enough toe box to accommodate the forefoot without pinching or rubbing. Wearing shoes that are too restrictive in the forefoot can irritate a bunion and cause it to become inflamed and painful (bursitis), and can be a contributing factor in Morton's neuroma, a painful thickening of the the nerve that runs between the metatarsals. The *wide forefeet lacing technique* allows the front section of the shoe to widen in order to accommodate a bunion or wider forefoot.

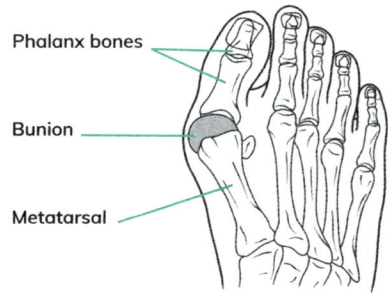

Phalanx bones

Bunion

Metatarsal

Bunion

Different types of shoes

Road shoes

These have a shallow tread with lots of rubber-to-ground contact to give good grip on road and hard surfaces. The midsole needs to offer enough cushioning to cope with the repetitive impact of a regular stride on a consistent hard surface. The upper doesn't need to offer much protection but needs to hold the foot securely.

Trail shoes

These have a deeper tread than road shoes but still offer plenty of rubber-to-ground contact to provide good grip on gravel, rock and surfaced trails. They will also work well on dry grass and dirt but will normally start to struggle in mud. The midsole needs to offer enough cushioning to cope with hard trails. A stiffened rock plate is sometimes used to protect the foot from sharp rocky ground. The upper must protect the foot from kicking stones so will often have a toe bumper of some type.

Fell shoes

These are designed for off-road and off-trail running. They have deep, well-spaced tread to provide good grip in mud and on wet, grassy surfaces. The softer compound rubber that they use will also grip well on rock but will wear out quickly if worn on harder trails or the road. The midsole doesn't need much cushioning because these shoes are designed to be worn on soft ground. A low stack height and low drop is often used to prioritise stability and lower weight – the drop of a shoe doesn't make as much difference to running gait when running on soft ground. The upper of a fell shoe needs to protect the foot from the uneven, rocky and pathless terrain it is designed for so they will often feature a toe bumper and some increased foot protection around the sides.

All weather, all-terrain shoes

Some running shoes have a waterproof lining, often Gore-Tex, which is usually a full sock membrane that is fixed between the inner and outer layers of the upper and under the insole. A waterproof shoe will be warmer, heavier and more expensive than a non-waterproof shoe. It will often have a slightly snugger fit than the non-waterproof version of the same shoe due to the extra layer of material. A waterproof shoe can be good in the winter when running on roads, trails and through short grass, but it's not so good if water is likely to go over the top and into the shoe. A waterproof shoe can't drain so once you have wet feet you will continue to run with your feet in a puddle which is heavy and uncomfortable. For this reason, fell shoes are very rarely waterproof. Waterproof shoes will take longer to dry after your run.

Snow and ice shoes

Shoes designed for use on snow and ice have small metal studs incorporated into the tread to add grip on icy surfaces. They work very well if you do regularly find yourself running on icy roads or trails, but you can't really use them in any other conditions so **microspikes** or **nanospikes** (detachable spikes, a bit like a lighter-weight version of crampons) may be more versatile for most runners. The uppers of these shoes tend to be waterproof and have slightly more insulation than normal trail shoes to help keep your feet warm. You will probably wear thicker normal or waterproof socks with this style of shoe so you may need to size up – it's best to try them with your preferred socks.

Super shoes

Running shoe design is evolving all the time, as brands in a highly competitive industry strive to get the edge over all the others. In 2017, Nike brought its 'super shoe', the Vaporfly 4%, to market, leaving other brands – and any runners not wearing the shoes – trailing in its wake. All three male medallists in the 2016 Olympic marathon wore a prototype of the Vaporfly 4%.

Nike's claim that the shoe's design improves the running economy of highly trained runners by four per cent – equating to an improvement in performance of between two per cent and three per cent – seems to have been borne out by results over subsequent years. Since 2016, top 50 male marathon runners' times have improved by about two per cent on average, while for the women it's closer to 2.6 per cent.

In 2019, Kenyan legend Eliud Kipchoge broke the two-hour marathon barrier, albeit under highly controlled non-race circumstances. The following day, compatriot Brigid Kosgei smashed the women's marathon record, which had been held by Paula Radcliffe since 2003. Both athletes were wearing the shoes. Calls for the shoes to be banned for their potentially unfair performance advantages echoed around the industry, but few would argue against sports technology being allowed to develop with the aim of improving performance.

At the time of writing, most of the major footwear brands have brought out their own version of the super shoe and Nike is no longer dominating the medal tables. Even some trail running shoes now come with an integrated carbon plate. Love them or hate them, there's no doubt the recent innovation in shoe design has changed running, but how do they work?

There's still research to be done on both the potential performance benefits and injury risks involved in wearing super shoes. It's thought their performance enhancement is generated by enhancing athletes' running economy, i.e. reducing the energetic cost of running at a given speed, as an integrated carbon plate acts like a springboard, deforming and then springing back to propel the foot forwards. Instead of the main flex point being at the ball of the foot, it shifts backwards – like rolling the wheel of a diving board backwards in order to increase its bounce – therefore increasing the lever-arm through which force is applied. Super shoes are also extremely lightweight, and use a soft, bouncy foam which returns more energy to the runner than traditional foam, and may reduce fatiguing impact forces through the lower limbs.

As with any similarly dramatic innovation, it's likely the performance advantages of super shoes aren't completely risk-free for all runners. There is some concern that moving the flex point backwards could be putting more stress on parts of the foot that are less able to flex and absorb impact, including the tightly packed joints around the navicular bone. If you're trying out super shoes for the first time, build up wear time gradually to allow your body to adapt to the altered stresses. If you experience unusual pain or recurrent injuries when you're wearing the shoes, it may be that they're not right for you.

Socks

Socks are an essential but often-underappreciated part of running kit. They protect, support and cushion your feet, reduce rubbing and blisters, wick sweat away from the skin and regulate temperature. Running socks are made in the shape of your foot with extra padding under the forefoot, heel and around the ankle and often some support through the midfoot. The top of the sock is usually thinner and more breathable. Look for seamless toe construction to reduce the risk of rubbing.

Socks need to be durable, quick drying and stretchy, so they're usually made of nylon or polyester with elastane for stretch. Merino blended in with the synthetic fibres improves comfort, alongside Merino's naturally antimicrobial and thermoregulating properties.

Toe socks are increasingly popular, designed to produce a close fit that reduces moisture and friction between the toes. Some runners love them and others hate them, but if you do suffer from interdigital (between the toes) blisters, they're well worth a try.

Twin layer socks are designed to promote movement (and therefore friction) between the two layers of fabric, rather than between the foot, sock and shoe. This can be a good way of reducing the likelihood of blisters, but can also result in ruckling of the fabrics. Choosing a separate liner and oversock, specific to your requirements, is almost always a better option.

Waterproof socks can keep your feet dry more successfully than waterproof shoes as they come much further up your leg and it's not as easy for water to splash into them. They are often worn with thin liner socks but can be used on their own. Waterproof socks are also warm and windproof, so they can be useful in cold and dry environments as well as in the wet.

TOP TIPS FOR CHOOSING SUSTAINABLE RUNNING KIT

* **Choose fabrics carefully:** synthetic fabrics such as polyester and nylon are usually oil-based and don't biodegrade at the end of their life. They also tend to smell quickly. Recycled versions are only better if they're made by recycling old polyester clothing or fishing nets rather than using plastic bottles (which means new plastic bottles need to be made) and then recycled into new clothing at the end of their life.
* **Merino wool** is naturally antimicrobial – so doesn't smell – and biodegrades at the end of its life. Check it's from responsibly reared sheep.
* **Buy good quality kit** that you'll use a lot and which will last a long time. Care for your kit and it'll last even longer and perform better, too. Aim for versatility in your wardrobe, using a layering system to get the most out of every garment all year round.
* Rather than buying new, **buy and sell kit second-hand** through Facebook groups such Outdoor Gear Exchange UK and Running Gear Buy and Sell.

Equipment

Running packs

When you need to carry more than can fit in a pocket, a running-specific pack is the most comfortable and convenient way of carrying kit on a run. Usually designed in a vest-style that feels somewhere between clothing and a rucksack, they feature a combination of larger and smaller compartments and stretch holders on the back with zipped and open pockets on the front. Many also have zipped waist pockets for extra, easy-access storage. Available in storage volumes from 0.5 litres up to around 30 litres, there's a pack to suit every shape and need.

Well-designed packs will be adjustable to fit different body sizes and are often also available in different back lengths and those designed specifically for the female body. Good fit is really important for comfortable carrying, especially when you're running with heavier loads, and to reduce the risk of chafing.

If you're only carrying minimal kit, a soft, waistband-style pack with stretch and/or zipped pockets will allow you to carry food, a phone and sometimes even a lightweight jacket and poles. These are comfortable, packable and versatile.

Larger waist packs are also available, which carry up to around five litres of kit. This keeps the back free and will carry mandatory race kit of waterproofs, hat, gloves and nutrition; however, if you want to be able to carry liquid or much weight it's hard to stop them bouncing annoyingly.

You can run with a more traditional rucksack and some brands make rucksack-style packs designed for running, like Ultimate Direction's Fastpack series. The advantage of this style of pack is the larger capacity and ability to carry larger objects. These bags will often have zipped hip pockets which are accessible while running and you can add your own front-mounted chest pockets if the pack doesn't have them. Make sure that the pack has a chest strap if you want to be able to run with it.

With all packs, a variety of zipped and stretch pockets as well as a larger rear storage area allow you to organise your kit and reach important regularly used items on the go. Stretch stash pockets are useful for quickly stowing away a jacket or other items that you are likely to want again soon. If you use poles or if you run in winter conditions when you need to carry an ice axe, make sure that the pack can store these easily and accessibly.

Many packs use waterproof fabrics but almost none will have taped seams, so it is always a good idea to store anything that needs to stay dry in a plastic bag or waterproof dry bag. Super-light roll-top dry bags are durable, reliable and available in a range of sizes.

Carrying water

Having the ability to carry water (or other drinks) on the go is useful and, on longer, more remote runs, essential. The main options are soft flasks, which fit into the front pockets of a running pack, or a hydration bladder, which fits into a sleeve in the back and delivers water via a tube. Which option you go for depends on personal preference and the amount of water you need to carry.

Soft flasks are best suited to carrying up to a litre of water and come in sizes from 150 up to 750 millilitres. They're easy to access and drink from, and easy to refill without the need to remove your pack in order to do so.

Hydration bladders carry between one and three litres and sit in a sleeve within the pack. Water is heavy, so carrying larger volumes is more comfortable on the back. Bladders are less convenient to refill than soft flasks, as they require the drinking tube to be detached and the bladder removed from your pack. However, because they carry more water, you'll probably need to refill less often. In very cold weather, the water in the drinking tube can freeze, making it impossible to drink. Insulated tube covers are available, which help. Another top tip is to blow the water out of the tube and back into the bladder after each use, preventing it from freezing in the tube. The larger volume of water carried against your (warm) back in your pack means the water in the bladder itself is unlikely to freeze.

Another handy way to access water on the run is by using a purifying or filtering system, which can be a very portable bottle with an integrated filter, or a filter that can be attached to a bottle or soft flask. These are particularly useful if you're heading into areas where there's plenty of water in the landscape, such as lakes and streams, as you can drink safely and carry less water with you. Most filters will remove over 99.999 per cent of bacteria, parasites, microplastics, chemicals and organic matter. A water filter like this is also a good back-up for long-distance adventures or trips to areas where clean drinking water isn't always available.

Debris gaiters

If you're running on trails, especially if you're running or racing longer distances, debris gaiters are well worth considering. Made from super-lightweight fabric, they're held up by elasticated ankle cuffs and attach on to the laces of your shoes – and sometimes underneath the shoes too – creating a debris-proof seal around the tops of your shoes. When you're running anywhere with sand, grit, mud or even snow, they're a brilliant way to keep it out of your shoes and well away from your feet.

Poles

Running poles are made from aluminium or carbon fibre. Aluminium is cheaper and tough, but can bend. Carbon fibre is usually lighter and is very strong but will snap if stressed too much. Poles designed for trail running are telescopic or have a Z-fold system to allow them to be stashed away and carried when not in use. Telescopic poles slide into themselves which is neat and cheaper but results in a longer packed length, more weight, less reliability and slower deployment. Z-fold poles fold up quickly when the locking mechanism is released and deploy almost instantly; the poles can't collapse unless you release the locking mechanism, so they are very reliable.

Pole handles are made from foam, cork, rubber or a mixture. They offer an ergonomic design for comfort over many hours, insulation in cold weather and some shock absorption, but the specifics of the material and shape of the handles varies and will suit individual people differently. As the consequences of the wrong handle include discomfort, rubbing and an insecure grip, it's essential you get this right when choosing a set of poles. Some poles have a handle that extends down the shaft a bit; this is useful when climbing steep hills and stops you having to adjust the length of the pole.

Poles are available in a variety of lengths to suit your height and intended use. Some also have a degree of height adjustment to fine-tune the fit or to allow more than one person to use them effectively. To find the length you need, stand in your normal running shoes with your arm by your side and your elbow bent at 90 degrees to your body, then measure the distance from the ground to the top of your hand.

Should I use running poles?

Poles have gained popularity with runners in recent years, driven by the rise of mountain and ultra races. Used properly and in the right circumstances, running poles are invaluable, and can save your knees and quads a lot of battering on steep ground. While they do make you slightly less efficient – runners burn more calories overall when using poles than when not using poles – poles can aid balance and propulsion, as well as spread the load that would normally be carried by the lower body over the upper body as well.

Poles are most useful in runs or races with a substantial amount of ascent and descent, allowing you to use your arms to pull you up hills, and reduce the magnitude and the rate of forces experienced on the way back down. Additionally, poles can help with balance on rough terrain, especially when you're tired and liable to trip towards the end of a long run. If you're going to use poles in a race, train regularly with them for the six weeks beforehand in order to build the arm strength and technique required to use them effectively and efficiently. As well as practising poling on similar terrain to that you'll experience in a race, it's important to practise folding, unfolding and storing your poles on the go.

To store your poles on the go, they can be attached to a pack using the pack's pole loops; stashed in a quiver, which attaches next to your pack and is accessed over your shoulder; or

threaded through carry loops on a waistbelt. Practise running with your poles stored to make sure they're comfortable.

How to use poles

When using poles for propulsion, they can either be used alternately, driving back with the opposite arm to the leg, or together. The first method works best on less steep terrain, whereas the second is great for really steep climbs, when you can effectively haul yourself up using your arms. Using the wrist loops or, with some poles such as Leki's trail running range, the clip-in gloves, enables a secure attachment without needing to over-grip the handles. It also helps to avoid leaving a pole behind you when it gets stuck in mud, or accidentally dropping one off a mountain.

> For descending or crossing very technical ground and streams, it's often a good idea to unclip/loop the poles so they can be dropped safely in the event of a fall rather than being attached to you. This also allows you to shift your hand position to the top of the handle for descending, which is particularly useful with poles that don't have length adjustment.

Navigation

For information on the different smartphones, GPS watches and handheld GPS devices, see page 205.

Emergency kit

For longer runs and when you are off into more serious mountainous or remote areas, it's sensible to carry a few items of emergency kit just in case. These items often correspond to mandatory race kit.

Sim says:
'I carry a lightweight waterproof, basic first aid kit and an energy bar on almost every run, adding more kit if I'm out for longer or going somewhere more remote.'

Mandatory race kit

Some races require you to have certain items of kit – requirements designed to keep you safe and get you back to civilisation if something goes wrong. They are a good example of the minimum you should carry for your own running adventures of a similar distance over similar terrain. Road races don't normally have any kit requirements because if an emergency was to occur you are never far from help. At the other end of the scale, a multi-day, self-supported off-road race held in winter conditions, like the infamous Montane Winter Spine, could require around 30 different items. The Fell Runners Association has a mandatory minimum kit requirement for most of their medium or long races comprising:

* Waterproof whole-body cover (with taped seams and integrated attached hood)
* Hat and gloves
* Map of the route and compass (magnetic rather than electronic)
* Whistle
* Emergency food

This feels like a sensible minimum for most runs off road and away from easy emergency access.

Here are some other items of emergency kit you might want to consider, depending on the length, location and weather conditions of your run.

* It's worth carrying a basic **first aid kit** with you so that you can patch up cuts and dress blisters while you're out. Most outdoor first aid companies produce a small first aid kit designed for active sports. Once you have one you can often lighten it further by removing multiples of the same items and anything you're unlikely to need.

Sim says:

'My basic first aid kit weighs less than 90 grams; including its water-proof pouch.'

---

* If you get into trouble, then being able to call for and attract the attention of rescuers can make a bad situation better. Carry a **mobile phone** with enough battery to call for help. A mini **power bank** with enough power to charge your phone could be useful if you intend to use your phone while out on a run. A **whistle** will attract people's attention in any weather and light conditions; running packs often come with one attached. A **flashing torch** will guide people to you in the dark – very small and lightweight emergency lights are available with long battery lives.

The internationally recognised emergency signal is six blasts on the whistle or six flashes of a torch, repeated every minute.

* Even if you normally follow a route on an electronic device, or if you are following someone else or a marked route, carrying a **paper map and compass** and having the skills to use them could prevent problems.

* If something does go wrong when you're out running, and you have to stop and remain stationary for any length of time, some form of shelter can help prevent or delay hypothermia. A simple **foil blanket** is cheap, weighs about 50 grams and has a tiny pack size. If you're running in more exposed or remote conditions, a **foil bivvy bag** weighs about 100 grams – it isn't much bigger than a foil blanket but because you can get inside it will give much more protection than a blanket. If you're running with a group, more durable **survival shelters** or bothy bags are available from two-person up to 20-person sizes. These are great in an emergency providing protection from the elements and warming up the occupants quickly with the shared body heat; they are also useful if you take a break for food or navigation.

* A lightweight **waterproof jacket** is a good item to carry, as it will add the most protection and warmth for the weight. Other **spare clothes** can be handy too – a pair of waterproof trousers, an additional long-sleeve base layer, a microfleece or light insulated jacket. Storing your spare clothes in a lightweight waterproof bag means they stay dry until you need them.

Sim says:

'My lightest synthetic insulated jacket is lighter than my lightest micro-fleece and offers far more warmth – a useful thing to know as I didn't expect this until I weighed them.'

---

* Some **emergency food** – such as chocolate or an energy bar – stashed away in your pack can save a run from being a struggle, giving you a boost and picking you up from a low. High-energy food warms and cheers you up, an important boost if everything else is going wrong!

* A good **headtorch** means you can run when you want to and when life allows regardless of the light conditions and time of day. Headtorches need to be comfortable, and they mustn't bounce when running. The battery life needs to be long enough for anything you are likely to want to do. They need to be bright enough and have a beam pattern that allows you to run on the terrain you enjoy. If you're a road runner running on lit streets, then the primary aim is for you to be seen so you won't need as powerful a beam as an off-road runner navigating by torchlight.

The brightness of a headtorch is measured in *lumens*.

* For road or well-surfaced trails, around 200 lumens is perfectly adequate to see by.
* For off-road running on rough trails we prefer at least 400 lumens.
* If you also need to be able to navigate where it's useful to have a longer beam length, then we'd look for a torch with over 500 lumens.

Maintenance and repair

Taking good care of your kit and catching repairs early will give you the best return for your investment and help look after our planet.

Washing

In general, technical running kit washes best at 30 °C on a gentle cycle. Kit doesn't necessarily need washing after every run, especially if it's made from Merino wool or has an antibacterial treatment; simply hang it up to air and dry before the next run. Specific technical washing liquids are available which are particularly important to use with waterproof or weather-resistant fabrics. Once washed, reproofing waterproof fabrics with a non-toxic water-resistant treatment such as TX Direct from Nikwax or Repel from Grangers gives them a new lease of life. You don't need to tumble-dry running kit as it will dry quickly anyway, with the exception of down, which should be washed with a specialist down wash and then tumble-dried on low along with some tennis balls to encourage the down to reloft and regain its insulating properties. Shoes are best cleaned by hand with water and a brush; it's good to rinse out the inside as well to remove any grit.

Repairing at home

Repairing small holes or tears in normal running kit is fairly easy to do as long as you do it early; ignore them and they will get worse and become harder to mend. The strong fibres of polyester and nylon allow any holes to be sewn closed while wool or wool-mix fabrics will need darning. None of it is that hard to do, and there are plenty of videos available online to show you what will work best for the specific material you need to mend. It's a great feeling once it's done – you could even go with visible mending and show off your ingenuity with a contrasting colour patch or thread.

Waterproof fabrics are best fixed with tape or patches specifically designed for the type of fabric – these can be bought from outdoor shops. Holes in shoe uppers can be darned, patched or glued depending on the materials and position. ENGO patches – which are intended to prevent blisters – will repair worn-out heel linings. Soles can be glued back on using flexible shoe glue.

Repairing professionally

Many brands offer an in-house repair service for their own products. You can access these by contacting the brands directly or talking to the shop where you bought the kit. These repairs may be covered under warranty but in some cases you may be charged. There are some companies that repair outdoor kit from any brand for a reasonable charge. Several down clothing and sleeping bag manufacturers offer a wash and repair service. If the upper is in good condition some running shoes can be resoled either by the brand or by an independent repair company. Your local cobbler may be able to repair holes and soles on running shoes; they can also sew through tough fabric to repair packs.

End of life

If you have kit that is still in good condition but you no longer use, consider selling it on or giving it away to help out runners who would rather not buy new or are on a budget. Several companies and charities will take used clothing and reuse or recycle it for you.

14

Footcare for runners

Good footcare is paramount for runners. If our feet aren't in good working order, we won't be running anywhere. Getting into good habits, including caring for your skin and nails, and choosing the right socks and shoes for your feet, will keep you running comfortably for as many miles as you choose.

Blisters

Blisters are caused by friction, usually as a result of rubbing from your sock and/or shoe with forces generated by repetitively striking the ground with your foot. They occur when there's a large amount of friction over a relatively short time, with heat and moisture adding to the perfect conditions for blister development. Movement between the epidermis (the outer layer of skin) and the dermis (the inner layer of skin) causes loosening between the skin layers. Serum (a clear fluid), sometimes also containing blood, moves into the space created, resulting in the classic bubble of a blister that can range from tiny and inconsequential to huge and horrible.

Blisters start out as hotspots – that tingly sensation of discomfort from a rub point in a shoe – and can be caught in time, before they become blisters, if you stop and do something about them. Is there some grit in your shoe you can empty out, a crease in your sock you can remove, or do you need to tighten or retie your shoelaces to reduce movement of your foot in your shoe? Can you swap your shoes for a pair you know don't give you blisters? Are your socks too thick or too thin? Anything you can do at this point to prevent the rubbing from continuing will prevent an annoying blister from developing. If you develop a hotspot, remove the cause if you can, and cover the area with tape, a blister plaster or other adhesive skin protection such as moleskin. At the very least, apply some lubricant to the area before continuing.

Even if you take early action blisters can develop anyway, sometimes without us even noticing until they become painful. If you simply try to ignore a painful blister and keep running, you may end up with long-term skin damage, skin infections and even injuries caused by an altered running gait as you attempt to avoid the pain. Occasionally, there really is no choice but to grin and bear it, but always stop and deal with a blister at the earliest possible opportunity.

To pop or not to pop?

There's much debate over whether it's best to pop and drain blisters or leave them be. In general, if you're part way through a race and you can't remove whatever caused the blister in the first place, it's often best to pop and drain it. Leave it where it is and, even if you've covered it, it's likely the continuing friction will carry on damaging the skin, rupturing the blister in an uncontrolled and unhygienic way. Instead, clean the area with an alcohol wipe and, using a sterile needle or blade, make a tiny incision in the blister. Drain the fluid, clean the area again, cover with a clean, protective plaster and apply some lubricant. Once you're home, care for the blister by keeping it clean and regularly applying a fresh plaster until healed.

If a blister isn't going to be subjected to further trauma – for example if you've only found it at the end of a race and won't be running again for a few days, it's probably best to leave it alone. The bubble of the blister offers the perfect natural protection, cushioning the area and keeping its contents clean. Once the skin underneath has had time to heal, the outer layer of skin usually peels away, leaving the site as good as new.

Socks

Wearing two layers of socks – either a separate, lightweight liner sock with a normal running sock over the top or a twin-skin model – can help reduce friction on your skin by absorbing some of the movement that would otherwise occur at your skin between the two layers of fabric. Some people love this approach, while it doesn't work for others – it's worth a try.

Toe socks, such as Injinji, can help reduce interdigital blisters by reducing moisture and friction between your toes. If you're prone to this kind of blister, toe socks are well worth experimenting with, either as a lightweight liner under a 'normal' sock or as a standalone sock. Like twin-skin socks, toe socks divide opinion, so give them a good test before committing.

Top tips for preventing blisters

Take time perfecting the fit of your shoe, including buying the right shape and size, tying your shoelaces well, and choosing socks that offer sufficient protection without making the shoe too small. Classic blister locations caused by shoes are the little toes in shoes that are too narrow in the toe box, and at the heel in shoes that are too loose and therefore rub.

Practise good footcare in between runs, drying your feet well, including between your toes, and then applying a moisturiser such as shea butter to keep your skin flexible and in great condition.

Apply a good lubricant (we like Squirrel's Nut Butter) to your feet before long runs, paying particular attention to the higher-friction areas – usually the heels and the inside edge of the big toe and first metatarsophalangeal joint, as well as between the toes.

Act as soon as you feel a hotspot developing, applying a protective covering (such as a simple plaster) and some lubricant.

Never wear an untested pair of shoes, socks or a combination of the two on a long run or race. Try new things out on short training runs first.

Calluses

Along with blisters, calluses are also caused by friction. Calluses occur when there is intermittent friction over a longer period of time, usually regular running over weeks, months and even years. The pattern of calluses on your feet can tell you a lot about how your feet work during running. They're rarely symmetrical, giving a nice picture of which foot pronates or twists more as you run, and which toes curl over to weight-bear on the tips.

A callus is your body's way of protecting these hard-wear areas, reinforcing the skin to prevent future damage. This works well up to a point – you need to keep calluses in check to avoid them becoming sore and eventually developing blood blisters underneath the hard skin. Podiatrists remove calluses using a scalpel, but this can be a high-risk strategy if you're not trained in using a scalpel and/or trying to work on your own feet! The best way to gently remove a callus, without the risk of a surgical incision, is to soak your feet well in warm water and then scrape the callus off using a blunt scraper or even a fingernail. Doing this regularly, followed by applying a moisturiser (shea butter works brilliantly), will maintain your calluses so that they stay both protective and flexible.

Corns and verrucas

Corns are areas of thickened skin caused by intermittent friction. They tend to be flat against the outside of the skin but have a sharp point which digs into the lower layers of skin, causing pain. Corns can be painlessly removed by a podiatrist. Avoid corns by keeping your skin supple and moisturised.

Verrucas are caused by a virus and look like small, round areas, usually on the soles of the feet and often with dark spots in them. They are contagious, so should be covered when using communal areas such as swimming pools and changing rooms. If a verruca is troubling, visit a podiatrist who can offer treatment or advice. Otherwise, they usually go away on their own, but it can take several years.

Infections

The most common foot infection is athlete's foot – a fungal infection that tends to invade the dark, damp spaces between the toes – you'll usually notice itching and damage to the skin. Athlete's foot is easily treated with an antifungal cream, available from a pharmacist. Fungal nail infections are more difficult to shift, often requiring longer-term treatment.

Less common, but often more serious, are bacterial infections. Often occurring secondary to a fungal infection or other damage to the skin, and precipitated by the ideal bacterial breeding conditions of our shoes, bacterial infections can quickly spread and, if not treated quickly, can lead to sepsis. If you notice a painful, red, hot, swollen area on your foot, particularly if it's accompanied by red 'tracking' lines, seek urgent medical advice.

Trench foot

Trench foot occurs when feet are immersed in cold, damp, unsanitary conditions for long periods of time. Anyone who runs ultras in the UK is probably familiar with this scenario. As the foot gets cold, blood vessels constrict to preserve heat, depriving the foot and toes of blood flow and therefore nutrients and oxygen. Without good strategies to prevent and recognise the early signs of trench foot, the results can include numbness or heaviness, itching, white and deeply fissured skin, intense pain and a high risk of infection.

Trench foot was a huge problem in World War I. There were an estimated 75,000 cases amongst British soldiers; in severe cases it led to amputation and even death. Preventative measures were introduced once the condition was recognised as being different from frostbite, as trench foot occurs even without freezing temperatures. These included modifying footwear and applying grease to the feet to protect the skin from moisture.

Today, severe trench foot is rare, but long-term damage to the skin and nerves of the foot is common amongst those who undertake adventures in extreme environments. Long races in cold, damp weather, including the Winter Spine – and potentially even the Summer Spine – and ultras over the colder, damper months, can put you at risk. Notoriously damp music festivals like Glastonbury also see a few cases each year. But it's not something to take lightly: even mild trench foot can take many months for the skin to fully recover from, while nerve damage can be permanent.

How to prevent trench foot

If you know you're going to be spending an extended amount of time in cold, wet conditions, use a good barrier cream to protect your feet from moisture. Trench Foot Cream is specifically designed for runners, but other barrier creams, including those designed for nappy rash, also work well.

Apply the cream a day or so before the event to ensure the best protection, and then reapply at regular intervals during the event.

Waterproof socks can also add a highly effective barrier for lengthy wet-weather runs. Just make sure they're long enough so that water can't get in the top and, if you can, change them for dry pairs along the way.

If you are unlucky enough to develop trench foot, dry the area as soon as you can and rewarm it gently – rapid warming can cause intense pain and itching. Keep your feet clean, dry and warm and seek medical attention as soon as you can.

Toenails

In his excellent book *Fixing your Feet*, John Vonhof lists properly trimmed toenails as one of his three 'absolutes'. The others are moisture-wicking socks and wearing gaiters for running on trails. Trimming your toenails too little, too much or just badly can cause problems that really aren't worth the tiny bit of extra time it takes to do it properly. Toenails that are too long catch on your sock or the top of your shoe, causing painful, black and even ripped nails. Too short and your toes will lack protection and may get sore as you run, as well as increasing the risk of an ingrowing toenail.

A toenail turns black when repeated trauma from the front or top of the shoe has resulted in a blood blister beneath the nail. A nail often eventually falls off within a few weeks or months of going black, leaving a brand-new nail growing underneath. You may find repetitive nail trauma results in disfigured nails, which can be difficult to manage, in which case it's a good idea to visit a podiatrist. The same applies to ingrowing toenails, which can quickly become infected and extremely painful. Classic signs of an ingrowing toenail include heat, swelling and redness of the skin alongside the nail, and pain on squeezing the toe from the sides. When caught early, ingrowing toenails can be treated conservatively, but due to the risk of making things worse this is usually best done by a podiatrist. Advanced cases will need to have all or part of the nail removed under local anaesthetic by a specialist podiatrist.

How to cut your toenails

Invest in some trimmers specifically designed for toenails. These look a little like wire cutters, with long handles to give more leverage to cut thicker nails without damaging them.

Always cut nails straight across, leaving a small corner at each side. Don't cut the edges of the nail at an angle as this increases the risk of an ingrowing toenail.

Once you've finished cutting, give your nails a quick file – this is a great way to remove any rough edges or spikes, reducing the likelihood of catching and other damage.

15

Finding routes and giving something back

We've covered a lot of theory so far in this book. But, when it comes down to it, running is all about getting out there and experiencing the world. Running forges an entirely different relationship with the landscape than walking. Moving at speed, there's the leg-sapping nature of climbs; the exhilaration of a narrow ridge run; the thundering descents; the puzzle of crossing rocky, technical ground; and the pleasant softness of a forest path. A great running route not only takes you through beautiful, or at least intriguing, scenery; it thrills all your senses, challenges your strength and agility, and offers the opportunity for exploration – of a place and, often, of ourselves too. In this chapter, we offer some tips based on over a decade of researching and writing running routes for books, magazines and newspapers. We've also included some ideas for taking great running photos, and how to care for the beautiful places where we run.

Where to run?

Sim says:
> *'One of the many things that I love about running is exploration. I use running to find and link up the roads, cut-throughs and paths in my local town, to expand my knowledge of the local countryside, and to explore and immerse myself in a new place when I'm away from home. Over the years I've discovered wonderful places for family walks, interesting buildings and landmarks, shortcuts that I now use on my day-to-day journeys and beautiful pockets of nature, as well as some sections of trail that just feel amazing to run.'*

Finding routes has been an important part of our job for over a decade. Creating guidebooks on walking, running and other great adventures around Britain and further afield, devising enjoyable but ecologically sensitive routes for conservation organisations, and writing routes for magazines has taken us across the length and breadth of the UK in search of the very best. And, as we've gone, we've gradually got better at knowing where a good route might lie, glancing at a map to spot the telltale features we know will feel amazing on the run, knowing where to look for the best sources of information and inspiration. Here's our take on what makes a superb running route.

Underfoot terrain – this depends on what you're after; smooth uninterrupted tarmac or a track for concentrating on the kilometres and specific speed training. Gentle grassy trails for minimal impact, easy recovery running. Well-made mountain trails for amazing scenery without having to watch your feet. Or rough, rocky and muddy trails for fully engaged, step-by-step technical running.

Views – running somewhere spectacular can make the run memorable if the underfoot terrain allows you to look around.

Gradient – hills are great but sometimes you want a flatter run to bank some easy miles or train at specific speeds. You need to match the length, steepness and underfoot technicality of the hills to the type of run you fancy or what your training plan specifies.

Navigation – do you want to just run or is a bit of route finding a bonus? A run chosen for difficult navigation might be a good route if you're training for self-navigation races or challenges. Maybe the navigation function on your GPS watch means you can run a new route without worrying about navigation – just watch out for your battery life.

Practicalities – how do you get to the start and how do you get home when you finish? How important is a cafe or shop en route and do you need to make sure there is a toilet stop available?

Tips for finding great running routes
Local runners and running clubs
Joining a club or running with a knowledgeable local is a great way to find the best routes. Local runners, more so than local walkers, will know which roads or trails are most fun to run and where the best places for specific training sessions are.

Guidebooks
Running guidebooks should point you in the direction of some of the best trails in the local area. Walking and cycling guides are useful and will give more route suggestions but their authors won't have been thinking about the specific terrain and gradient requirements that make a route brilliant to run.

Magazines
Most running and in particular trail or off-road running magazines include a routes section in each issue. These are normally archived online and are a great resource for finding running routes.

Online mapping apps
Most online mapping programmes and apps allow you to search for routes created by organisations and other users. Some like OS Maps, Komoot and Strava allow you to search for running-specific routes and highlight popular sections or points of interest along the way.

Paper maps
A detailed map of the local area should show you the layout of the roads and trails. Rights of way across the countryside will be shown as well as waymarked trails and landscape features like rivers, valleys and hills that could create good running routes.

Race routes
Routes used for running races are often available from the race website and are fun to run in training. Do make sure that the route doesn't cross private land as the race may have permission to use land that isn't normally accessible.

Classic routes
Well-known long-distance trails like the Pennine Way and the South West Coast Path in the UK or the Tour du Mont Blanc in the European Alps are good places to find amazing running. Also look for the classic ascent paths of hills and mountains for tough but rewarding out-and-back adventures.

Homemade routes
Devising your own routes is all part of the fun and adventure of running. It could be as easy as following the road or path from your door and seeing where you end up, but there are landscape features and tips to help make finding a good route more likely. We look for features to circumnavigate like running around a lake or a strong linear feature like a section of coast or river

path to follow. You can then return the same way or look for an alternative way of getting back to the start. Try picking a local hilltop or mountain summit and find a route that takes you there. Valleys often provide an obvious horseshoe-shaped route where you follow one of the ridgelines up to the head of the valley and then the opposite ridgeline back to the start. You could start somewhere accessible by public transport and run back. Sometimes it's fun to run to a point of interest and back or create a route that passes a series of these; this can be a great way of sightseeing in a city.

Tips for taking great running photos

* **Get the light right:** light is everything in photography – get this right and you're almost guaranteed a great picture. The best times for that lovely, luminous light that makes colours sing but doesn't overexpose your image are mornings and evenings on clear days.
* **Dress for the occasion:** runners wearing brightly coloured clothes look good in photos and stand out – or 'pop' in photographer speak – against the background. Red and orange are usually winners.
* **Take lots of photos:** there's a strange thing that happens when you photograph runners throughout the running gait cycle. At some points, usually during the airborne or propulsive moments, they look great – strong, athletic, adventurous. One frame later, however, and things couldn't be more different as gravity sucks everything downwards and our previously dynamic runner better resembles a sack of potatoes. To get the best out of your running photos (and stay friends with your models), use a camera with a rapid-fire mode to allow you to capture those fleeting moments of awesomeness. Then delete the rest!
* **Consider a tripod:** to shoot the best selfies, especially in places where the terrain is rugged and uneven, a tripod is a great investment. From a larger, heavier version, which will give you the best view and

stability but is harder to carry, to lightweight pocket-sized versions, they'll save you time compared with trying to prop your phone or camera up somewhere that works, and you'll get far better results.
* **Find a new angle:** it's easy to stand at the side of a trail and take out-and-back shots, but the most magical photos often come from getting inventive. Lie on the trail, get runners to jump over the camera, find an interesting plant or rock for the foreground, frame your runner away from the easy centre spot, and play with focus to create some really interesting and different photos.

Running and reciprocity

Each time we run on a beautiful trail, admire a view or encounter the generosity of others in some way during our running, we're taking from the people and places around us and benefiting from it. It's easy to view the world as being ours to run in; ours to experience as we choose to. But if we don't reciprocate – give something back now and then – why should we assume things will always remain this way? If everyone simply continues to take, eventually there will be nothing left.

Giving back, whenever we can, is essential. Whether it's a friendly word or smile to another runner, helping out with conservation work on a trail, volunteering at a race or contributing funds or a signature to a campaign to make things better, each action helps to make running better. Pick up litter, have compassion for the people you meet – you've no idea what kind of day they're having, rescue an insect, appreciate your surroundings. As runners we can be the eyes and ears of the wild places we love, taking action when we see potentially damaging behaviours and raising awareness of issues as we come across them.

16

Navigation

The main aim of navigation while running is to be able to follow a pre-set route or reach a destination safely and efficiently. You must weigh up the advantages of precise navigation with the disadvantage that it will slow down your pace. Therefore, the majority of navigation used on a run could be termed as *rough navigation*; it can still be fairly accurate, but it is a constant evaluation of all the factors affecting your movement across the terrain rather than concentrating on the straightest line or most accurate following of your route.

To navigate well on a run, you need to practise using a map and compass regularly, so navigation and route choice becomes intuitive. You'll learn to make quick decisions about the best route choice from one point to the next based on the relevant factors at the time.

There's a host of electronic mapping devices and apps available, which we will discuss later. But, to travel safely and confidently in the hills, you still need to be able to navigate with a paper map and compass. Some races and events allow electronic aids, and some don't, but if you're out on your own adventure, having the skills to use a paper map which doesn't rely on batteries, a phone signal or a touchscreen that functions with freezing wet hands is essential. If you aren't able to pre-plan the route, a paper map is also often the quickest and easiest way of navigating as the size of the screen on electronic devices means you can't see all of the route options easily.

METRIC OR IMPERIAL?

In the UK, all maps use metric measurements so many people find it easiest to do the same: if you can start out measuring everything in kilometres and metres rather than miles and yards, learning to navigate is much easier. Set the units on any electronic devices to metric as well so that everything matches. If you still prefer miles for logging training – like Jen does – that's of course fine!

Maps

In the UK there are four main paper-based maps to choose from – see the table below for a summary.

	Scale	1km in real life is equivalent to	Contour line spacing	Index contour interval
OS Explorer	1:25,000	4cm	5m (10m on high land)	50m
OS Landranger	1:50,000	2cm	10m	50m
Harvey British Mountain Map and Ultramap	1:40,000	2.5cm	15m	75m
Harvey Superwalker	1:25,000	4cm	15m	75m

Types of maps available in the UK.

Ordnance Survey (OS) Explorer maps include a lot of detail and are very good to run with. OS Landranger maps have less detail and crucially for runners don't include some smaller paths or field boundaries and fence lines – all of which are extremely useful. We don't recommend using the Landranger series to run with. Harvey maps have fewer symbols and wider contour line spacing – which means they look a little less cluttered – and the features they do have are useful, so these maps are good for running with. Many races and mountain marathons use Harvey maps, so it is good to be familiar with them.

Grid references

All these maps use the standard British grid system – it allows you to give someone an exact location anywhere in the British Isles which they can then navigate to. Or it allows you to check with an app like OS Locate or a GPS device exactly where you are and then find that on a map. In some races, checkpoint locations will be given to you in the form of a grid reference which you will then need to plot before you can decide on the best route to get there.

A **six-figure grid reference** (e.g. SK 246 844) is made up of the following elements:

* two letters (in this case SK), which identify the area on the National Grid in the UK (these are shown in the corner of all maps),
* six numbers (the first three showing eastings – which represent the west–east location – and the second three showing northings – which represent the south–north location), to give you the exact location on the map.

Six-figure grid references (which identify a 100-metre square) should give you enough information to find a checkpoint and you can still accurately identify them on a normal-scale paper map.

All types of UK maps we've discussed have one-kilometre grid squares marked on them – these enable you to roughly judge the distance between points. Over time you will learn roughly how long it will take you to travel that distance over a specific type of terrain so you should know roughly how long it will take you to travel from one point to the next. This is very helpful when out running – if you expect to reach a certain point in roughly 20 minutes and you reach it in 10 minutes check you are where you think you are. Or if you've been running for 30 minutes and still haven't reached it, stop and check, as you may have missed it. Catching navigation errors early can save a lot of time and distance in the long run.

Contour lines

These are shown on maps as continual lines of equal height. The numbers written on the contour lines show the height above sea level and always 'read uphill' – i.e. the top of the number faces uphill. There are darker *index contours* (every 50 or 75 metres) shown too. The contour lines show both how high and how steep a slope is; you can count the number of contour lines on a slope to measure its height. A steep slope is represented by close contour lines; widely spaced contours represent a shallow slope. With time and practice you will become able to visualise a landscape from the contour lines drawn on a map, a skill that is very handy when planning a running route.

Symbols

While you are getting used to a map check the key for any symbols that you don't know the meaning of – you will soon get to know all the relevant ones and it helps make map reading more intuitive when you know what the symbols all mean. Key symbols for runners in the UK include:

* Designated rights of way (footpaths, bridleways and byways).
* Other trails (tracks, roads and paths).
* Walls, fences and field boundaries.
* The boundary of open access land (this is handy as when you are on open access land you aren't restricted to rights of way).

* Trig points (usually on the summits of hills).
* Types of terrain (trees, cliffs, scree and bog) – these are useful clues as to the ease of running across an area and can help with route choice.
* Landmarks that can be seen from a distance (masts, wind turbines, telegraph poles and churches with towers or spires) can be useful to locate yourself on a map.

Carrying your map

A map is only useful if it's to hand, either literally in your hand or in a pocket that you can access without breaking stride. You therefore need your map to be weatherproof so that you continue to use it in bad weather. Harvey maps are printed on lightweight waterproof paper which is excellent. OS maps are available in a waterproof version, but the laminate is stiff and much bulkier than Harvey maps. Map cases can be annoying, as you will soon run off the edge and have to remove and refold the map to continue to use the case. If you subscribe to OS Maps online, you can print the sections of map that you need for a run. You can laminate these and then you have small, relevant and weatherproof maps ready for any adventure.

Compass

You also need a compass, and like the map it needs to be easily available, ideally in your hand. A standard baseplate-style compass is perfectly serviceable for the runner, but specialist running compass are also available and can make life easier. Running compasses have a wider needle which is both more obvious to look at and has a stronger magnet making the needle faster and more stable (it will point to north more quickly with less swinging). A thumb compass can be worn over the thumb and wrist which means the compass is always visible; it also keeps your hands free for holding the map and doing other things like eating. See page 204 for advice about how to take a compass bearing.

Map reading as you run

Now you've chosen your map and compass, studied the map key and worked out how to carry them, you need to get out there and use them. Typically, you will have a pre-planned route to follow – this could be a race route, a guidebook suggestion or one of your own making (see pages 196–197 for some tips). It's a good idea to draw the route on to your map or print the map with the route already plotted. This means you can follow where you are on the route more easily as you run.

The most important thing when map reading is orientating your map so that it is pointing in the correct direction. This means that the features in front of you should match the features displayed on the map. The top of the map is always north and all normal words are written west to east. The vertical grid lines drawn on the map run south to north, so you simply have to align these lines with the north arrow of your compass. Turn the map in your hand so that the map is pointed towards north and the features in front of you should match the map.

> Always keep the map orientated when you are looking at it. Failure to do this results in most navigation errors.

When you are running it's important to know where you are on the map; it's much easier to keep track of this rather than having to work it out whenever you look. You should know where you started from so keep track of your position by moving your thumb along the route as you move, this way your thumb is always pointing to your current position on the map. If you also keep the map orientated, you will make navigation much easier for yourself.

Following a route

When following a pre-planned route, you will have to deal with the terrain that you encounter – the most important things are to know where you are on the route and to stay on the route. The map will show you features that you will pass or follow as symbols on the map, the shape of the ground represented by contour lines, and the distance that you need to travel between points worked out roughly from the one-kilometre grid squares.

When following a route and keeping your position on the map, look for obvious features that you should come across like a stream, track, wall, summit, path junction or slope. Mentally tick these off as you pass them, moving your thumb on the map as you move to keep track of where you are.

> Think of these features as **checkpoints** on your route – use them to regularly confirm where you are and that you are still on route. Make sure you know roughly how far they are from the last point and if you should be running uphill, downhill or on the flat between them. All of this information will help you stay on route and also help you spot any errors quickly.

If something doesn't feel right don't just carry on hoping it will be OK; stop and check the map more carefully, work out where you are and then carry on with confidence. A simple app on your phone or a GPS device that gives you your grid reference (this is not allowed in some races and events) will allow you to double-check exactly where you are which can be very helpful to ensure that you are still on route.

Route planning for self-navigation events

If you are competing in an event where navigation is part of the challenge, you may be given a map of the checkpoints you have to visit but no specific route to follow, or you may simply be given the location (probably a grid reference) of the checkpoints or finish point. You will then have to decide on your route between specified points. Here are some factors you'll want to consider.

* Height gain or loss on the section – speed decreases and effort increases with ascent.
* Availability of fast roads or trails – if surfaced trails are close by and heading in the correct direction the extra distance taken to reach them can be made up by the speed and ease of running on them.
* The underfoot terrain – choosing a route that avoids slow terrain like bogs and favours easier terrain like close-cropped moorland grass could make the leg faster even if the distance is further.
* The weather, in particular wind speed and direction – you may need to avoid exposed areas or ridges due to high winds. More sheltered valley running may stop you getting cold and allow you to run faster overall.
* Very steep ground – at some point, however fit you are, you will have to walk when a slope (either uphill or downhill) becomes too steep. Steep slopes can also cause greater fatigue than making the same ascent on shallower longer slopes.
* Ease of navigation – if one route option is easy to navigate (e.g. following a fence line) it can be quicker than a shorter route that requires more concentration and accurate navigation.

* Any obstacles that cannot be crossed – e.g. rivers, cliffs or private land – which force route choice.

Rough navigation

Most running navigation could be termed as *rough navigation* – you follow fairly accurate but not exact directions between features, making use of the information on the map and what you can see around you. With practice you can route plan and follow the directions while running or at the least walking, so you maintain a good average pace. In some cases when you need to find a hidden or exact point, you need to slow down and navigate more precisely – this is *micro navigation* (see page 204). This can also be the case in bad weather when visibility is poor or on more dangerous terrain where straying off the route could be problematic.

To follow your route and make navigation as easy as possible, there are several features and techniques you can employ using the information shown on OS Explorer or Harvey maps.

Handrails are physical features that you can follow while running. It could be a path, road, stream or wall. Or the edge of an area of woodland, a lake or the coast. Also, it could be a landscape feature like a ridge line or valley bottom. In some cases, it could simply be running downhill or uphill.

Catch features are physical features that you will reach either on the way to a checkpoint or shortly after a checkpoint. A good example would be a road or river running across your direction of travel. You may not know exactly where on the catch feature you are, but you should be very confident of hitting it at some point. The catch feature then gives you a reference point to work from, or, if it is after the checkpoint, it prevents you from going too far wrong.

Tick-off features are points on your route that are easily identifiable and therefore give you a precise location on the map. These could be things like a trig point, a lake or pond, a bridge or a path junction. Another example is a significant corner in an otherwise straight fence, path or river. Tick these off as you run between two points to ensure that you are on route.

Attack points are points that you intend to reach when you move from rough navigation to accurate micro navigation. An attack point is often used if you can follow a handrail for the duration of a section between checkpoints but a short final section has no handrail or catch features, so you have to be very accurate to find it. Once you reach the catch feature or point you have identified as your attack point you stop and take an accurate bearing from there to the checkpoint and run on a compass bearing for the last section.

Aiming off is where it makes sense to aim to one side of the point you are attempting to reach. It's most useful in bad weather when visibility is poor. For example, if you need to reach a wall corner, aim to the right of the corner. Then, when you hit the wall (a catch feature), you'll know to turn left and follow the wall (a handrail) to reach the wall corner. If you aimed straight at the corner but missed and strayed slightly left, you may miss the wall altogether and therefore find it much harder to get back to the correct place.

Micro navigation

When rough navigation is not accurate enough, switch to micro navigation. Micro navigation is most accurate over short distances (less than one kilometre and ideally less than 500 metres) when any small inaccuracies are not amplified by distance. It involves following compass bearings from one point to the next. Remember to continue to look at distances, timings and things like catch features as a backup in case you miss the checkpoint.

TAKING A COMPASS BEARING

* Align the side of a baseplate compass on the map from where you are to where you want to go. This could be the final destination, if it isn't too far away, or an attack point between your current position and the end point. Make a mental note of the rough distance to this point so that you know how long it should take – remember you will be travelling more slowly than normal when moving on a bearing.
* Keeping the edge lined up, turn the bezel so that the north–south lines on the compass face match the north–south grid lines on the map.
* Take the compass off the map and turn the whole compass (not the bezel) until the red north needle is pointing exactly at the north point marked on the bezel.
* The direction that you need to travel is now indicated by the big arrow on the baseplate.
* Look along the arrow to spot a feature in the landscape that you can move towards – this is easier than trying to travel by following the bearing by looking at the compass. If you have good visibility this could be a feature on the horizon; in poor visibility it could be a tuft of grass 10 metres away. Keep the compass in your hand and follow it until you reach the next known point where you can take another bearing. Remember the distance and roughly how long it should take to help find the next point. Continue like this to your destination.

Electronic navigation aids

The skills to use a paper map and compass are very important but you don't have to use them for every run. There are a host of electronic navigation aids that can help you follow a route or make it easier to work out exactly where you are if you get a bit confused when out for a run. At home, computer-based mapping software is easy to use and provides an amazing resource for route planning and inspiration.

OS Maps online mapping is available for the whole of the UK at 1:25,000, 1:50,000 and smaller-scale regional overview levels, as well as satellite images and basic street view mapping. It's relatively cheap and allows you to plan your own routes or view routes created by other people, organisations and races. There is also a 3D fly-through feature, so you can enjoy the ultimate in armchair-based route planning! You can then save the route as a GPX file and put it on to an electronic mapping device, or print it out and take it with you.

There's a range of other mapping and navigation apps available. The ever-popular **Strava** allows you to compare your times on local Segments with other runners. Strava's Heatmap is also a great feature, offering an insight into the most popular running routes in any given area.

Komoot is a mobile app that allows you to plan your own route, find existing routes and navigate on the go. Highlights, top tips and recommendations mean you can tap into shared community knowledge, but the emphasis is far more on adventure and exploration, rather than Strava's more competitive, comparative nature. Komoot offers worldwide coverage, with over 35 million users, so it's a great choice if you're heading somewhere new and looking for recommended routes to run, complete with things to see and places to stop to refuel, terrain information and beautiful photos for each adventure.

Smartphones

When out running a smartphone makes a great handheld navigation aid. You can view and download maps and view your current location – we tend to use a combination of the OS Maps app for its detailed 1:25,000 mapping and Komoot for its voice directions, local recommendations and clever route-finding algorithms. You can download maps and routes on to the phone so that it still works if you run out of signal. This works very well but it can drain your battery fast, so if it runs out you have no mapping and no way of calling for help. We always take a portable power pack with us on longer adventures so we can recharge our phones on the go. Smartphones are also very expensive and not really designed for bad weather; if you are reluctant to get your phone out because it's raining and it's your main navigation tool, then you're quite likely to go the wrong way. If you're using your phone for navigation in bad weather, invest in a good-quality shockproof and waterproof phone cover to keep your phone safe and dry.

GPS watches

You can load a GPX file on to a GPS watch and then use it to help you to follow a route. A very simple map is displayed on the watch face, typically with an arrow following the route line. These are very useful for a quick check to make sure you are following the pre-set route but don't give you very much extra information. You can normally set an alarm to warn you if you are going off route which can be very helpful if you are following a marked course where navigation shouldn't be necessary, but you manage to miss a marker and make a wrong turn. Watches will also record where you have been along with your speed, distance and elevation data which can be useful for training.

Handheld GPS units

These tend to have a better battery life and weather resistance than a smartphone. The screens are normally designed to be used with gloves and they often have buttons which are much easier to use than touchscreens with cold and wet hands. They also separate your phone from your navigation device so you can keep your phone warm, dry and charged – ready for an emergency. Most handheld GPS units allow you to load mapping software on to them, and therefore view a useful map of your location enabling informed route choices. You can upload GPX files on to the device and follow a pre-planned route, and also record a route you run for future use.

VI

Training plans and workouts

17

How to build your perfect training plan

It's easy to find generic training plans in books and online. But this one-size-fits-all approach doesn't work for everyone, and may not work perfectly for anyone. By taking all the essential ingredients of a great training plan, and tailoring it to your specific requirements, you can make sure you're maximising your available time and energy in pursuit of your individual running goals. This section will take you through how to create a training plan that's uniquely designed for you. You'll find some completed examples of one week of a training plan for different distances on pages 216–217.

Training phases

An effective training plan combines your **training volume** (the total distance or duration you run) with training sessions of varying intensities to create an overall **training load**. This load is distributed over time, ensuring you get the key training sessions and rest/recovery at the best times to stimulate the adaptations you need to achieve your running goals – all in a way that fits around the rest of your life.

If you're training for a specific race or races, the concept of **periodisation** means your training is shaped in a way that builds in both volume and specificity as you approach your race, so you're as prepared as you can be when you line up at the start. Training is divided into separate *phases*, with each phase having a specific purpose in the grand plan of peaking both fitness and readiness to race on race day. Here are the phases.

Base phase: beginning 16 weeks before your goal race, your base phase begins wherever you are when you start the programme. The purpose of this phase is to get you used to running regularly again if you've had some time off, and to begin the process of mental and physical preparation for racing. During this phase, establishing a good strength and mobility routine (two or three days each week) is also essential, creating a resilient base on which to build your training.

Build phase: With 12 weeks to go, and a good base of fitness established, you'll move into your build phase, which gradually and systematically increases your training load over the next six weeks. Increases in volume (duration or distance) and intensity are addressed in separate weeks, to avoid increasing overall load (and therefore risk of injury or burnout) too rapidly over too short a time. While there are many exceptions, the 10 per cent rule is a good guide – increasing your overall training load by no more than 10 per cent each week.

During this phase, *specificity* for your race also increases. If you're training for a marathon or ultra, your long runs will gradually increase in distance to reflect this. If you're training for a new 5K or 10K personal best, you'll be doing more time trials and tempo runs, ensuring you're building the readiness for the specific demands of race day.

Strength and mobility work two or three days each week supports the stresses and adaptations your body is going through during this phase.

Peak phase: with six weeks until race day, you'll switch to the weeks that combine your highest mileage with the sessions that are most specific to race day. For marathon and ultramarathon runners, this is when you'll run your longest long runs and, if you're aiming for a race with a lot of climbing and descending, your hilliest hilly runs. It's also when the non-running aspects of good rest, recovery, nutrition and hydration also really come into their own.

Strength and mobility workouts twice a week continue to provide resilience during these highest volume weeks.

Taper phase: preferences for the amount and duration of the taper phase vary between individuals and depending on the race you're preparing for. However, to optimise the hard-won adaptations from your weeks of training, and maximise your recovery and readiness to race, a two-week taper that reduces training volume by 40 per cent of your peak phase in the first week, and 60 per cent in the second week, has good evidence to back up its efficacy.

Prioritise reducing volume rather than intensity during this time, especially if you're training for a shorter, faster race, in order to maintain the speed of muscle recruitment and leg turnover. Continuing with some light strength and mobility work during your taper is also beneficial.

Easy weeks: throughout your 16-week training plan, it's important to include some weeks where you drop back your training a little to allow for some extra recovery and adaptation time as the stresses on your body increase. Many off-the-shelf training plans schedule in a recovery week every third or fourth week, but in reality this rigidity isn't often beneficial. As you go through your training, listen to your body and its cues that you're pushing just a little too hard, or not quite recovering enough.

SIGNS YOU NEED TO TAKE AN EASY WEEK

If you're getting pain or niggles, dreading training for several days in a row, struggling to sleep or struggling to wake up, being grumpy or irritable, or if your metrics suggest it (consistently elevated resting heart rate and/or consistently low resting HRV taken first thing in the morning before getting up), make it an easy week. This reactive, rather than prescriptive, approach, based on listening to your body's signals rather than following a generic plan set by someone who's never met you, is the most effective for optimising both training and recovery.

Figure 1 shows a typical training cycle. The four phases are shown, along with the percentage of maximum **training volume** each week.

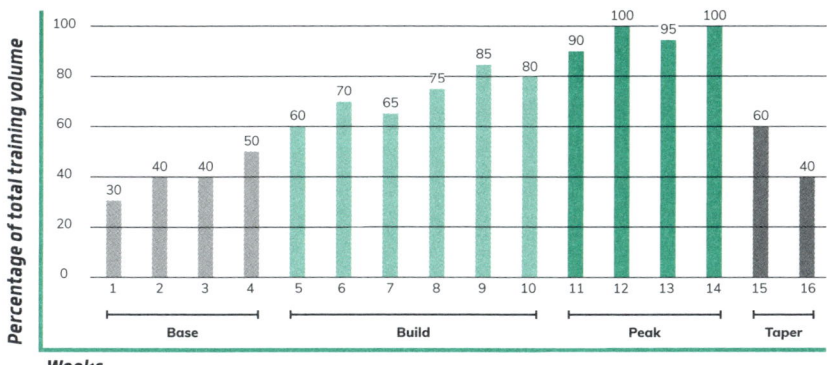

Figure 1 – a typical training cycle showing training volume over the four phases (base, build, peak and taper) leading up to race day.

Training load

Your training load is the total stress of all your training – running and otherwise. It's a combination of your **training volume** (the total distance or duration) and **training intensity** (including faster running and elevation gain) and varies over the various phases of your training programme, increasing gradually during your build phase and peaking during the final weeks before your taper down to race day. We'll go into the specifics of training volume and training intensity later on in this chapter.

Training load is the main factor to consider when you're planning your training. Too much and you risk injury and depletion; too little and you won't stimulate the desired adaptations to training. Don't forget that walking the dog, commuting to work, physical jobs and running after kids all add to your overall load.

Quantifying training load

Once you're in the midst of your training, you can 'feel' the effects of your training load both physically and psychologically, and adjust accordingly, increasing it if you're feeling sprightly and decreasing it if you're feeling fatigued. This is similar to using RPE (rate of perceived exertion – see page 82) for individual training sessions, but applied to your overall sense of how your training load is affecting your body and mind.

Apps and wearable devices quantify training load differently, all with the aim of offering advice on when you should be pushing harder and when to back off and take extra rest. The most common metric used for quantifying training stress, used by Garmin, TrainingPeaks and other platforms, is Training Stress Score (TSS). TSS was originally developed for cyclists, using power data easily obtained from bikes. The running version – rTSS – uses pace instead of power. Calculated using data on the duration, pace and elevation of your run, recorded by your watch or other device, an algorithm designed to account for the specific physical demands of running determines an appropriate rTSS score for each workout. Based on this, and depending on the platform you're using, recommendations for how your training should progress will be made. Weekly rTSS scores can range from 220 for a low-volume 5K runner to over 1,000 for a high-volume ultrarunner.

Training stress scores can be helpful in judging overall training load, especially if you train on terrain with significant elevation, when the distance and duration of your training alone doesn't provide an accurate picture of physical work undertaken. However, as with any digital metric, numbers are only approximations of real life, and so should always be taken into account alongside subjective measures of how you're feeling.

Training volume

Your training volume is the total time or distance you train each week. Whether you record this in miles, kilometres or hours and minutes, or a mixture of these, is up to personal preference. Your training volume will necessarily be determined by:

* How much you *should* run, based on the phase of training you're in and your personal running, health and injury history.
* How much you *want* to run, based on your motivation and goals.
* How much you *can* run, based on everything else you've got going on in your life.

Typically, training volume will increase as you move through the phases of your training, peaking during the final few weeks before your race and then reducing substantially during your taper.

Table 2 gives you an idea of the training volume you can expect to need to put in during the build and peak phases of your training for different goal distances. Be realistic about how much time you can devote, and build your training plan accordingly. Don't forget to factor in time for strength and mobility work (see page 215).

Race distance	Training volume	Distance per week (miles)	Time per week (hours)
5K	Low	8–10	1.5–3
	Medium	15–25	3–4
	High	40–50	5–8
10K	Low	10–15	2–3
	Medium	20–30	4–5
	High	50–60	7–9
Half marathon	Low	15–25	3–5
	Medium	30–40	5–7
	High	60–70	8–10
Marathon	Low	25–35	6–7
	Medium	35–60	7–10
	High	80+	10+
Ultramarathon	Low	30–40	6–8
	Medium	50–60	8–12
	High	80–120	12+

Table 2 – suggested distance and time per week (i.e. your training volume) for different race goals.

If your current training volume is significantly lower than the training volume suggested in table 2, it's essential that you build up gradually in order to minimise the risk of injury and maximise adaptations to the new training load. Going from zero to the suggested volume for an advanced runner in the space of a week won't make you an advanced runner, only an injured one, but building up gradually over months and years will. The table shows running only, and doesn't include time spent doing other activities such as cross-training or strength and mobility, which can add a significant number of extra hours to your overall training load.

Percentage of training at:	Low intensity	Moderate intensity	High intensity
Base	80%	15%	5%
Build	80%	10%	10%
Peak	70%	10%	20%
Taper	50%	10%	40%

Table 3 – suggested intensity distribution for 5–10K.

Percentage of training at:	Low intensity	Moderate intensity	High intensity
Base	80%	15%	5%
Build	80%	10%	10%
Peak	70%	15%	15%
Taper	50%	20%	30%

Table 4 – suggested intensity distribution for a half marathon.

Training intensity

Including a range of different intensities in your training stimulates adaptations across the body's different energy systems and muscle fibre types. This makes you a more efficient, adaptable, resilient runner and avoids the common pitfall of running all your runs at the same mid-range pace. The suggested training intensity distributions in this section are guided by the 80:20 principle, which says that for optimal improvements, 80 per cent of your training should be lower intensity, and 20 per cent should be higher intensity. You can judge the intensity of your training by feel – using RPE or the talk test (see page 82) – or by heart rate (see page 83).

As with your training volume, your training intensity should change over the course of your training programme, varying in the percentage of training you undertake at lower and higher intensities depending on the phase of training you're in, and the race you're training for.

Tables 3–6 suggest the percentage of time you should spend at each intensity according to training phase and race distance.

Percentage of training at:	Low intensity	Moderate intensity	High intensity
Base	80%	10%	10%
Build	80%	10%	10%
Peak	70%	20%	10%
Taper	50%	25%	25%

Table 5 – suggested intensity distribution for a marathon.

Percentage of training at:	Low intensity	Moderate intensity	High intensity
Base	80%	15%	5%
Build	70%	10%	20%
Peak	90%	5%	5%
Taper	50%	25%	25%

Table 6 – suggested intensity distribution for an ultramarathon.

Workouts at different intensities

An effective training plan includes a range of different workouts that keeps things interesting, and therefore keeps you engaged in your training, while varying the stresses on your body. Workouts at different intensities target different energy and physiological systems like muscle fibre recruitment, making you a stronger, faster and more efficient runner. This incorporates the **periodisation** necessary to reach your race goals. Introduce some **specificity** too (e.g. if your race is on trails, do plenty of training on trails).

All running workouts should start with a thorough **warm-up** and end with a thorough **cool-down** to allow your body to cope with the stresses being placed upon it, improving the quality of your run and reducing injury risk. Depending on individual factors (some runners feel they need longer to warm up than others) and the conditions and intensity of your run (you'll need longer to warm up and cool down in colder weather and for higher-intensity sessions) this could vary from 10 to 30 minutes.

Table 7 shows the various workouts you can choose from, along with which intensity they are and the page number for a full description.

Workout	Intensity	Page
Long slow run	Low	219
Steady-state run	Moderate	220
Interval training	High	221
Hill repeats	High	222
Fartlek	Variable	223
Strides	High	223
Tempo run	High	224
Progression run	Variable	224
Time trial	High	225
Easy/recovery run	Low	226
Cross-training	Variable	227

Table 7 – the workouts.

Building your perfect training plan

This guide will take you through the step-by-step
process of creating a 16-week training plan, culmina-
ting in a goal race. Using the information from earlier
on in this chapter, you'll design a plan that takes you
from your base starting point, through a gradual build
that increases in both training load and specificity,
peaking ready for your race. If you have fewer than 16
weeks to go, you can see where your training volume
should be using figure 1 on page 211. This plan can be
used for a single goal race, or multiple times in a year.

Step 1: calculate your availability – for those of
us who aren't full-time athletes, how much we can
train is often determined by how much time we
have available in our busy lives without negatively
impacting anything else. Based on the suggested
training time commitment for your goal race distance
(see table 2 on page 212), and the amount of time you
have available in your week to train, write down the

maximum number of hours (or equivalent distance)
you're able to run each week. Don't forget to add two
to three 20–30-minute strength and mobility sessions,
plus any cross-training you'd like to do on to this total.

Step 2: calculate your training volume for the week
– as you move through the phases of your training
plan, your weekly running volume will increase from
30 per cent of the maximum you determined in step 1
during your base phase up to 100 per cent in the final
weeks before race day. You'll need to be comfortable
running the distance or duration that equates to 30
per cent of your maximum when you start your base
phase, so pick your goal race with this in mind.

Step 3: enter your key workouts – using tables
3–6 on page 213 to find your suggested intensity
distribution, along with the workouts in chapter 18,
choose three key workouts, making sure you include:
* one longer run, mostly undertaken at a lower
  intensity, and
* two higher-intensity runs, for example, one tempo
  run and one interval session.

You can mix up your intensities within the same
workout, for example, by including a tempo run (page
224) or strides (page 223) within a longer, lower
intensity run.

Step 4: add in your remaining workouts –
depending on how many hours and days you're
available to train, add in mostly lower-intensity runs
until you've reached your goal distance/time for the
week. Add in your strength and mobility workouts,
ideally planning these for non-running or easy run
days to optimise both your running and strength
training.

Example weeks of training plans

Example 1
* Race: 5K.
* Training volume: medium (i.e. 3–4 hours per week – see table 2 on page 212).
* Week 12 of a 16-week training plan, therefore in the peak phase of training.

Using figure 1 (see page 211), during week 12 (peak phase) runners will be undertaking 100 per cent of their maximum training volume, i.e. 3–4 hours (180–240 minutes – in this example we'll use 240 minutes), plus two strength and mobility sessions.

Using the appropriate suggested intensity distribution table for the race distance (in this case this is table 3 – see page 213), your training should be *approximately* split into:
* 70 per cent low intensity (i.e. 165 minutes),
* 10 per cent moderate intensity (i.e. 25 minutes),
* 20 per cent high intensity (i.e. 50 minutes).

(Numbers have been rounded for ease of use.)

Table 8 shows week 12 of this training plan, illustrating the workout to be undertaken on each day and the approximate intensity distribution of each workout.

	Workouts	Approximate intensity distribution
Monday	20-minute strength and mobility session	
Tuesday	Mile reps interval session: * 20-minute easy warm-up; * Four sets of: 1 mile at goal 5K race pace with 2.5-minute jog recoveries; * 10-minute easy cool-down	40 minutes low intensity 30 minutes high intensity
Wednesday	Rest day	
Thursday	60-minute steady-state run with strides: * 20-minute easy warm-up; * 30 minutes at marathon pace with six sets of 30-second strides; * 10-minute easy cool-down	30 minutes low intensity 25 minutes moderate intensity 3 minutes high intensity
Friday	20-minute strength and mobility session	
Saturday	30-minute recovery run	30 minutes low intensity
Sunday	90-minute long run with fast finish: * 60 minutes easy running then 20 minutes at 10K race pace; * 10-minute easy cool-down	70 minutes low intensity 20 minutes high intensity

Table 8 – week 12 of a 5K training plan.

Example 2

* Race: trail marathon.
* Training volume: medium (i.e. 7–10 hours per week – see table 2 on page 212).
* Week 12 of a 16-week training plan, therefore in the peak phase of training.

Using figure 1 (see page 211), during week 12 (peak phase) runners will be undertaking 100 per cent of their maximum training volume, i.e. 7–10 hours (420–600 minutes – in this example we'll use 570 minutes), plus two strength and mobility sessions.

Using the appropriate suggested intensity distribution table for the race distance (in this case this is table 5 – see page 213), your training should be *approximately* split into:

* 70 per cent low intensity (i.e. 400 minutes),
* 20 per cent moderate intensity (i.e. 115 minutes),
* 10 per cent high intensity (i.e. 55 minutes).

(Numbers have been rounded for ease of use.)

Table 9 shows week 12 of this training plan, illustrating the workout to be undertaken on each day and the approximate intensity distribution of each workout.

	Workouts	Approximate intensity distribution
Monday	**20-minute strength and mobility session**	
Tuesday	**3-minute hill repeats:** * 20-minute easy warm-up; * Ten sets of 3-minute hills (incline should be runnable but feel hard towards the top; jog easily back down to recover); * 20-minute easy cool-down	75 minutes low intensity 30 minutes high intensity
Wednesday	**45-minute recovery run**	45 minutes low intensity
Thursday	**60-minute easy run with strides:** * 20-minute easy warm-up; * Over the next 30 minutes, include ten sets of 20–30-second strides; * 10-minute easy cool-down	55 minutes low intensity 5 minutes high intensity
Friday	**Steady-state run:** * 20-minute easy warm-up; * 120-minute run at just below marathon pace; * 10-minute easy cool-down	30 minutes low intensity 120 minutes moderate intensity
Saturday	**20-minute strength and mobility session**	
Sunday	**210-minute off-road run with fast finish:** * 180-minute run at an easy pace; * For 15 minutes, increase pace every 5 minutes up to 10K pace; * 15 minutes easy cool-down; * Run this on similar terrain to the race	195 minutes low intensity 15 minutes high intensity

Table 9 – week 12 of a marathon training plan.

How long should my longest run be?

The distance or duration of your longest runs should be dictated both by your race distance/duration and what works for you. Those training for a fast 5K probably don't need to run for more than 30–40 minutes at a time (unless they want to), while those training for marathons and ultras should include a weekly long run that peaks at 20–22 miles/3–4 hours for marathons and perhaps a little more than this for ultras. Some ultrarunners, especially those who race relatively often, rarely run further than 20 miles in training, whereas others enjoy spending long days of five hours or more out in the hills at a time. Whatever your preference, make sure your runs allow you to practise your race-day strategy, including the kit, nutrition and hydration you'll use on the day.

18

Running workouts in detail

In this section we describe the fine details of various running workouts. For how to incorporate these exercises into your training plan, see chapter 17.

Long slow run

Intensity: low; **RPE:** 3; **talk test:** able to hold a full conversation.

Purpose: building endurance; conditioning the body to the repetitive stresses of running; improving ability to utilise fat for fuel.

How to do it: run at a comfortable pace for an extended period that matches your race goals. If you're training for a marathon, long runs should build up from around 10–12 miles to peak at around 18–22 miles. Long runs when you're training for an ultra should reflect the terrain you'll be running on and not usually be more than four–six hours. Be aware of your running form, stopping if you find you're losing form and reducing the distance of your long runs until you can maintain good form throughout. Practise fuelling and hydrating as you go.

Example workouts
Basic long run
The longest run of the week, undertaken at a low intensity throughout.

Long run for ultramarathons
Slow running on terrain similar to the race for four–six hours. Practise hiking up hills – a key skill for hillier ultras. Practise with a pack and poles if you'll be using these in the race. Eat regularly – every 20–30 minutes – and drink to thirst.

Long run with strides
In the final hour of your long run, add in eight–10 bursts of faster running to loosen up the legs and recruit different muscle fibres.

Long progression run
Increase your pace towards the end of your long run, starting out at low intensity and building to moderate intensity towards the end of your run.

Fast finish long run
Do your long run at a low intensity until the final five–10 kilometres, then ramp it up to a harder effort. This is a great way to get the legs moving again after they've been working in the same way for several hours, and to bring some fast-running fun into your long runs. It's great practice for sprint finishes in races, too!

Steady-state run

Intensity: moderate; **RPE:** 4–6; **talk test:** able to talk in short sentences.

Purpose: conditioning your body to higher stresses over a longer period of time, so are important when training for half marathon and marathon-distance races. Moderate-intensity runs are all the rage right now, but these mid-paced workouts should be treated with care as they apply a reasonably high level of stress on the body for an extended period of time.

How to do it: run at a pace that's at or just below your marathon pace, or that you could keep up for two hours at the most. You should be able to speak in short sentences, but not hold a full conversation. They're nowhere near all-out, but they are definitely not easy runs.

Example workouts
Basic steady-state run
The duration should be between 90 minutes and two hours for maximum benefit while minimising injury risk. Warm up well for 20 minutes, then increase your pace to at or just below your marathon race pace. Hold this steady for the duration of the workout.

Steady-state run with strides
Add faster bursts of running into a steady-state run, returning to your marathon race pace in between the harder efforts. This is a hard session, but helps marathon pace to feel more manageable, as you're accumulating time at a faster pace in between steady-state running.

Progression/steady-state long run
Increase your pace as you progress through a long run – this will accustom you to working harder later on in a run, which is great race preparation. Your steady-state run should form the mid-to-late portion of the run, during the final 30 per cent of the distance.

Interval training

Intensity: high; **RPE:** 9–10; **talk test:** single words only.

Purpose: improving speed and cardiovascular fitness; targeting different energy systems; accumulating time at higher intensity with breaks in between efforts.

How to do it: intervals alternate between short, high-intensity bursts of running and brief recovery periods. Have a fixed plan for your interval sessions and try to stick to it. Try to run your final reps at the same pace as your first ones – even though they'll undoubtedly feel harder! Interval sessions are also great to do on a treadmill; often these will allow you to pre-set your session, so you don't need to think about it.

Example workouts

3x3-minute interval
Run three minutes hard then jog for three minutes to recover. This is a great interval session for those training for half marathons and longer, as these longer intervals improve running economy and lactate threshold. If you're new to intervals, start out with three–four reps and increase to eight–10 as you progress. Try to pace the session so that the final three minutes are run at the same (hard) pace as the first.

Pyramid intervals
Run for one minute hard with one minute recovery; then two minutes hard with two minutes recovery; then three minutes hard with three minutes recovery ... carry on until you're on five minutes, and then reverse back down to one minute. Pace each effort so you're consistent throughout – your shortest efforts should be fastest, and your longest efforts slowest.

400-metre reps
Great to do on a track – run 400 metres at your goal mile pace then take 1 minute of active rest, walking or jogging slowly. Build up from five to 10 reps as you progress. Alternatively, try 800-metre reps with two minutes of active rest.

Mile reps
Great for those training for 5K or 10K races. Run one mile at goal 5K or 10K race pace, take two and a half minutes of active rest, walking or jogging slowly. Repeat two–four times.

Hill repeats

Intensity: high; **RPE:** 8–10; **talk test:** one or two words at a time.

Purpose: strengthening leg muscles; improving aerobic capacity and, if done at high intensity, increasing speed. Running intervals on a hill also reduces impact forces compared with running intervals on the flat, so you get the benefits with a lower risk of injury.

How to do it: find a hill with an incline varying from shallow to steep, depending on the terrain you're training for. Those training for faster, flatter races such as road marathons should run faster up a shallower incline, while those training for hilly or mountainous races should choose a steeper incline. Run up your chosen hill at a hard effort – you should be breathing hard and wanting to stop by the end of each rep – then jog or walk back down for recovery.

Example workouts
15-minute hills
Great for those training for hilly or mountainous ultras, these should be carried out on a slope that is steep enough to feel it in the legs, but not so steep that you can't keep running for the full 15 minutes. Take enough recovery time between efforts so that your breathing has returned to normal and you're ready to go again. If you don't live anywhere with long enough hills, these are great to do on a treadmill.

3-minute hills
Good for all runners, 3-minute hills strike a balance between faster-paced running and endurance. The longer and hillier the race you're training for, the more reps you should try to do. Marathon runners should choose a shallow incline, which boosts the effectiveness and reduces the injury risk of a standard *3x3-minute interval session* (see page 221) compared with carrying it out on the flat. Those training for a hilly and/or longer, slower race should do these on a steeper incline. Start out with four–five reps and build up to 10–12 as you progress.

Hill sprints
A great session for working on VO_2 max, leg strength, whole-body coordination and muscle recruitment, hill sprints are also easy to do anywhere where there's a short hill. Find a hill that takes between 10 and 30 seconds to run up, and repeat, giving maximum effort to each rep. Walk or slowly jog back down and repeat.

Efforts on a hilly run
If you're lucky enough to live somewhere undulating, hill sessions can be undertaken a bit like fartlek sessions, simply taking advantage of the changes in terrain as you go. Go easy on the flat and downhills, but push hard on each hill as you encounter it.

Fartlek

Intensity: variable – efforts should be high intensity; recovery should be low; **RPE:** 8–9 (efforts), 2–3 (recovery); **talk test:** one or two words (efforts), full sentences (recovery).

Purpose: combining speed and endurance training.

How to do it: meaning 'speed play' in Swedish, fartlek is a less-structured form of interval training that's enjoyable and flexible to fit in with the area you're running in. Run at a comfortable pace, but mix in random bursts of faster running for varying durations – perhaps between two trees or lamp posts. You can either run each effort hard throughout or use the 'peak and fade' approach, gradually building speed, peaking at the middle of each interval, and then decreasing pace. This approach avoids rapid changes in pace, reducing the likelihood of injury.

Example workouts
Lamp posts or trees
If your regular run takes you along paths or pavements with regular 'goals' such as trees, lamp posts or gates, use these to dictate your efforts. As you go, pick a start and finish point up ahead and run hard between them, then easy jog to recover in between.

Hilly fartlek
As for **Efforts on a hilly run**, if you're lucky enough to live somewhere undulating, fartlek sessions can focus on running hills, simply taking advantage of the changes in terrain as you go. Go easy on the flat and downhills, but push hard on each hill as you encounter it.

Strides

Intensity: high; **RPE:** 8–10; **talk test:** one or two words.

Purpose: strides have a similar function to fartlek or other types of speedwork, injecting bursts of faster running into a lower-intensity run. Instead of being a session in their own right, they're most often used within a longer, slower run, in order to improve leg turnover, work on VO$_2$ max, and target different muscle fibres and energy systems. Strides are usually based on time (e.g. 20 seconds fast) or a number of strides (e.g. 50) and should be done at a sprint. As with other intervals, using a peak-and-fade approach avoids sudden changes in pace, reducing the risk of injury associated with high-impact speedwork.

How to do it: during a lower-intensity run, such as a steady-state or long run, once you're thoroughly warmed up but not too fatigued, add in up to 10 bursts of faster running. As with other high-intensity intervals, strides work well as peak-and-fade efforts, rather than rapid changes in pace.

Example workouts
Long run with strides
See page 219 for details.

Steady-state run with strides
See page 220 for details.

Tempo run

Intensity: high; **RPE:** 7–8; **talk test:** short sentences.

Purpose: improving your lactate threshold and race pace.

How to do it: run at a 'comfortably hard' pace that is just below your 10K race pace. This pace should be challenging but sustainable for an extended period, usually 20–40 minutes.

Example workouts
Basic tempo
After a thorough warm-up of 20–30 minutes' running at an easy/moderate pace, run for 20 minutes comfortably hard. You should feel like you're working as hard as you can without things becoming unstable – a pace you can maintain for the full 20 minutes. As you progress, gradually build the duration of your tempo run up to between 40 and 60 minutes, but if you can run at this pace for more than an hour, you're not running hard enough, so increase your pace to reduce the time.

Long run with tempo
Adding a tempo run into a long run is a great way to break up the monotony, recruit different muscle fibres and use your muscles in a different way. It also increases fatigue, so your long run doesn't need to be as long to feel the same in terms of effort. Add your tempo about two-thirds through a long run, so you're tired but not too fatigued. Generally, 20 minutes at tempo pace is enough in the midst of a long run. You could progress to two lots of 20-minute tempo efforts.

Progression long run
This is a great session for marathon training, when you want to train yourself to run hard in the final hour of a marathon. Divide your long run into three (either by distance or time), running the first third easy, the second third moderate, and the final third at, or slightly faster than, your marathon race pace.

Progression run

Intensity: low progressing through moderate to high – ideally about 30 per cent each; **RPE:** building from 3 up to 7; **talk test:** building from full sentences to a few words.

Purpose: learning to pace yourself, and that you always have more left than you think!

How to do it: start at a very easy pace and gradually increase your speed as the run progresses. The goal is to finish strong, running faster than you started. Your hardest effort shouldn't be all-out though, as you'll be tired by this point and pushing too hard could lead to excessive fatigue.

Example workouts
Progression thirds
Whatever the planned distance/duration of your run, you can divide it up into thirds to make it a progression run. Run the first third easy, the second third moderate and the final third hard.

Progression tempo run
After a thorough warm-up, run for 10 minutes at your half marathon pace, then 10 minutes at your 10K pace, then 10 minutes between your 10K and 5K paces.

Progression long run
See left for details.

Time trial

Intensity: high; **RPE:** 8–9; **talk test:** one or two words.

Purpose: assessing your progress and setting new goals.

How to do it: run a specific distance (e.g. 5K or 10K) at your maximum effort to gauge your current fitness level and set benchmarks for future improvements. You could use your local parkrun, or a loop or out-and-back of a known distance. To allow accurate comparison, it's a good idea to use the same course for each time trial.

Example workouts
Parkrun
At an accurately measured 5K (although the ascent and underfoot conditions vary widely) your local parkrun is a perfect place to run a regular time trial. Run the same course each time if you want an accurate representation of your progress.

Race
Regular 5K and 10K races take place all around the world. Entering these from time to time will give you a good idea of your fitness, and opportunities to experience race-day nerves and pre-/post-race prep and routines without too much pressure.

Home-based 5K or 10K time trial
Using a watch, measure out a loop, linear or out-and-back route of an exact distance. It doesn't need to be five or 10 kilometres, but as these are popular race distances, they give you a good idea where your pace is in comparison with others – if that's something you're interested to know. After a thorough warm-up, run the measured route, timing yourself as you go. Note the times down, and repeat regularly, or whenever you want to check on your progress. Remember to cool down well after a longer, harder effort, too.

Easy/recovery run

Intensity: low; **RPE:** 2; **talk test:** full conversation.

Purpose: aiding recovery; improving aerobic fitness; increasing mitochondrial biogenesis; improving running form; headspace.

How to do it: run at an easy, relaxed pace to help your body recover from more intense workouts. It's important to keep this run slow and low in intensity. These runs are rarely more than an hour.

Example workouts
30–60 minutes easy run
Your breathing should be steady and you should be able to hold a full conversation.

Easy run with strides
Start out with 20 minutes of easy running. Over the next 10 minutes, add in bursts of faster running – not more than 20 seconds each – to loosen up the legs. Finish with 20 minutes of easy running.

Easy adventure run
Take some water and snacks and head off-road to explore somewhere new. Leave your watch at home, listen to the birds and admire the scenery.

Cross-training

Intensity: variable.

Purpose: adding variety to your training routine and applying different stresses to your body.

How to do it: incorporate other forms of exercise into your training plan. Especially in your off-season, including aerobic activities such as cycling, skiing and swimming can improve your VO_2 max and lactate threshold with far lower impact on your body than running. Using a StairMaster or similar exercise machine is also a great way to train for running in hilly or mountainous areas if you live somewhere flat or weather-affected.

Example workouts
Cycling, either indoors or outdoors
Cycling is a great, low-impact way to maintain and improve aerobic fitness. If you're happy on a bike, heading out for an adventure on two wheels is a fantastic way to explore, too. Whether you prefer road cycling, mountain biking or gravel, cycling is fun, sociable and a good compliment to running. If you prefer to avoid the possibility of falling off, or encountering bad weather or cars, there's a range of excellent indoor options, too. Zwift or spinning classes or simply getting a turbo-trainer for your own bike at home all offer the option of a safe, controlled environment. Group classes (in person at a gym or online from your home) are brilliant for motivation, and offer a set structure to each workout.

Yoga and pilates
Offering mobility-based movement, muscle strengthening (especially core and pelvic strength that's hard to build solely through running), relaxation and mindfulness, and a sense of connection with your body, yoga and pilates are wonderful for runners. These can also be a good social activity if you join in-person classes.

Walking and hiking
For longer races, such as ultras, when time on your feet is important, walking is a great way to build strength and stamina. It's also an essential part of many ultras – even elite ultrarunners hike the uphills. For all runners, walking is a great recovery activity, facilitating movement with very little impact.

Swimming
A whole-body activity, swimming is great for all-round strength and mobility, and also a good way to improve breath control and aerobic fitness. To be effective and enjoyable, swimming demands good technique, so if you're new to the sport or haven't done it for a while it's a good idea to work with a coach for a few sessions to make sure your stroke is as good as it can be.

19

Home-based strength and mobility exercises

In this section we describe some great exercises which will help strengthen your core, increase your mobility and optimise your running as part of a well-designed training plan. For more information on the theory behind strength training and running, see chapter 6; for how to incorporate these exercises into your training plan, see page 215.

Supine spine and pelvis mobilisation

Dead bug

Bird dog

Single-leg bridges

Supine spine and pelvis mobilisation

A nice exercise to start or end the day with. Choose a firm, flat surface – ideally a slim mat on a hard floor. Lie on your back and bring your knees up to a comfortable degree of hip/knee flexion; don't cross your ankles but if your feet overlap a little that's fine. Link your hands together and rest them on top of your knees. Focus on relaxation and breathing throughout this exercise.

Now rock gently from side to side, feeling the movement mobilising the joints in your hips, pelvis, spine and shoulders. You can increase the degree of rocking, but not to the point where you're overbalancing. The more relaxation you can maintain throughout this exercise the more effective the mobilisation will be, allowing the joints to move more freely. Continue rocking for about a minute, or until any stiffness and crunchiness in the joints has eased.

Dead bug

Lying on your back, slowly, and in control, extend your opposite arm and leg. Keep your pelvis level and core engaged throughout. Repeat on the other side.

Bird dog

From an all-fours position, extend the opposite arm and leg out in front and behind your body, keeping your shoulders, back and pelvis level by activating the stabilising muscles throughout your trunk. Concentrate on driving your arm forwards and foot back – the foot shouldn't be too far off the floor. Repeat on the other side.

Single-leg bridges

Keep your pelvis level and your core and glutes engaged as you lift your body by pushing down on your foot. Repeat on the other side.

In each strength and mobility session, carry out **eight–12 repetitions** of each exercise, **maintaining good form throughout**. Mix up the exercises if you don't have time for them all in each session.

INHALE EXHALE INHALE EXHALE INHALE EXHALE: 5 BREATHS INHALE EXHALE INHALE EXHALE

Sun salutations

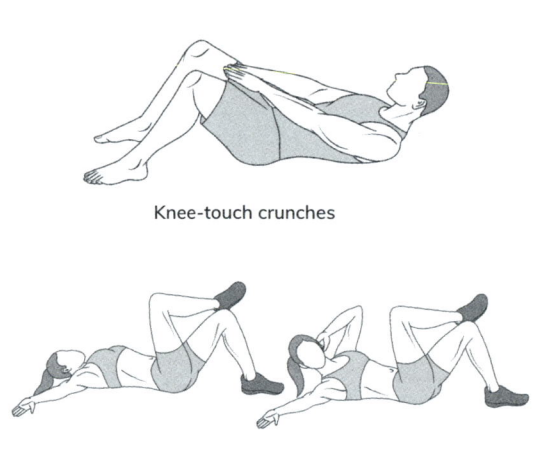

Knee-touch crunches

Deep crunches

Rotational crunches

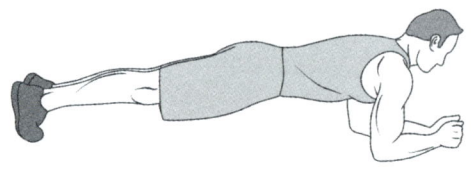

Front plank

Sun salutations

Another nice exercise to start the day with. Keep focused on your breath throughout and get as close to each posture as you comfortably can. Remember runners don't need to be super bendy – we need stiffness in our muscle–tendon units for efficiency – so never push past what's comfortable in any pose.

Knee-touch crunches

Lie on your back with your feet on the floor, knees bent and hands on thighs. Slide hands up to knees and return.

Rotational crunches

Lie on your back with your left foot on the floor with your knee bent. Bend your right leg out to the side at 90 degrees with your ankle resting on your left knee.

Put your left hand by your ear, with your elbow bent. Stretch your right hand out to the side. Bring your left elbow up towards your right knee and lower back down. Repeat on the other side.

Deep crunches

Lie on your back, with legs extended upwards at 90 degrees to your body. Stretch your hands up towards your feet and back down.

Front plank

Lower down on to your front with your body straight and weightbearing on your toes and your elbows or forearms. Hold for at least 20 seconds, but stop once form is lost. Build up to a minute.

Side plank

Rotating side plank

Resistance-band walking

Single-leg mini squats

(a)   (b)

Side plank

Lower down on to your side with your body straight and weightbearing on one forearm and the sides of your feet. Rest your non-weightbearing hand on your hip for balance. Hold for at least 20 seconds, but stop once form is lost. Build up to a minute. Repeat on the other side.

Resistance-band walking

Place a medium strength resistance band just above the knees, then walk to the side in both directions.

Rotating side plank

Start as for side plank but hold your non-weightbearing arm straight up. Rotate this arm underneath your body and return. Repeat on the other side.

Single-leg mini squats

Begin in standing and lift your left leg up. Squat down on your right leg, making sure your knee doesn't go to any more than 30–40 degrees of knee flexion (with 0 degrees being a straight leg and 90 degrees being a right angle at the knee). Keep your shoulders and pelvis level and activate the gluteal (bum) muscles all the way through the exercise. Make sure your knee is travelling over the top of your foot (a), not swinging inwards (b). Repeat on the other side.

Round-the-clock lunges

(a)   (b)

Step-ups/step-downs

Round-the-clock lunges

A great pre-run exercise for activating and mobilising the core, pelvis and legs. It's also helpful for balance, proprioception and multi-directional stability, all of which are essential for off-road running, and for improving protective support around the knees.

Begin in standing and do lunges every 45 degrees around you, starting on one leg and swapping to the other around the other side.

Try to make each movement both dynamic *and* controlled, lowering into each lunge and powering back out. Stop before you lose good form – this is one to start with just a few reps until you're used to the exercise and then build up gradually. Once you're really solid on the technique you can add a hand-held weight such as a dumbbell.

Step-ups/step-downs

Forward step-ups/step-downs (a) and lateral step-ups/step-downs (b) are a great way to train for hilly terrain if you live somewhere flat. Keep your pelvis level by keeping the glutes activated throughout, especially during lateral steps, driving your body upwards during the up portion and lowering slowly during the down.

Weighted running arms

(a)

(b)

Squat jumps

Squat jumps

The explosive part of this exercise helps develop power throughout the lower body, while the controlled lowering eccentrically loads the muscles, especially the quadriceps in the thighs, in a similar way to downhill running.

This exercise is all about generating power through your legs and glutes, so it's important not to use your arms to aid propulsion. You can either clasp your hands in front of your chest or place your hands behind your head.

Start in a squat position with your knees bent to about 90 degrees. Activate the glutes and explode upwards into a jump. Land on soft knees and control the downward motion back into the squat. You can either do single-pulse squat jumps (a) or double-pulse squat jumps (b), where you start in a squat position, lift up slightly, squat back down, then jump.

Weighted running arms

This is a great exercise to strengthen your arms for using poles while running. If you're not used to using poles – or live somewhere flat where it's hard to train with poles regularly – simulating the arm motion used during running with poles, with a weight in each hand, helps strengthen your arm muscles in a running-specific way. The action should be more exaggerated than normal running arms, with an increased lifting of the hands and bending at the elbows both in front and behind the body. Keep the weights light and the reps high– you're training to run with poles for many hours, so fatigue-resistance is as important as improving strength.

Bibliography
and references

Abdi, F., Rahnemaei, F.A., Roozbeh, N., *et al.*, (2021), 'Impact of phytoestrogens on treatment of urogenital menopause symptoms: A systematic review of randomized clinical trials', *European Journal of Obstetrics & Gynecology and Reproductive Biology*, Volume 261, pp. 222–235, doi: 10.1016/j.ejogrb.2021.03.039.

Adamczyk, J.G., Gryko, K. and Boguszewski, D. (2020), 'Does the type of foam roller influence the recovery rate, thermal response and DOMS prevention?', *PLOS ONE*, doi: 10.1371/journal. pone.0235195.

Altini, M. and Plews, D. (2021), 'What is behind changes in resting heart rate and heart rate variability? A large-scale analysis of longitudinal measurements acquired in free-living', *Sensors*, Volume 21(23), Article ID: 7932, doi: 10.3390/s21237932.

Baxter, N. and Jefferson Lenskyj, H. (2021), *Running, Identity and Meaning: The Pursuit of Distinction Through Sport*, Emerald Publishing Limited.

Bosquet, L., Montpetit, J., Arvisais, D., *et al.* (2007), 'Effects of tapering on performance: a meta-analysis', *Medicine & Science in Sports & Exercise*, Volume 39(8), pp. 1358–1365, doi: 10.1249/mss.0b013e31806010e0.

Bramble, D. and Lieberman, D. (2004), 'Endurance running and the evolution of *Homo*', *Nature*, Volume 432, pp. 345–352, doi: 10.1038/nature03052.

British Soft Drinks Association (2020), *Annual Report*, available at: www.britishsoftdrinks.com/write/MediaUploads/BSDA_Annual_Report_2020.pdf

Chen, J., Zhang, F., Chen, H., *et al.* (2021), 'Rhabdomyolysis after the use of percussion massage gun: a case report', *Physical Therapy*, Volume 101(1), doi: 10.1093/ptj/pzaa199.

Clear, J. (2018), *Atomic Habits*, Random House.

Cohen, S., Doyle, W.J., Alper, C.M., *et al.*, (2009), 'Sleep habits and susceptibility to the common cold', *Archives of Internal Medicine*, Volume 169(1), pp. 62–67, doi: 10.1001/archinternmed.2008.505.

Davis, H.L., Alabed, S. and Chico, T.J.A. (2020), 'Effect of sports massage on performance and recovery: a systematic review and meta-analysis', *BMJ Open Sport & Exercise Medicine*, Volume 6, Article ID: e000614, doi: 10.1136/bmjsem-2019-000614.

Dridi, R., Dridi, N., Govindasamy, K., *et al.* (2021), 'Effects of endurance training intensity on pulmonary diffusing capacity at rest and after maximal aerobic exercise in young athletes', *International Journal of Environmental Research and Public Health*, Volume 18(23), Article ID: 12359, doi: 10.3390/ijerph182312359.

Eiken, O., Mekjavic, I.B., Babič, J., *et al.* (2022), 'Effects of vision on energy expenditure and kinematics during level walking', *European Journal of Applied Physiology*, Volume 122(5), pp. 1231–1237, doi: 10.1007/s00421-022-04914-6.

Emig, T. and Peltonen, J. (2020), 'Human running performance from real-world big data', *Nature Communications*, Volume 11, Article ID: 4936, doi: 10.1038/s41467-020-18737-6.

Fensham, N.C., Heikura, I.A., McKay, A.K.A., *et al.* (2022), 'Short-term carbohydrate restriction impairs bone formation at rest and during prolonged exercise to a greater degree than low energy availability', *Journal of Bone and Mineral Research*, Volume 37(10), pp. 1915–1925, doi: 10.1002/jbmr.4658.

Filipas, L., Bonato, M., Gallo, G., *et al.* (2022), 'Effects of 16 weeks of pyramidal and polarized training intensity distributions in well-trained endurance runners', *Scandinavian Journal of Medicine & Science in Sports*, Volume 32(3), pp. 498–511, doi: 10.1111/sms.14101.

Fitzgerald, M. (2014), *80/20 Running: Run Stronger and Race Faster by Training Slower*, Berkley.

Garcia, L., Asano, R.Y., Silveira, R., *et al.* (2023), 'Psychophysiological responses to self-selected exercise intensity over the menstrual cycle: a randomized crossover phase trial', *Research Quarterly for Exercise and Sport*, Volume 94(3), pp. 646–654, doi: 10.1080/02701367.2022.2036316.

Goulet, E.D.B. and Hoffman, M.D. (2019), 'Impact of ad libitum versus programmed drinking on endurance performance: a systematic review with meta-analysis', *Sports Medicine*, Volume 49(2), pp. 221–232, doi: 10.1007/s40279-018-01051-z.

Haghighat, F., Ebrahimi, S., Rezaie, M., *et al.*, (2021), 'Trunk, pelvis, and knee kinematics during running in females with and without patellofemoral pain', *Gait Posture*, Volume 89, pp. 80–85, doi: 10.1016/j.gaitpost.2021.06.023.

Hanley, B., Bissas, A. and Merlino, S. (2020), 'Men's and women's world championship marathon performances and changes with fatigue are not explained by kinematic differences between footstrike patterns', *Frontiers in Sports and Active Living*, Volume 2, doi: 10.3389/fspor.2020.00102.

Heikura, I.A., Burke, L.M., Hawley, J.A., *et al.* (2020), 'A short-term ketogenic diet impairs markers of bone health in response to exercise', *Frontiers in Endocrinology*, Volume 10, doi: 10.3389/fendo.2019.00880.

Husserl, E. (1936), *Die Krisis der Europäischen Wissenschaften und die Transzendentale Phänomenologie*, Kluwer [*The Crisis of European Sciences and Transcendental Phenomenology*, Northwestern University Press (1970)].

Jeukendrup, A.E. (2017), 'Periodized nutrition for athletes', *Sports Medicine*, Volume 47, pp. 51–63, doi: 10.1007/s40279-017-0694-2.

Joyner, M.J. and Coyle, E.F. (2008), 'Endurance exercise performance: the physiology of champions', *The Journal of Physiology*, Volume 586(1), pp. 35–44, doi: 10.1113/jphysiol.2007.143834.

Kaufman, K.A., Glass, C.R. and Arnkoff, D.B. (2009), 'Evaluation of mindful sport performance enhancement (MSPE): a new approach to promote flow in athletes', *Journal of Clinical Sport Psychology*, Volume 3(4), pp. 334–356, doi: 10.1123/jcsp.3.4.334.

Kerksick, C.M., Arent, S., Schoenfeld, B.J., *et al.* (2017), 'International society of sports nutrition position stand: nutrient timing', *Journal of the International Society of Sports Nutrition*, Volume 14, Article ID: 33, doi: 10.1186/s12970-017-0189-4.

Konrad, A., Glashüttner, C., Reiner, M.M., *et al.* (2020), 'The acute effects of a percussive massage treatment with a hypervolt device on plantar flexor muscles' range of motion and performance', *Journal of Sports Science & Medicine*, Volume 19(4), pp. 690–694.

Laborde, S., Allen, M.S., Borges, U., *et al.* (2022), 'Effects of voluntary slow breathing on heart rate and heart rate variability: a systematic review and a meta-analysis', *Neuroscience & Biobehavioral Reviews*, Volume 138, Article ID: 104711, doi: 10.1016/j.neubiorev.2022.104711.

Lee, D.C., Brellenthin, A.G., Thompson, P.D., *et al.* (2017), 'Running as a key lifestyle medicine for longevity', *Progress in Cardiovascular Diseases*, Volume 60(1), pp. 45–55, doi: 10.1016/j.pcad.2017.03.005.

Lee, D.H., Rezende, L.F.M., Joh, H.K., *et al.*, (2022), 'Long-term leisure-time physical activity intensity and all-cause and cause-specific mortality: a prospective cohort of US adults', *Circulation*, Volume 146(7), pp. 523–534, doi: 10.1161/CIRCULATIONAHA.121.058162.

Lepers, R., Burfoot, A. and Stapley, P.J. (2021), 'Sub 3-hour marathon runners for five consecutive decades demonstrate a reduced age-related decline in performance', *Frontiers in Physiology*, Volume 12, Article ID: 649282, doi: 10.3389/fphys.2021.649282.

Li, G., Li, J. and Gao, F. (2020), 'Exercise and cardiovascular protection'. In: *Physical Exercise for Human Health*, Springer, doi: 10.1007/978-981-15-1792-1_14.

Locke, E.A. and Latham, G.P., (1990). *A Theory of Goal Setting and Task Performance*, Prentice-Hall.

Longman, D.P., Wells, J.C.K. and Stock, J.T. (2023), 'Human energetic stress associated with upregulation of spatial cognition', *American Journal of Biological Anthropology*, Volume 182(1), pp. 32–44, doi: 10.1002/ajpa.24820.

McCormick, A., Meijen, C. and Marcora, S. (2015), 'Psychological determinants of whole-body endurance performance', *Sports Medicine*, Volume 45(7), pp. 997–1015, doi: 10.1007/s40279-015-0319-6.

McIntyre, R.D., Zurawlew, M.J., Mee, J.A., *et al.* (2022), 'A comparison of medium-term heat acclimation by post-exercise hot water immersion or exercise in the heat: adaptations, over-reaching, and thyroid hormones', *American Journal of Physiology: Regulatory, Integrative and Comparative Physiology*, Volume 323(5), pp. R601–R615, doi: 10.1152/ajpregu.00315.2021.

Malta, E.S., Dutra, Y.M., Broatch, J.R., *et al.* (2021), 'The effects of regular cold-water immersion use on training-induced changes in strength and endurance performance: a systematic review with meta-analysis', *Sports Medicine*, Volume 51(1), pp. 161–174, doi: 10.1007/s40279-020-01362-0.

Marcora, S.M. and Staiano, W. (2010), 'The limit to exercise tolerance in humans: mind over muscle?', *European Journal of Applied Physiology*, Volume 109(4), pp. 763–770, doi: 10.1007/s00421-010-1418-6.

Martela, F. and Riekki, T.J.J. (2018), 'Autonomy, competence, relatedness, and beneficence: a multicultural comparison of the four pathways to meaningful work', *Frontiers in Psychology*, Volume 9, Article ID: 1157, doi: 10.3389/fpsyg.2018.01157.

Martínez-Ramírez, I., Carrillo-García, A., Contreras-Paredes, A., *et al.* (2018), 'Regulation of cellular metabolism by high-risk human papillomaviruses', *International Journal of Molecular Sciences*, Volume 19(7), Article ID: 1839, doi: 10.3390/ijms19071839.

Maughan, R.J., Burke, L.M., Dvorak, J., *et al.* (2018), 'IOC consensus statement: dietary supplements and the high-performance athlete', *British Journal of Sports Medicine*, Volume 52(7), pp. 439–455, doi: 10.1136/bjsports-2018-099027.

Mosley, E. and Laborde, S. (2022), 'A scoping review of heart rate variability in sport and exercise psychology', *International Review of Sport and Exercise Psychology*, doi: 10.1080/1750984X.2022.2092884.

Ndahimana, D. and Kim E.-K. (2017), 'Measurement methods for physical activity and energy expenditure: a review', *Clinical Nutrition Research*, Volume 6(2), pp. 68–80, doi: 10.7762/cnr.2017.6.2.68.

Oswald, F., Campbell, J., Williamson, C., *et al.* (2020), 'A scoping review of the relationship between running and mental health', *International Journal of Environmental Research and Public Health*, Volume 17(21), Article ID: 8059, doi: 10.3390/ijerph17218059.

Paavolainen, L., Häkkinen, K., Hämäläinen, I., *et al.* (1999), 'Explosive-strength training improves 5-km running time by improving running economy and muscle power', *Journal of Applied Physiology*, Volume 86(5), pp. 1527–1533, doi: 10.1152/jappl.1999.86.5.1527.

Paludo, A.C., Paravlic, A., Dvořáková, K., *et al.* (2022), 'The effect of menstrual cycle on perceptual responses in athletes: a systematic review with meta-analysis', *Frontiers in Psychology*, Volume 13, Article ID: 926854, doi: 10.3389/fpsyg.2022.926854.

Parry, D. and Micklewright, D. (2014), 'Optic flow influences perceived exertion and distance estimation but not running pace', *Medicine & Science in Sports & Exercise*, Volume 46(8), pp. 1658–1665, doi: 10.1249/MSS.0000000000000257.

Podlogar, T. and Wallis, G.A. (2022), 'New horizons in carbohydrate research and application for endurance athletes', *Sports Medicine*, Volume 52, pp. 5–23, doi: 10.1007/s40279-022-01757-1.

Pontzer, H., Durazo-Arvizu, R., Dugas L.R., *et al.* (2016), 'Constrained total energy expenditure and metabolic adaptation to physical activity in adult humans', *Current Biology*, Volume 26(3), pp. 410–417, doi: 10.1016/j.cub.2015.12.046.

Rhim, H.C., Kwon, J., Park, J., *et al.* (2021), 'A systematic review of systematic reviews on the epidemiology, evaluation, and treatment of plantar fasciitis', *Life (Basel)*, Volume 11(12), Article ID: 1287, doi: 10.3390/life11121287.

Rønnestad, B.R. and Mujika, I. (2014), 'Optimizing strength training for running and cycling endurance performance: a review', *Scandinavian Journal of Medicine & Science in Sports*, Volume 24(4), pp. 603–612, doi: 10.1111/sms.12104.

Scheer, V., Janssen, T.I., Vieluf, S., *et al.* (2019), 'Predicting trail-running performance with laboratory exercise tests and field-based results', *International Journal of Sports Physiology and Performance*, Volume 14(1), pp. 130–133, doi: 10.1123/ijspp.2018-0390.

Schulkin, J. (2016), 'Evolutionary basis of human running and its impact on neural function', *Frontiers in Systems Neuroscience*, Volume 10, doi: 10.3389/fnsys.2016.00059.

Selinger, J.C., Hicks, J.L., Jackson, R.W., *et al.* (2022), 'Running in the wild: energetics explain ecological running speeds', *Current Biology*, Volume 32(10), pp. 2309–2315, doi: 10.1016/j.cub.2022.03.076.

Senefeld, J.W., Wiggins, C.C., Regimbal, R.J., *et al.*, (2020), 'Ergogenic effect of nitrate supplementation: a systematic review and meta-analysis', *Medicine & Science in Sports & Exercise*, Volume 52(10), pp. 2250–2261, doi: 10.1249/MSS.0000000000002363.

Shcherbina, A., Mattsson, C.M., Waggott, D., *et al.* (2017), 'Accuracy in wrist-worn, sensor-based measurements of heart rate and energy expenditure in a diverse cohort', *Journal of Personalized Medicine*, Volume 7(2), doi: 10.3390/jpm7020003.

Stankiewicz, J. and Todd, N. (2020), 'A deep-tissue massage with unintended consequences', *Critical Care*, Volume 158(4), doi: 10.1016/j.chest.2020.08.680.

Stanley, J., Halliday, A., D'Auria, S., *et al.*, (2015), 'Effect of sauna-based heat acclimation on plasma volume and heart rate variability', *European Journal of Applied Physiology*, Volume 115(4), pp. 785–794, doi: 10.1007/s00421-014-3060-1.

Taipale, R.S., Mikkola, J., Nummela, A., *et al.* (2010), 'Strength training in endurance runners', *International Journal of Sports Medicine*, Volume 31(7), pp. 468–476, doi: 10.1055/s-0029-1243639.

Tan, R., Cano, L., Lago-Rodríguez, Á., *et al.*, (2022), 'The effects of dietary nitrate supplementation on explosive exercise performance: a systematic review', *International Journal of Environmental Research and Public Health*, Volume 19(2), Article ID: 762, doi: 10.3390/ijerph19020762.

Thorpe, R.T., Strudwick, A.J., Buchheit, M., *et al.* (2016), 'Tracking morning fatigue status across in-season training weeks in elite soccer players', *International Journal of Sports Physiology and Performance*, Volume 11(7), pp. 947–952, doi: 10.1123/ijspp.2015-0490.

Tiller, N.B., Elliott-Sale, K.J., Knechtle, B., *et al.* (2021), 'Do sex differences in physiology confer a female advantage in ultra-endurance sport?', *Sports Medicine*, Volume 51(5), pp. 895–915, doi: 10.1007/s40279-020-01417-2.

Tiller, N.B., Wheatley-Guy, C.M., Fermoyle, C.C., *et al.* (2022), 'Sex-specific physiological responses to ultramarathon', *Medicine & Science in Sports & Exercise*, Volume 54(10), pp. 1647–1656, doi: 10.1249/MSS.0000000000002962.

Van Hooren, B., Fuller, J.T., Buckley, J.D., *et al.* (2020), 'Is motorized treadmill running biomechanically comparable to overground running? A systematic review and meta-analysis of cross-over studies', *Sports Medicine*, Volume 50(4), pp. 785–813, doi: 10.1007/s40279-019-01237-z.

Venturini, E. and Giallauria, F. (2022), 'Factors influencing running performance during a marathon: breaking the 2-h barrier', *Frontiers in Cardiovascular Medicine*, Volume 9, Article ID: 856875, doi: 10.3389/fcvm.2022.856875.

Vonhof, J. (2000), *Fixing your Feet*, Wilderness Press.

Wakefield-Scurr, J., Sanchez, A. and Jones, M. (2023), 'A multi-stage intervention assessing, advising and customising sports bras for elite female British athletes', *Research in Sports Medicine*, Volume 31(5), pp. 703–718, doi: 10.1080/15438627.2022.2038162.

Wiewelhove, T., Döweling, A., Schneider, C., *et al.* (2019), 'A meta-analysis of the effects of foam rolling on performance and recovery', *Frontiers in Physiology*, Volume 10, Article ID: 376, doi: 10.3389/fphys.2019.00376.

Yoshimura, A., Sekine, Y., Furusho, A., *et al.* (2022), 'The effects of calf muscle self-massage on ankle joint range of motion and tendon-muscle morphology', *Journal of Bodywork and Movement Therapies*, Volume 32, pp. 196–200, doi: 10.1016/j.jbmt.2022.05.009.